# Access® 2007 Forms & Reports For Dummies®

Cheat Sheet

## Types of Access Queries

| Type | Description |
|------|-------------|
| Append | Adds records to an existing table. |
| Crosstab | Calculates and displays summary results using a spreadsheet-like layout. |
| Delete | Permanently removes a specified set of records. |
| Make-Table | Creates a new table and adds records to the new table. |
| Parameter | Prompts for the record selection criteria whenever the query is executed. |
| Select | Displays records that match a specified set of criteria. |
| SQL-specific | Queries that can only be created using SQL statements. |
| Update | Modifies existing records in a database. |

## Access Form and Report Tools

| Tool | Name | Description | Tool | Name | Description |
|------|------|-------------|------|------|-------------|
| | Logo | Inserts a picture as a logo. | | Button | Adds a button that executes a macro or a VBA procedure. |
| | Title | Inserts a title. | | Combo box | Enables you to add a box where the user can select from a list of options or enter a new value. |
| | Page number | Inserts page numbers. | | List box | Enables you to add a list box where a user can select from a set of pre-existing values. |
| | Date & time | Inserts the date or time. | | Subform/ Subreport | Adds a subform or subform that is tied to a different table than the main table used as the source of data for the form or report. |
| abl | Text box | Adds a text box to your form or report. | | Line | Adds lines to the form or report. |
| Aa | Label | Adds a text label to your form or report. | | Rectangle | Enables you to draw a rectangle on the form or report. |

*(continued)*

## For Dummies: Bestselling Book Series for Beginners

# Access® 2007 Forms & Reports For Dummies®

| Tool | Name | Description | Tool | Name | Description |
|------|------|-------------|------|------|-------------|
| | Image | Adds a digital image to a form or report. | | Insert hyperlink | Adds a hyperlink. |
| | Option group | Creates a set of option buttons that function as a group so that only one option can be selected at a time. | | Attachment | Adds an attachment. |
| | Checkbox | Adds a check box that can be selected or deselected. | | Line thickness | Controls the width of lines. |
| | Option button | Adds an option button to your form or report. | | Line type | Controls the style of lines. |
| | Toggle button | Adds a button that has two states — up for off and down for on. | | Line color | Sets the color of lines. |
| | Tab control | Enables you to create a form that has two or more tabs that group related objects. | | Special effect | Sets the appearance of objects. |
| | Insert page | Adds a new page. | | Set control defaults | Sets the default values. |
| | Insert chart | Adds a chart. | | Select all | Selects all objects. |
| | Unbound object frame | Enables you to add objects such as text or images that don't change when moving between records. | | Select objects | Selects objects that you've added to a form or report design. |
| | Bound object frame | Enables you to add objects that change when moving between records. | | Control wizards | Enables wizards that help you add objects (such as combo boxes) to your forms and reports. |
| | Page break | Enables you to add a page break to force multiple pages to appear on the form or report. | | Insert OLE object | Enables you to add OLE objects. |

## For Dummies: Bestselling Book Series for Beginners

# by Brian Underdahl and Darlene Underdahl

Authors of *iPAQ For Dummies*

BICENTENNIAL
1807
WILEY
2007
BICENTENNIAL

Wiley Publishing, Inc.

**Access**™ **2007 Forms & Reports For Dummies**®

Published by
**Wiley Publishing, Inc.**
111 River Street
Hoboken, NJ 07030-5774
www.wiley.com

Copyright © 2007 by Wiley Publishing, Inc., Indianapolis, Indiana

Published by Wiley Publishing, Inc., Indianapolis, Indiana

Published simultaneously in Canada

For general information on our other products and services, please contact our Customer Care Department within the U.S. at 800-762-2974, outside the U.S. at 317-572-3993, or fax 317-572-4002.

For technical support, please visit www.wiley.com/techsupport.

Wiley also publishes its books in a variety of electronic formats. Some content that appears in print may not be available in electronic books.

Library of Congress Control Number: 2006936765

ISBN: 978-0-470-04659-3

Manufactured in the United States of America

10  9  8  7  6  5  4  3  2  1

1O/RU/RS/QW/IN

WILEY

# *About the Authors*

**Brian Underdahl** is the well-known, bestselling author of over 70 computer books on a broad range of subjects. He has appeared on a number of TV shows, including the *Computer Chronicles,* and several *TechTV* programs, and is the subject of an hour-long interview on the syndicated *Computer Outlook* radio program. One of his titles was recently recommended to viewers by Scott Gurvey, Bureau Chief, on the *Nightly Business Report* on PBS, and his books have won awards including an Award of Merit from the Northern California Technical Communications Competition and the Referenceware Excellence Award for best title in the Graphic Design and Multimedia category.

Brian has been involved in personal computers from their beginning and has a background in electrical engineering. His last "real" job was as a Senior Programmer/Analyst for a large company, where he worked hard to bring the power and freedom of PCs to the desktops.

Brian figures that it's the author who should do the work so that readers can get their money's worth. That's why his books are different — he takes the time to explain what's going on so that readers can understand the subjects easily.

**Darlene Underdahl** spent many years as a Quality Assurance expert. She is applying that "attention to detail" in the writing she does today. In addition to technical writing, she has written a memoir of her early years and is gathering notes for future projects. She works and lives with her husband, the bestselling author Brian Underdahl, in the mountains above Reno, Nevada.

# Dedication

**Darlene:** For Brian . . .

# Author's Acknowledgments

No book is the product of one person, even if one person has the title of author and gets to have his or her name on the cover. I'm very lucky to have a lot of people I can thank for all the hard work and effort they put into this book. They include Kyle Looper and Pat O'Brien.

I'd also like to thank the many people who provided me with the wonderful Access tools and add-ons so that I could give you an idea about how you can get even more from Access. Please do check out the Web sites I list for these great products — you owe it to yourself to see how much more productive you can be.

We can't work without a functioning computer, so special thanks go out to Allison Wagda at ZoneLabs for providing ZoneAlarm Internet Security Suite. I sleep a lot better at night knowing that I don't have to worry about viruses and spyware, and I hope all my readers realize the importance of this type of protection.

Finally, many thanks to Fred Holabird of Holabird Americana, www.holabird americana.com, for allowing me to use samples from the Holabird Americana databases in order to be able to show some real-world examples in this book. Fred is a good friend and I'll always be grateful for his help!

## Publisher's Acknowledgments

We're proud of this book; please send us your comments through our online registration form located at www.dummies.com/register/.

Some of the people who helped bring this book to market include the following:

### Acquisitions, Editorial, and Media Development

**Project Editor:** Pat O'Brien

*(Previous Edition: Nicole Haims)*

**Acquisitions Editor:** Kyle Looper

**Copy Editors:** Andy Hollandbeck, Mary Lagu

**Technical Editor:** Michael Alexander

**Editorial Manager:** Kevin Kirschner

**Media Development Specialists:** Angela Denny, Kate Jenkins, Steven Kudirka, Kit Malone, Travis Silvers

**Media Development Coordinator:** Laura Atkinson

**Media Project Supervisor:** Laura Moss

**Media Development Manager:** Laura VanWinkle

**Media Development Associate Producer:** Richard Graves

**Editorial Assistant:** Amanda Foxworth

**Sr. Editorial Assistant:** Cherie Case

**Cartoons:** Rich Tennant (www.the5thwave.com)

### Composition Services

**Project Coordinator:** Jennifer Theriot

**Layout and Graphics:** Claudia Bell, Carl Byers, Lavonne Cook

**Proofreaders:** Susan Moritz, Techbooks

**Indexer:** Kevin Broccoli

---

**Publishing and Editorial for Technology Dummies**

**Richard Swadley,** Vice President and Executive Group Publisher

**Andy Cummings,** Vice President and Publisher

**Mary Bednarek,** Executive Acquisitions Director

**Mary C. Corder,** Editorial Director

**Publishing for Consumer Dummies**

**Diane Graves Steele,** Vice President and Publisher

**Joyce Pepple,** Acquisitions Director

**Composition Services**

**Gerry Fahey,** Vice President of Production Services

**Debbie Stailey,** Director of Composition Services

# Contents at a Glance

# Table of Contents

## Part V: Way Cool Advanced Queries, Forms, and Reports .................................................... 273

# Introduction

**M**icrosoft Access 2007 can be an incredibly useful application, but it can also be very frustrating if you don't know how to make it do what you want it to do. In a perfect world, you'd have a guru around, 24/7 — someone who knows Access 2007 inside and out and is willing to guide you along the way, showing you handy little tricks and useful techniques that help you get the results you need.

Well, I may not be there with you, but this book is the next best thing. I've gathered the really useful pieces of information that you need to create powerful queries, very easy-to-use forms, and reports that actually tell the story of what is going on inside your data. Along the way, I make sure to show you the special tricks and techniques that I use.

## About This Book

*Access 2007 Forms & Reports For Dummies* is a hands-on guide that uses real-world examples to show you just what you need to know about Access and why you need to know it. You won't find a bunch of buzzwords and jargon. Rather, you do find the solid information you really need and can't find elsewhere about creating queries, forms, and reports. Yes, I do give you good, solid information about queries in addition to forms and reports because queries are an essential element that will help you create better forms and reports.

*Access 2007 Forms & Reports For Dummies* is also a reference that you can use as you like. If you have a specific problem you need to solve right now, you can jump directly to the related topic and skip around as much as you want. But if you really want to make Access work for you, I suggest that you read through the entire book because you will discover many things you don't already know.

Finally, *Access 2007 Forms & Reports For Dummies* is specifically for users of Access 2007. Although the basics of queries, forms, and reports haven't changed much from the earlier versions of Access, there are enough important changes in Access 2007 so you'll find this book very useful even if you've used previous versions of Access.

# Conventions Used in This Book

We've used a few conventions in this book to make it easier for you to spot special information. Here are those conventions:

- ✔ New terms are identified by using *italic*.

- ✔ Web sites addresses (URLs) are designated by using a `monospace` font.

- ✔ Any command you enter at a command prompt is shown in bold and usually set on a separate line. Setoff text in italic represents a placeholder.

- ✔ Command arrows, which are typeset as ⇨, are used in a list of menus and options. For example, Tools⇨Options means to choose the Tools menu and then choose the Options command.

- ✔ Key combinations are shown with a plus sign, such as Ctrl+F2. This means you should hold down the Ctrl key while you press the F2 key.

- ✔ All Access properties and fields are set apart in `monospace` font, as well, like this: Use the `Input Mask` property of the Data tab to create an input mask.

- ✔ Wherever I instruct you to use a snippet of code, I set it apart like this:

```
INSERT INTO LIVEWINBID
SELECT [Auction 67].*
FROM [Auction 67];
```

# What You Don't Have to Read

I always have a hard time telling people that they don't have to read certain parts of a book if they don't care to. You can find some really useful information hidden away in things like the text next to Technical Stuff icons, but I understand if you feel that there isn't room in your brain for one more bit of technical information. Maybe the best thing that I can recommend is that if you don't want to read the whole book now, start by reading what looks the most interesting and then, after you've discovered how much really cool stuff I include, go back and have a look at what you missed the first time. You'll be glad you did!

# Icons Used in This Book

*Access 2007 Forms & Reports For Dummies* includes icons that point out special information. Here are the icons I use and what they mean:

This icon makes you seem like a real Access expert in no time. It highlights special tricks and shortcuts that make using Access even easier. Don't miss any of these!

This icon reminds you of important information that can be far too easy to forget and that can cause a lot of frustration when you do forget.

Be careful when you see this icon. It points out an area where you'll want to be extra cautious so that you don't cause yourself problems. It also tells you how to avoid the problems.

Technical Stuff is information for folks who want to know all the geeky details.

Real World Examples tell you about actual ways to apply your new Access techniques. Don't miss any of these because they're sure to give you a lot of ideas you can adapt and use.

# Foolish Assumptions

Making assumptions is always a gamble because assumptions can quickly come back to haunt you. That said, in writing this book I made some assumptions about you. This book is for you if:

- ✔ You have Access 2007 and want to know how to use it more effectively.

- ✔ You don't yet have Access 2007, but are wondering if getting Access 2007 can help you organize all of that data you're currently trying to manipulate with Excel or some other spreadsheet.

- ✔ You have a bunch of data that you want to turn into useful information.

- ✔ You want to see how you can create more efficient Access reports and quit wasting so many trees.

- ✔ You would like to know how to use data from an external database without having to get down on your knees to beg permission every time you need to run a report.

- ✔ You have finally realized that you are a *5th Wave* cartoon addict and simply can't pass up the chance to see what is hidden in these pages.

# How This Book Is Organized

*Access Forms & Reports For Dummies* has six parts. Each part is self-contained, but all the content is somewhat interconnected. That way you'll see the most useful information without a lot of boring repetition.

## Part I: Accessing Both Ends: Getting Data In and Info Out

This part shows you the basics of queries, forms, and reports. You see how these pieces fit together, and I make sure that you have the fundamentals down pat so that you have a good foundation for the rest of the topics.

## Part II: Creating Effective Queries

Queries enable you to work with sets of data instead of simply dumping everything into the pot. This part shows you how to create effective queries that enable you to pick and choose what shows up in your forms and reports. You even see how you can step beyond simple queries by having a look underneath the fancy face that Access throws onto your queries.

## Part III: Building Really Useful Forms

Forms make data entry and editing into a much easier task. This part shows you how to create forms that really are useful, and it tells you how to create forms that tackle data from more than one table at a time — for even greater efficiency.

## Part IV: Designing Great Reports

With Access reports you can turn data into useful information. This part shows you how to create great reports that look good and that provide a wealth of understandable information.

## Part V: Way Cool Advanced Queries, Forms, and Reports

Ordinary techniques are for ordinary people. This part takes you well beyond the ordinary and shows you how to get so much more from your queries, forms, and reports. This part also shows you some great tools you can use to make Access into an even more powerful partner for your database needs.

## Part VI: The Part of Tens

This part tells you about some places on the Web where you can find even more information about Access. It concludes with some vital tips to remember as you work with Access.

# Part I
# Accessing Both Ends: Getting Data In and Info Out

The 5th Wave    By Rich Tennant

"Ms. Lamont, how long have you been sending out bills listing charges for 'Freight', 'Handling', and 'Sales Tax', as 'This', 'That', and 'The Other Thing'?"

# In this part . . .

You need a good foundation if you're going to build anything useful and long lasting. In this part, I make sure that you have a good foundation for the topics in the rest of the book. Here you discover the basics of queries, forms, and reports that you really need but that you may have missed up until now.

# Chapter 1

# Getting to Know Forms and Reports

*W*ithout forms and reports, an Access database is just a jumble of hard-to-use information. But with really good forms and reports, that same database becomes both informative and a joy to use. Well-designed forms and reports make your Access databases into something that's far beyond the ordinary in utility, ease of use, and flexibility.

If you've been playing around with Access for a while, you have probably at least tried to create some forms and reports. Maybe some of your efforts didn't seem too bad, but you've probably had your share of frustration, too. Creating forms and reports that really do what you want them to do can be an awfully exasperating experience.

In this chapter, I show you a number of interesting things about forms, reports, and their sidekick queries so that you can see what each of them can do and why they're all important. You see how queries can greatly enhance the capabilities of forms and reports. I finish up the chapter by very briefly mentioning some really cool tools (find out even more about them in Chapter 20).

## Finding Forms Fascinating

In order to understand the importance of forms in an Access database, begin by looking at the alternative. Figure 1-1 shows the *Datasheet* view of a typical

Access table. (A *table* is the structure in which Access stores information in your database.) The Datasheet view looks an awful lot like an Excel worksheet. You are likely pretty familiar with this view of a database because it seems as though almost everyone's first attempt at a database is to just create a list in a spreadsheet. Welcome to the "if the only tool you have is a hammer, everything looks like a nail" club!

Each field is in a column

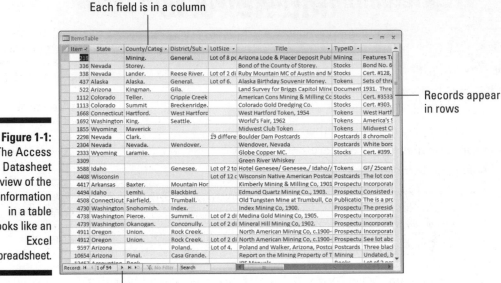

Records appear in rows

Record navigation tools

**Figure 1-1:**
The Access Datasheet view of the information in a table looks like an Excel spreadsheet.

In Datasheet view, each record is displayed in a single row, with columns for each of the database fields. Even though this view of the data is probably pretty familiar, it isn't very convenient. For one thing, unless you're keeping track of only a little information about each item, it's really hard to see an entire record in Datasheet view because everything has to fit into one row. That means you have to scroll back and forth to see all of the fields. Depending on the length of each field, sometimes you can't even see the entire contents of a single field on-screen. And don't even think about seeing a single record wrap around and take up multiple rows — making everything fit on-screen simply is not an option.

Of course, some other factors make the Datasheet view pretty inconvenient for most purposes. Can you imagine how little fun it would be to scroll through screen after screen trying to find a specific record in Datasheet view? Now imagine that instead of finding a single record, you want to find a dozen or so related records in a table containing 10,000 or more records. It's almost enough to make you want to move to a desert island where there aren't any computers, isn't it?

Fortunately, there's a good solution at hand in the guise of *forms*. Access forms provide a much more convenient way for you to interact with your database. Learning to create great forms is certainly going to be a lot easier than packing up your stuff for that move to a desert island. The following sections give you a look at some of the ways forms can help you.

## Streamlining data input with forms

No database has much value until it contains information. You wouldn't be able to get any useful data from an empty database, so a very important task in creating a database is inputting your data. Sure, you might have some existing data that you can import, but even that data required input at some point.

Entering data into a table in Datasheet view really isn't much fun. You first have to open the table and then locate the record where you want to enter your data. Maybe you're adding to an existing record, or perhaps you're adding a new record right after the last existing one in the datasheet. When you've selected the correct record, you have to move the insertion point to each field in turn and type in the information. It's easy to accidentally start typing into the wrong field — especially if the table layout doesn't quite match the layout of the information you're entering (and how often do you see data on paper that doesn't match the layout of the table?).

Forms can make inputting data much easier in several ways.

- ✔ **Forms typically have labels that make seeing exactly which field you're filling in far easier.**
- ✔ **Forms can have drop-down lists so that you simply choose the proper information from the list without worrying about mistyping the data.**
- ✔ **Forms are usually laid out with plenty of room to see all the fields in a record.** That makes keeping track of which record you're entering a much easier task.
- ✔ **You can easily create forms for special purposes, such as entering data in specific sets of fields.** In this case, the form might not need to include all of the fields; when you use only what you need, you end up with a simpler, less confusing form.
- ✔ **Forms don't have to be laid out using the same field order as the table.** This is an especially handy feature if you're inputting data that is laid out quite differently than your table.
- ✔ **You can set up forms to validate the data so that users can't mess up your database by entering bogus information.**

Even if some of these form features seem a little bit beyond your interests or immediate needs right now, don't worry — you'll find out about all of them and get many more great ideas in the chapters that follow.

## Entering data with the Form Wizard

Using a form to enter data into an Access database is much easier than entering data directly into a table in Datasheet view. Figure 1-2 shows a simple form you might create with the Form Wizard in Access. In this case, the form is not optimized in any way — it appears the way the wizard created it.

Enter data in the fields

Field labels

Use drop-down list boxes to choose from a list

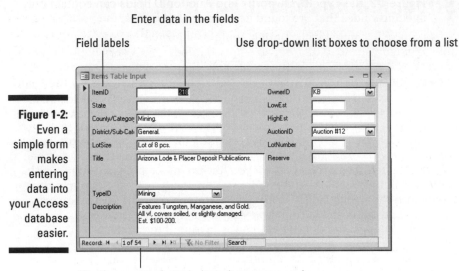

**Figure 1-2:**
Even a
simple form
makes
entering
data into
your Access
database
easier.

Use these controls to navigate between records

If you compare the form shown in Figure 1-2 with the Datasheet view shown in Figure 1-1, you can see pretty easily how much more convenient the form is for entering data. Each of the fields is clearly labeled (even if the Form Wizard didn't quite figure out the proper size for a couple of the labels). Here are a couple of ways that the Form Wizard makes entering data easier:

✔ **Easy movement between fields:** You can move between the fields by clicking the field you want or by pressing the Tab key. Because the fields are labeled, you can easily move to specific fields, skipping the fields you don't want to use for now.

✔ **Easy movement between records:** You can use the navigation controls at the bottom of the form to navigate between records. This feature is just like the navigation controls you commonly use, but with a notable exception: In forms, pressing Page Down moves you to the next record, and Page Up moves you to the previous record. In Datasheet view, Page Down and Page Up move you to a new screen page of records. (The number of records you jump depends on how many records are visible on the screen, and this can change depending on how you display the datasheet window. Don't you just love the inconsistency?)

In Datasheet view, you can use the Up-Arrow and Down-Arrow keys to move a single record at a time, but in a form, the arrow keys move the insertion point between fields.

✓ **Customizable drop-down lists:** Because you can modify the underlying table with *lookup fields* (fields that enable a user to select from a list of predefined values — see Chapter 17), you can ensure that the fields contain specific values that are found in related tables. For example, in Figure 1-2, the TypeID, OwnerID, and AuctionID fields can contain only specific values that are found in some related tables; the possible values for these fields appear in the drop-down lists in these boxes. Rather than typing an entry in these fields (and risking errors due to mistyping), you simply choose a value from the drop-down list.

✓ **Larger input areas:** To make entering longer values easier, the wizard provides larger input areas (in this case the Title and Description fields). In fact, if you type more information than can fit into the on-screen display of one of these fields, Access automatically adds a scrollbar along the right side of the field so that you can view the entire value. How's that for handy?

The database I use in these examples contains some features, such as lookup fields, that you might not yet be using in your Access databases. I explain all of the special features in later chapters as appropriate so that you will be able to incorporate them into your databases.

## Editing information with forms

Forms are also much handier than the Datasheet view for editing existing database information. When you're editing information, forms retain all of the advantages they offer when you're first entering data, of course, but some additional features are especially useful for editing. As Figure 1-3 shows, if you right-click a form field, Access pops up a very handy context menu that provides some really cool options.

The pop-up menu commands are extremely helpful for editing the filters.

✓ **Sort A to Z:** Choose this option to sort the records of a selected field in ascending alphabetical order. For example, if you originally decided to view the data shown in the State field and chose to sort the results in ascending alphabetical order, Alabama appeared first. This and the next option are best used in a secondary field after you have applied a filter (note the many filter variations that appear in the context menu) because these options won't have any effect in a filtered field.

✓ **Sort Z to A:** Choose this option to sort the records in descending order.

✓ **Text Filters:** To filter the data, select the field you want filtered and right-click. Access then proposes a set of appropriate text filters. (Other types of fields, such as number fields, will have different filters.)

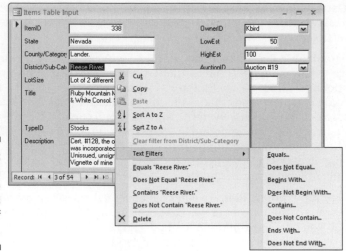

**Figure 1-3:**
Right-click a
form field to
display this
menu of
options.

Be sure to use the Clear Filter command (from the pop-up menu) when you finish editing records. Otherwise you may find yourself confused later when the form doesn't display all of the records that you know should be in your database.

## Viewing data by using forms

You can use a form when you simply want to view the data without entering new information or editing existing records. The same pop-up menu that appears when you right-click on a form field is just as handy when you simply want to view the records, too.

# Recognizing Why Reports Rock

Okay, so forms are great, but what about reports? The following sections look at some of the ways that you can use reports; they're well worth the effort it takes to create them.

## Using reports to show results

One very useful purpose for reports is to show results that aren't otherwise displayed in a table format. You can create a report to see important details at a glance. Figure 1-4 shows an example of a report that summarizes results from an auction database created in Access. In this case, the report summarizes by state, with sum, average, minimum, and maximum results.

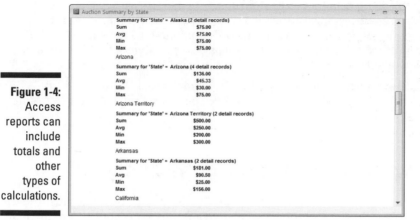

**Figure 1-4:**
Access
reports can
include
totals and
other
types of
calculations.

Figure 1-4 provides a good example of how a report can provide information that simply doesn't appear on its own in an Access table. Tables don't summarize the data from a collection of records, so unless you want to sit down with a calculator to figure out such details, you should create reports to get this kind of information from your database.

## Using reports to present data in a professional format

You might not need all the information Figure 1-4 includes. You might, for example, simply want a list that provides a snapshot of what's in your database. This is especially true if you want to distill complex information quickly and efficiently for your boss or client. If you just want to check things over for yourself, open a table and click the Print button (choose a small table so you won't waste paper). If you want to show off your data for others, the extra effort of creating a report makes sense for several good reasons:

✔ **Providing a professional layout:** Unless you're printing the data from a very small and simple table, the results of printing directly from a table's datasheet view probably won't fit the width of your paper. Good luck trying to make sense of the resulting printout!

✔ **Easing report navigation:** You can easily include page numbers and dates on your reports — in fact, the Access Report Wizard adds this information automatically. Keeping track of a report that has dates and page numbers printed on it is much easier — especially if you have a limited amount of time to orally guide others through your exhaustive 100-page report.

✔ **Presenting data in a logical format:** You can use as much or as little room as necessary for the fields on a report to accommodate the amount of data that's in each record. Compared to the single line for each record on a printout of a table's Datasheet view, this feature alone is worth the effort.

✔ **Adding a title:** Including a title on a report is easy. With a title, you'll be able to figure out the purpose of the report early on a Monday morning before your first cup of coffee kicks in.

## Using reports to show data analysis

Of course, you can summarize data in an Access report, but that's just the tip of the iceberg in terms of the types of data analysis you can do. Here are just a few examples of some other ways you can use a report to analyze the information in an Access database:

✔ **Compare similar results:** You can produce a report that shows how each salesperson's results compare to the average of all of your company's representatives.

✔ **Compare data over time:** You can use a historical sales report to determine which ice cream flavors to stock at each of your ice cream stands.

✔ **Predict opportune moments:** You can use a report to show how temperature patterns affect the populations of various types of pests and use this information to predict the best time to send out flyers for your extermination business.

✔ **Determine the best course of action:** You can create a report that tells you whether it's worthwhile to set up a calling committee for your club's annual meeting based on an analysis of the results from several past meetings.

## Using reports to preserve the moment

In most cases, an Access database is constantly changing as new data is entered, existing data is edited, and old data is deleted. Sometimes, though, you may have good reasons to preserve a record of exactly how things were at a particular moment in time. Consider these possibilities:

✔ If you maintain the membership list for the local branch of your favorite club, you know that sometimes members can be a bit slow about renewing their memberships. I've seen instances in which members have come back after several years away. Keeping all of the past members in the database may not always be reasonable, but having an end-of-year membership report stored away is a useful way to keep the data in case you need it again in the future.

✔ If you run a small business, you probably want to keep track of your exact inventory at various times of the year. A dated report of your inventory stored offsite could be extremely valuable if you ever needed to file an insurance claim after an untimely disaster or did a one-on-one with the tax man.

✔ If you go into business with someone else, an Access report showing exactly which items you contributed to the business could save some arguments in the event you later split up. (Sure, you both know now that the extremely rare Babe Ruth baseball card is yours, but wouldn't it be nice to be able to prove it when your former partner tries to sell it for $10,000?)

Even if you do keep the printouts, it's also a good idea to keep backup copies of your database in case of an emergency. But be very careful that you don't accidentally overwrite your current database file with an old copy if you do need to open your old file; you can easily destroy months or even years of work if you're careless.

# Seeing Why Both Forms and Reports Have a Place

Forms and reports seem somewhat similar in that they both provide ways to look at data that aren't available in the datasheet view of a table. Do you really have to learn how to create both of them? Yes. Using forms and reports isn't an either/or proposition.

Even though forms and reports share some characteristics, they do have important differences, and your databases will lack a little something if you use one (and not both) of these tools.

Here's a list of things you should know about choosing reports or forms:

✔ **If you want to add, remove, or change data in a table, use a form.** Sure, you can filter the data that appears in a report so that it appears as though some of the data has been removed from the database, but that's not the same as actually deleting data.

✔ **Use reports to view data in more than one record in a more permanent format.** In general, forms display only a single record at a time. In addition, because reports typically are meant to be printed, and they often include the date, reports provide a permanent record of the information.

It's not *strictly* true that forms can display only a single record at a time. As you find out in later chapters (such as Chapter 10), some forms that are based on multiple tables can include a section called a *subform* that can display multiple records from the second table in Datasheet view.

✔ **Both forms and reports depend on a table (or a query, as discussed in the next section) to provide the information that they display.** You can't create a form or a report unless you first have a table or query to use as a basis for the form or report. One important result of this fact is that Access forms and reports can exist only within an Access database file.

Access forms and reports are usually tied to an Access table (but they can also get their data from a query). When you create a form or a report, the name of the table is saved along with the form or report. If you (or someone else) delete the table, you can't open the form or report associated with it unless you have associated the form or report with a different table.

# Understanding the Value of Queries

I know, the title of this book doesn't mention *queries,* but queries are a fundamental and vital part of making your Access forms and reports really useful. Queries are nothing to be afraid of, and they might end up being your favorite part of Access!

## Introducing the query concept

So just what is a query? In its simplest form, a query acts like a filter; you can use a query to choose specific information that you want to see from a table. A more complex query takes you well beyond the scope of a filter (see Chapter 5). Figure 1-5 shows an example of a basic query, known as a *select query.*

When you run a query, Access displays the results in Datasheet view, as shown in Figure 1-6. In this example, I set the criteria value in the State field to Nevada, and this is reflected in the results shown in Figure 1-6.

The query results in Figure 1-6 are shown in a Datasheet view that looks almost identical to the Datasheet view of an ordinary Access table, with only the title bar as a tip-off that this is really a query. You can, indeed, use a query as a substitute for a table as the basis for a form or a report . . . or for another query!

The table that is the source of the data

The fields that will be included in the results

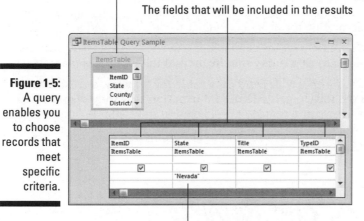

**Figure 1-5:**
A query
enables you
to choose
records that
meet
specific
criteria.

The criteria used to filter the results

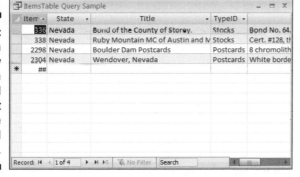

**Figure 1-6:**
Running a
query
results in a
filtered
display that
matches the
specified
criteria.

# Using queries to enhance forms and reports

Because you can use a query as the basis for an Access form or report, you now have a powerful tool that enables you to do otherwise impossible things with those forms and reports. Consider these possibilities:

✔ You can create a form that's based on a query that selects records that fall within specific date ranges. For example, say you want to follow up with customers who placed an order last year but who haven't ordered in several months. Use a query.

> ✔ You can create queries that combine data from several tables to produce information that is a composite of the information from those tables. You might want to use this data to create form letters that include new product information for products similar to those ordered in the past by specific customers.
>
> ✔ You can easily create a query that includes only the orders placed by a specific customer. This is a great tool if the customer wants a record of all its orders in the several months or years.

Because queries are so important, I put information about them throughout the book. In fact, Chapter 2 digs right in to give you a solid basis in queries so that, when you create forms or reports, you know what your options are.

# Queries, Forms, and Reports Basics You Need to Know

In Access, all of your data is stored in *tables*. You can create totally self-contained tables or relate multiple tables so that you can consolidate data efficiently. Databases that work from a single, self-contained table are often called *flat file* databases. Databases that include two or more related tables are called *relational* databases. Fortunately, you use the same tools in Access no matter which type of database you use.

As I mention earlier in this chapter, forms and reports are based on either a table or a query. Queries can be based on tables or even on other queries — although queries based on queries can be kind of confusing to work with.

Access provides two primary methods of creating queries, forms, and reports. You can start with a wizard, as shown in Figure 1-7, or you can create the query, form, or report from scratch by using *design mode*.

Whether you start with a wizard or in design mode, you begin the process of creating a query, form, or report by choosing the table (or tables) you want to use, and then you choose which fields to include. Remember that you can also choose an existing query in place of a table.

In most cases, you can choose as many or as few fields as you like. You are likely to find that some fields in a table (or query) are simply unnecessary. For example, if you want to create a report that summarizes the values of the items in your collection, you don't need to include the field that tracks when you received each item.

**Figure 1-7:**
Access has
wizards like
this one to
help you
create
queries,
forms, or
reports.

After you select the fields you want to use, the next step depends on which task you're performing. If you're creating a query, you may want to specify criteria or a sort order. If you're creating a form or a report, specify the layout of the form or report. If you're using a wizard to create the form or report, you simply choose from a set of predefined layouts. If you're working in design mode, you need to manually place the fields where you want them.

When your query, form, or report is finished, you name and save the final layout. If necessary, you can always return to the query, form, or report in design mode to make additional changes.

It's easy to become confused when you save objects in Access. Even though you use the standard File⇨Save command to save queries, forms, and reports, you aren't saving those items outside of Access. The objects are all saved within the Access database file, and you can view those objects only from within Access.

# Access Add-Ons and Extra Cool Tools

You may not realize this, but quite a few add-ons and extras are available to help you work with Access. These tools aren't built in to Access, but they do offer an awful lot of help when you're developing an Access database. Most of these add-ons come from third-party developers, although Microsoft does offer a few, too.

Just what can you do with these add-on tools? Here's a sampling:

- ✔ **Document the various objects in your Access database** so that you can easily maintain and correct the database.

- ✔ **Compare Access databases to see how they differ.** You'll find this opportunity invaluable for databases that were created by multiple people on multiple computers.

- ✔ **Repair database corruption** so that you can recover from the problems that always seem to occur just before you plan on doing your backup.

- ✔ **Locate and correct problems that slow down your database.**

- ✔ **Create better forms** using options that you can automatically add to the forms without a bunch of programming.

- ✔ **Turn existing paper forms into electronic ones** that you can use to enter data into an Access database without having to learn a whole new way of working.

- ✔ **Share Access reports with someone who doesn't have Access installed on his or her PC.**

- ✔ **Send Access data to a PowerPoint slideshow.**

I'm certain that at least one of these possibilities has you interested. I'm sure you'll find Chapter 20 to be very useful.

# Chapter 2

# Getting Started with Queries

*U*nderstatement alert: Queries are important facets of forms and reports. In fact, queries are so important that we originally debated about whether to include them in this book's title. Suffice it to say that they are important keys that can help you create the types of forms and reports that you want.

You use a query to control how Access actually functions. For example, you can specify which records a form or report will display or which records an action query will modify (action queries are ones that can change data). Queries put an awful lot of truly awesome power into your hands!

You can use several different types of queries in Access. The *select* query is by far the simplest and most common type of query, but Access also has many others. In this chapter, I explain each query type so that you can begin to use each of them in your databases. In addition, I show you how to create queries both by using a wizard and from scratch. Finally, you see how to modify queries so that you get even better results from them.

## Understanding the Types of Queries

Face it — trying to figure out what type of query to use can be downright confusing. Oh sure, the default type of query — the *select* query — is by far the most popular. You use it when you want to select a specific set of records to display in a form or report.

To go beyond the basics with Access, you want to get a little more sophisticated; that's where things can seem about as clear as mud. Well, don't worry. In the next few pages, you can gain a far better understanding of what the various types of queries do and how you can use them. Here's a list of the other (besides Select) commonly used queries:

- **Crosstab queries**

- **Make-table queries**

- **Update queries**

- **Append queries**

- **Delete queries**

- **Parameter queries**

  A parameter query is actually just a normal query that is set up so that it asks for the criteria used in the query before the query is executed. Chapter 15 shows you how to create parameter queries.

- **SQL queries**

  You form a SQL query by using *Structured Query Language* — SQL. Chapter 7 introduces you to SQL queries.

Although you can use the Query Wizard to create queries, you use the Query editor to edit any existing queries — even those created using the Query Wizard. You can also use the Query editor (aka Design View) to create queries from scratch. Whenever you open a query in Design View (by right-clicking from the Navigation Pane, or right-clicking the title bar if the query is already opened, and choosing Design View), you actually open the Query editor.

## *Introducing select queries*

Select queries are the most basic and common type of query. A select query uses the criteria that you specify to choose a subset of the records to display in a Datasheet view. Figure 2-1 shows an example of a simple select query as it appears in the Query editor.

In essence, the select query says to Access, "Show me these files." The specific criteria you set up specify what *these* means. For example, in Figure 2-1, the select query says, "Show only files for customers from Nevada and California."

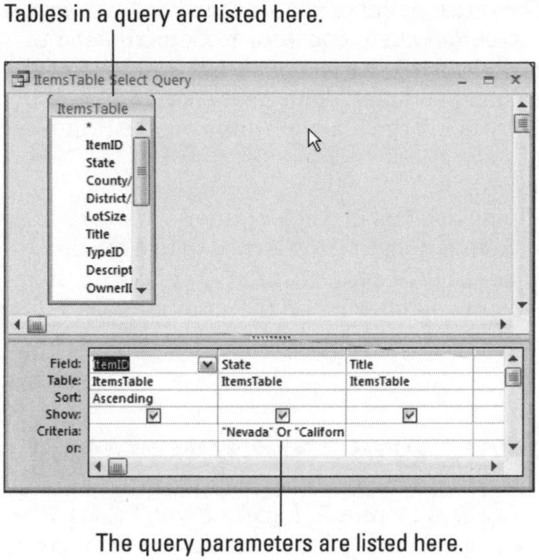

Tables in a query are listed here.

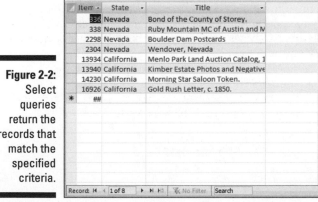

**Figure 2-1:**
This select
query has
two criteria
specified.

The query parameters are listed here.

From there, of course, you can make all sorts of specifications. For example, I included only three fields in this query, ItemID, State, and Title. These are the only fields that will have any effect on the results that are returned by the query. All three fields have their Show check box selected, so all three will appear in the datasheet after the query is run. In this case, the results will be sorted in ascending order according to the values in the ItemID field because I selected the Ascending option in that field's Sort row. Because I have specified Nevada or California as the criteria for the State field, records with states other than those two won't be included in the results. Figure 2-2 shows the result of running the query.

**Figure 2-2:**
Select
queries
return the
records that
match the
specified
criteria.

In addition to simply returning a set of records, as shown in Figure 2-2, the select query can also provide additional information. You can set up a select query to group the records using the values in the first field of the query, and then you can find the sum, average, minimum, maximum, or count of the records in each group by using the many options on the Home section of the Ribbon.

To use any of the grouping options in a select query, it's very important to make sure that you make the field that you want to use for the grouping the first field in the query because Access uses the first field as the primary grouping field. For instance, by filtering on the number 13934 (first field) you can retrieve only those records that are 13934 or greater.

## Getting to know crosstab queries

Crosstab queries (similar in structure to Excel's Pivot Table) are probably the least understood of all of the query types. A crosstab query groups data by using two types of information. One type of information is shown down the rows of the Datasheet view, and the other type of information is viewed across the columns. Each intersecting row and column cell displays a sum, an average, a count, or a similar type of analysis based on the values in the row and column headers.

This explanation actually sounds a lot more complicated than it is, and this is a case in which a picture really is worth a thousand words. Figure 2-3 shows an example of a crosstab query.

**Figure 2-3:** A crosstab query is used to analyze data using rows and columns.

| OWNER | Total Of ID | 0 | 1 | 2 | 3 | 5 | 10 | 15 |
|---|---|---|---|---|---|---|---|---|
|  | 820 | 820 |  |  |  |  |  |  |
| 0 | 402740 | 152711 | 298 |  |  | 1493 | 8340 | 6290 |
| 1 | 1000 |  |  |  |  | 1000 |  |  |
| 3 | 113751 | 62181 |  |  |  | 9166 | 25794 | 8908 |
| 19 | 944 |  |  |  |  |  |  |  |
| 44 | 937 |  |  |  |  |  | 937 |  |
| 75 | 39581 | 11630 |  |  |  |  | 22715 | 2690 |
| 87 | 1176 |  |  |  |  |  | 1176 |  |
| 93 | 3955 |  |  |  |  |  |  | 1308 |
| 111 | 105108 | 17265 |  |  |  | 16771 | 24701 | 12821 |
| 122 | 12627 | 7390 |  |  |  |  | 2867 | 1307 |
| 127 | 6426 | 2575 |  |  |  |  | 1346 | 2505 |
| 168 | 2380 | 1349 |  |  |  |  |  | 1031 |
| 206 | 1359 |  |  |  |  |  |  |  |
| 222 | 4417 | 4417 |  |  |  |  |  |  |
| 231 | 32850 | 5644 |  |  |  |  | 8457 |  |
| 233 | 1472 |  |  |  |  |  |  |  |
| 234 | 3969 | 3969 |  |  |  |  |  |  |
| 243 | 959 |  |  |  |  |  |  | 959 |
| 251 | 2991 | 956 |  |  |  |  | 2035 |  |
| 259 | 1394 | 1394 |  |  |  |  |  |  |

LIVEWINBID_Crosstab1

Record: 1 of 29    No Filter   Search

The first column in Figure 2-3 (Owner) lists the ID numbers of owners for items in an auction database. The second column (Total of ID) lists the total value of all auction items for each owner. The remaining columns to the right list the total values of the items by bid amount. So, for example, Owner Number 3 has a total of $113,751 worth of items listed for auction. Of that amount, $62,181 worth of items have not yet received any bids. Moving farther to the right, $9,166 in bids are in the 0 to $5 category; and $25,794 in bids are in the $5 to $10 category. In the $10 to $15 category, Owner Number 3 has received $8,908 in bids.

## Make-table queries

As the name implies, make-table queries create new tables from data in one or more existing tables. The new table typically contains a specially selected set of information that matches criteria that you specify. For example, you might want to use a make-table query to create a table of items that will be included in a specific sale. Figure 2-4 shows an example of this type of query.

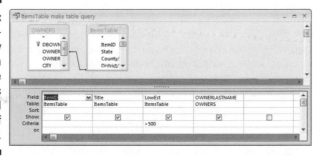

When you create a make-table query, you specify a name for the new table that Access creates when the query is executed. It's very important to make sure that the name you specify is actually a new table name and not the name of an existing table. If you don't create a unique name, Access will delete the original table when you run the make-table query and will replace it with the new table you created. Access warns you if you try to overwrite another table, as shown in Figure 2-5, but it's very easy to click that Yes button and do a lot of damage without giving much thought to what you're doing.

**Figure 2-5:**
A make-
table query
replaces
any existing
table that
has the
name you
specify for
the new
table.

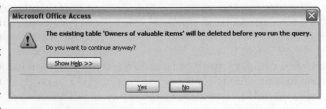

Even though make-table queries are useful for creating new tables, they're not very handy if you want to change information in an existing table or add new information to a table. See the following sections on update queries and append queries if you want query tools that will help you perform such tasks.

## Using update queries

An update query modifies the values in an existing table. You specify how to modify the records by using *expressions.* These expressions are similar to the formulas you create in a spreadsheet and can consist of mathematical expressions, string manipulation expressions, or even specific values — depending on the field type. Figure 2-6 shows an example of an update query that increases the value in the LowEst field by 25 percent (for Auction 35 only).

**Figure 2-6:**
Use an
update
query to
modify
existing
values.

When you create an update query, it's important to understand which table the query will modify. Unlike a make-table query, an update query changes the existing table — the one that is shown in the query. This can be a little confusing because a make-table query uses the records from the listed table (or tables) to create a new table, while an update query actually modifies the listed table.

When you create an update query, you only need to include fields that you want to update and any fields that you use to select the records to update. In Figure 2-6, only two fields were required in the query: The LowEst field is the field that is updated, and the AuctionID field is the field used to limit the update to records for Auction 35.

## Introducing append queries

The aptly named append query adds new records to the end of an existing table. They're pretty similar to make-table queries because both types of queries add records to tables; the difference is that an append query doesn't delete the existing table before adding the records — those changes are made to the original table. Figure 2-7 shows an example of an append query. In this case, I want to add the items that were slated for Auction 36 to Auction 35, so the append query is set up to select records in which the AuctionID value is 36 and then add those records to the existing Auction 35 table.

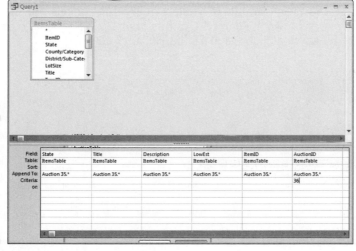

**Figure 2-7:**
You use an append query to add records to an existing table.

TIP

## Using the asterisk to add fields without fuss

To include all of the fields from the source table in the query, you can choose the asterisk (*) at the top of the field list. This shortcut works with any query type, but is probably most useful for select queries and append queries because these two query types typically don't suffer any ill effects from accidentally including extra or unnecessary fields.

If you look carefully at Figure 2-7, you may notice a subtle difference between the append query and the make-table query shown in Figure 2-4. The append query doesn't give you the option to include fields in the query that won't be included in the results of the query. The reason for this is simple, but it might throw you for a loop until you understand it: In an append query, only those fields that already exist in the destination table can actually be used when the query is run. If you include fields that aren't in the destination table, Access simply ignores those fields when it adds the records to the table.

## *Getting to know delete queries*

Delete queries remove selected records from an existing table. These queries are most helpful for trimming out records you no longer need in the table. Figure 2-8 shows an example of a delete query that cancels the effect of the append query shown in Figure 2-7. In this case, I decided that I didn't want to include the Auction 36 items in Auction 35 after all.

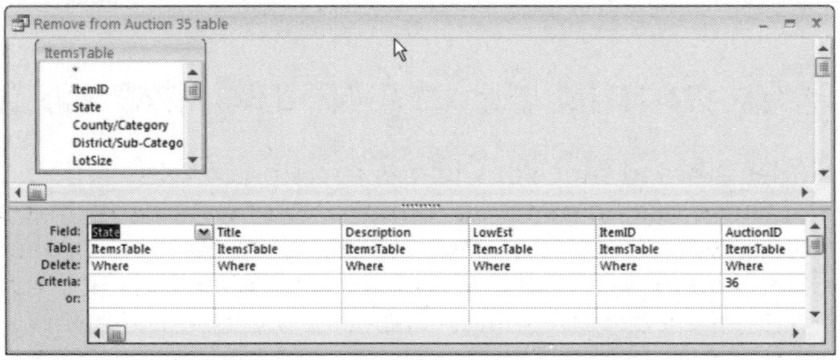

**Figure 2-8:**
You use a delete query to remove records from an existing table.

## Backing up your records just in case

If you're nervous about the permanence of the delete query, you might want to create a make-table query that uses the same criteria you intend to use for your delete query and then run the make-table query before you run your delete query. By doing so, you create a copy of the records that you're going to delete so that you can restore those records with an append query in case you later realize that you messed up in deleting the records and needed them all along.

You might also want to back up (or *archive*) the entire database file after you've made a backup table of the records you're deleting from the main table. Be sure to give your database file backup copy a different name so that you don't accidentally open it instead of your working copy in the future.

# Creating Queries Using a Wizard

You can create queries in two ways. In this section, you see how to use the Query Wizard to build a query. Later in this chapter, I show you how to start from scratch and create a query in Design View.

You can save yourself a lot of grief by creating a copy of your favorite Access database and using the copy to practice creating and running queries. By using the copy, you can experiment with different types of queries as wildly as you want without worrying about destroying any live data. You might want to add something like "practice copy" to the name of the copied file just to be sure you don't get confused.

## Why you should be off to see the wizards

Access includes a broad range of wizards to help you with various tasks. If you're one of those macho users who thinks, "We don't need no stinking wizards," you're welcome to skip over this section, but be forewarned — even the experts (database managers) sometimes find that the wizards can cut down on the drudgery of common Access operations. Letting a wizard do some of the work lets you get more done with less effort (and fewer mistakes).

Some people always seem to have the answers right at their fingertips. Ask one of those people how to do something that he or she is expert on and you'll instantly hear the whole process rattled off to you. Most of us, though, have too many different interests to make it worth our time to become experts on everything. That's one reason why the Access tools called *wizards,* are so useful. When you create a query by using a wizard, the wizard steps you through the process so that you don't have to remember everything up front. As each new piece of information is required, you can depend on the wizard to ask for it. And if, along the way, you need to change something, you can also back the process up, effectively telling the wizard, "Wait. I need to change something a few steps back."

If used correctly, a wizard is a valuable learning tool. For example, when you create a query by using a wizard, the wizard builds the query in the same Query editor you use to create a query in Design View. So if you watch what the wizard does, you can easily discover how to create your own queries from scratch.

## Understanding the limitations of the wizards

The Access Query Wizards may be awfully handy, but they can't do everything. Access doesn't include wizards to build every type of query, so if you want to create a make-table query, an update query, an append query, or a delete query, you'll have to do at least part of the work yourself in Design View.

If you already know what you're doing, using a wizard to create a query can take a bit more time than creating the query manually. In real-world terms, the difference is pretty small . . . but then, some people just prefer to do things for themselves.

## Creating your first query with the wizard

Creating a query with a Query Wizard is pretty easy stuff. You simply answer a few questions, and in a very few moments, you have a new query that's ready to use. It's this easy:

1. **Open the Access database in which you want to create a new query.**

2. **Click the Create tab on the Ribbon.**

    The Ribbon appears as shown in Figure 2-9.

**Figure 2-9:**
Open the
Queries list
to work with
queries.

3. **Click the Query Wizard option.**

   The New Query dialog box appears, as shown in Figure 2-10.

**Figure 2-10:**
Select the
type of
Query
Wizard you
want to
use in the
New Query
dialog box.

4. **Select the type of Query Wizard you want to use and then click OK.**

   For this example, I chose Simple Query Wizard to display the Simple
   Query Wizard dialog box, as shown in Figure 2-11.

**Figure 2-11:**
Use the
Simple
Query
Wizard to
select the
table and
fields for
your query.

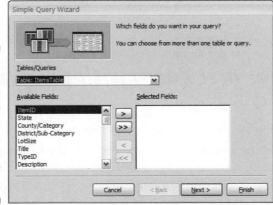

5. **Select the table or query you want to use as the basis (record source) for the query from the drop-down Tables/Queries list box.**

   You must choose the table or query first before you can select the fields because the list of fields depends on the table that you select.

6. **Select the fields you want to include in the finished query (you can choose from multiple Tables/Queries) and then click the > button to move the field from the Available Fields box to the Selected Fields box.**

   You can select as many or as few fields as necessary. If you select fields individually, the fields appear in the Selected Fields list in the order that you added them — an important point to remember if you decide to apply grouping to the records. You can also click the >> button to add all of the fields to the query. You can use the left-pointing arrows to remove fields you don't need.

7. **Click the Next button to display the options shown in Figure 2-12.**

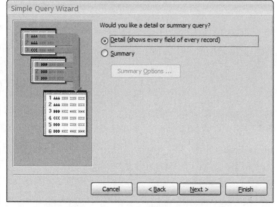

**Figure 2-12:** Choose the detail or summary option for your query.

8. **Select the Detail option to show all of the records in the result or Summary to show just the summarization of the results.**

   If you choose Summary, you must also click the Summary Options button and then select the types of summary values you want to see. For this example, select Detail.

9. **Click the Next button to display the options shown in Figure 2-13.**

10. **Enter a name for your query in the text box near the top of the dialog box.**

    Generally, it's a good idea to enter a descriptive title so that you can easily identify the query later.

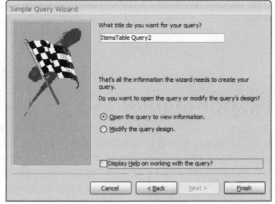

**Figure 2-13:**
Enter a
name for the
query and
choose an
option for
opening the
query.

11. **Choose whether you want to open the query to view the results or to modify the query in the Query editor and select the corresponding radio button.**

12. **Click the Finish button to close the wizard and create your query.**

Figure 2-14 shows the query I created using the selections in this example.

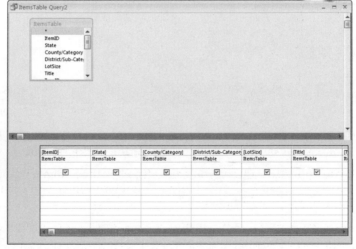

**Figure 2-14:**
The finished
query as it
appears in
the Query
editor.

After you finish creating the query, you can view the results of the query by clicking the Run button (it looks like a fat exclamation point) on the Access

Ribbon. In this case, the results probably won't seem like much because you haven't yet specified any criteria for selecting specific records. You can find out how to modify your query to specify criteria in the section, "Modifying Queries for Better Results," later in this chapter.

# Creating Queries in Design View

As handy as the Query Wizards may be, you eventually do have to use Design View to create truly effective queries. The reason for this is pretty straightforward — you need to work in the Query editor (otherwise known as Query Design View) in order to specify criteria. Until you specify criteria, your queries don't really do any record selection; they return all of the records from the source table.

## Getting to know the Design View

You have already seen most of the important elements that you use in Design View, but now it's time for a more formal introduction. Figure 2-15 identifies the Query Design View objects that you will use most often.

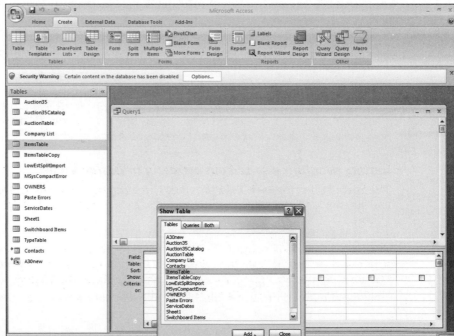

**Figure 2-15:**
You use the Query editor to create queries in Design View.

The Query editor window has two panes that you use to build a query. The upper pane shows any tables that you have added to the query. The lower pane shows any fields you are using in the query along with any parameters you have specified. As Figure 2-15 shows, the Query editor starts out empty after you select the Create section of the Ribbon, and then Query Design (you are in Design View at this time). You use the Show Table dialog box to add tables to the Query editor so that you can use the fields from those tables in the query.

For the sake of simplicity, the query examples in this chapter use fields from a single table. Chapter 5 shows you how to use multiple tables in queries.

### Getting your fields straight in Design View

When you add fields from a table to one of the columns in the lower pane of the Query editor, the fields appear in the same order that you placed them. Although the order of the fields isn't really important for many queries, it becomes important when you select a sort order or when you summarize the results by grouping. Access sorts and groups fields from left to right. So, for example, if you place a State field first with a City field second and then select an ascending sort order for each field, your records will be sorted by state and then by city within each state. But if you place the City field first and the State field second, results would be sorted by city and then by state — probably not a very useful sort order in most cases.

You can add fields to the columns by using any of several different methods:

 ✔ Drag-and-drop fields from a table in the upper pane of the Query editor.

 ✔ Click the down arrow on the right side of the Field list box to display a list of the fields and then select the fields you want.

 ✔ If you like to do things the hard way, type the field name in the box. Even if you choose this method, Access tries to help by filling in the name that matches what you're typing. When you have added a field name, Access automatically enters the table name for you.

### Getting everything sorted out correctly in Design View

The Sort list box for each field provides three options: Ascending, Descending, and Not Sorted (you will need to click inside the Sort box to obtain a down arrow).

The Show check box controls the display of the field in the final results. You might want to include a field in the query for sorting or grouping purposes but not have the field appear in the final results (Datasheet View). If so, simply deselect the Show check box for that field.

### *Getting your criteria set in Design View*

The Criteria boxes let you specify conditions for selecting records. The conditions you enter must be appropriate for the field type. For example, if you want to specify a numeric value such as >500 to select only those records in which the field value is greater than 500, the field where you enter the criteria must be one of the numeric field types. You can enter additional conditions in the Or boxes. Access then selects records that match any of the criteria you specify.

# Creating an example query in Design View

Creating a query in Design View is pretty easy, but it does require just a bit more thinking about the process because you don't have the wizard prompting you to make the correct choices. Here's how to create a simple select query in Design View:

1. **Open the Access database in which you want to create a new query.**

2. **Click the Create tab on the Ribbon.**

3. **Click Query Design.**

   The Query editor and the Show Table dialog box (shown in Figure 2-16) both appear.

**Figure 2-16:**
Use the Show Table dialog box to select the tables to use in your query.

4. **Select the tables you want to use in your query and click the Add button.**

   You can either hold down the Shift key to select multiple tables or choose them one-by-one.

5. **Click the Close button to close the Show Table dialog box so that you can work in the Query editor.**

   If you close prematurely, choose Show Table from Query Setup in the Design section of the Ribbon to add more tables.

6. **Add fields to the lower pane of the Query editor.**

   You can drag and drop them or choose them from the drop-down Field list box.

7. **Optionally, choose a sort order for any of the fields.**

8. **Leave the Show check box selected for any fields you want to display in the results and deselect it for any fields you don't want to see in the results.**

9. **Enter any criteria you want to use to select the records to include in the results.**

10. **Repeat Steps 6 through 9 until you have added all of the fields and criteria that you want to include.**

    Figure 2-17 shows the completed query I created for this example.

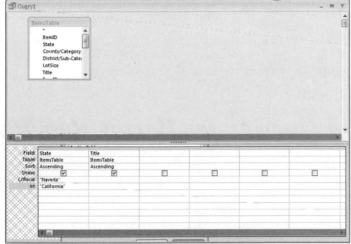

**Figure 2-17:** The completed query is now ready to run.

11. **Click the Run button to run the query.**

    Figure 2-18 shows the results of running the query shown in Figure 2-17.

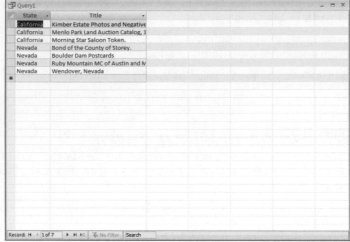

**Figure 2-18:** The completed query displays the results when it is run.

12. **If you want to save your query for future use, click the Save button.**

The Save As dialog box appears; enter a filename and click OK to save the query. If you don't save the query, Access prompts you to do so when you attempt to close the query.

The query shown in this example is very simple, but you'll probably discover that most of the queries you create will be quite simple. In later chapters, you find out how to create queries that do a whole lot more.

# Modifying Queries for Better Results

As you work with queries, you may find that the queries you create could use a bit of fine-tuning. Maybe you want to pare down the results so you don't have to wade through so many records, or maybe you've discovered that it really is a pain to slog through a whole bunch of unsorted data. Whatever the reason, being able to modify existing queries, rather than starting from scratch, can be a real time saver.

When you're experimenting with modifying queries, be sure to heed any warning messages that Access displays when you attempt to run the modified query. Remember that *select* queries and *crosstab* queries are always safe because they don't modify any of your data, but the other types of queries can modify data.

## Deleting a query

Sometimes, the easiest, safest, and smartest thing to do with a query is to get rid of it entirely and start over. If something has gone wrong and you're not sure what it is, go ahead and delete the query. Just highlight it in the list of queries and press Delete.

## Modifying an existing query

No matter which method you used to create a query, you really have only one option for modifying an existing query. That option is to open the query in Design View and make your changes in the Query editor. Access doesn't offer any wizards to help you modify existing queries.

To open an existing query in Design View, select the query in the database window, right-click it, and then choose Design View. When you open a query this way, the Query editor looks exactly the way it does when you're creating a query in Design View. That is, there aren't separate creating and editing modes to confuse you.

In some cases, you may find that fields you added to a query don't appear in the Query editor when you edit the query. The reason for the mysterious disappearing fields can't be attributed to aliens or ghosts; it's simply that Access drops any unused fields when you save a query. If you had fields in the query that didn't serve any purpose in the query, those fields are gone when you reopen the query.

After you open the query in Design View, you can click the Show Table button on the Ribbon. The Show Table dialog box appears so that you can add additional tables to the query. You can also add additional fields to the query by using the same methods you use when you're first creating a query in Design View. Likewise, you can add or modify any of the query criteria in exactly the same way you do when creating a query.

## Rearranging and deleting fields in a query

The one query-editing task that you might find a little confusing at first is rearranging the fields in the query. You can change the order of the fields by

 - ✔ **Dragging and dropping new fields:** To drag and drop a field, you need to drag the very small gray bar that's just above the Field row. When you drag and drop a field onto the column of an existing field, the existing field and any fields to its right shift to the right so that the new field is inserted before the existing field.

## Some examples of query modifications

Just in case you need a few ideas about the types of query modifications you might want to try, consider these options:

✔ Add a sort order to make it easier to understand the data that appears when you run the query.

✔ Specify some criteria to limit the amount of data that results from the query.

✔ Rearrange the columns in the query to produce more logical groupings when you sort on more than one field.

✔ Add additional fields to the query to show data that didn't appear in the original query.

✔ Simplify your query by removing fields that don't add any value to the results.

✔ If you have already created table relationships, add fields from the related tables to the query.

✔ Change the type of query by selecting a different type from the Ribbon options.

✔ **Clicking the Field box of a column and selecting a different field for the column.**

✔ **Deleting existing fields:** To delete a field, position the mouse pointer at the top of the field's column just above the Field row and then click when the pointer becomes a solid black down arrow. Choose the appropriate Delete button from the Ribbon or press the Delete key to remove the field. The remaining fields to the right shift to the left to fill the empty column.

# Chapter 3

# Creating Simple Forms

• • • • • • • • • • • • • • • • • • • • • • • • • • • • • • • • • • • • • • • • • •

• • • • • • • • • • • • • • • • • • • • • • • • • • • • • • • • • • • • • • • • • •

**Y**ou could argue that forms are an unnecessary luxury because you can, after all, enter information into a database table directly. To make that argument, though, you'd have to ignore the fact that if it weren't for forms, most people would probably think of databases as some strange and difficult application best left to some guys stuck away in a climate-controlled room with a bunch of mainframe computers. Forms really give PC database applications like Access their friendly face.

In this chapter, you see how to create simple Access forms by using both the Form Wizard and Design View. After you master the basics, I show you how to improve the forms that you've created by using some simple techniques to improve the layout of your forms and also to make your forms a bit more compact for easier use.

## Creating Forms with the Help of a Wizard

Just as it does with queries, Access provides you with two primary methods of creating forms: You can use a Form Wizard, or you can create forms from scratch in Design View. In addition, of course, you can use a combination of the two methods by starting your form in a wizard and then using Design View to fine-tune it.

Compared with creating a query, creating a form in Access is somewhat complicated. (See Chapter 2 for more information about creating queries.) The reason for this added complexity is that for a form, you have additional considerations that you don't have with queries. These important points make form design a bit more complex than query design:

✔ A form might be used by someone who isn't familiar with the database, so you need to provide visual clues regarding the purpose of the form and the layout of the fields.

✔ Forms are often used for data input, so you may need to go to greater lengths to adjust the order in which the fields appear on the form. Making sure that field order matches the data source makes data entry faster and reduces errors. It's certainly preferred over making users jump around the form to enter data in an inconvenient order.

✔ Field names that are convenient in a table often look strange in a form. You might need to edit the field labels to make them more understandable for the humans who will use the form. For example, "Low Estimate" is more readable and obvious than "LowEst."

✔ People are creatures of habit. Because most users are accustomed to seeing certain layouts, such as name, address, and city stacked vertically, you may throw users off if you use an unfamiliar layout, such as name, address, and city spread horizontally across the form or stacked vertically, but out of order, such as city, address, name.

These few points aren't the only ones to consider, but they do highlight some of the reasons why creating forms takes a bit of conscious effort to do right.

Forms can be based on tables or on queries (or both). This is also true of queries and reports, of course. The examples in this chapter use forms that are based on tables, but that's simply to focus on the task at hand without the additional complication of first creating an appropriate query.

## Meeting the Form Wizard

The Access Form Wizard is similar to the Access Query Wizard. You begin using the wizard by selecting the tables or queries that you want to use as the basis for your new form or query, and then you choose which fields you want to include (click More Forms on the Ribbon to activate the Form Wizard). In the dialog box that appears (see Figure 3-1), you have several options for form layout and appearance.

The wizard enables you to make some simple choices regarding how the basic form is built, although you'll probably still want to use Design View to touch up the form in most cases.

The Form Wizard creates forms by using fields from tables or queries. To use the Form Wizard, you simply choose it from the Ribbon and select the tables or queries to use as the basis for the form. As Figure 3-2 shows, the resulting form isn't going to win any awards for appearance (notice that many of the labels are cut off), but this is certainly the easiest method for creating a quick-and-dirty form.

**Figure 3-1:**
The Form
Wizard
offers
several
choices.

For all their benefits, wizards have their downsides. However, they give you an idea of what a particular type of form looks like in the least number of clicks.

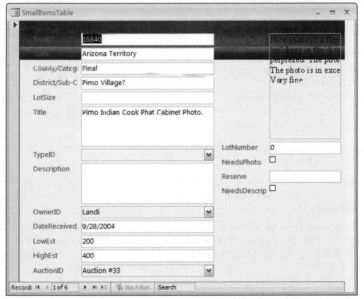

**Figure 3-2:**
This form
was created
with the
Form
Wizard.

# *Befriending the Form Wizard*

In the following example, I show you how to create a simple form with the standard Form Wizard.

The following example uses a single table to keep the example easy to understand. Chapter 10 shows you how to build forms that use multiple tables.

Follow these steps to create a simple form with the Access Form Wizard:

1. **Open the Access database that contains the table you want to use as the source for the new form.**

2. **In the Create section of the Ribbon, click More Forms (see Figure 3-3).**

   The forms list appears.

3. **Click Form Wizard.**

**Figure 3-3:**
Access the
Forms
Wizard from
the Ribbon.

4. **For a form using a single table or query, follow these steps (for multiple tables or queries, repeat as necessary):**

   *a. Select the table or query you want to use as the basis for your form from the Tables/Queries/Forms/Objects list box on the left.*

   You must choose the table or query before you can select the fields.

   *b. Select the fields in the order you want them to appear in the form, clicking the > button after you select each field to move it from the Available Fields list to the Selected fields list.*

   You can click the >> button to move all remaining fields to the Selected Fields list.

   Repeat Step 4 if you want to add more tables or queries to the form.

5. **Click Next.**

   The form layout section of the Form Wizard, shown in Figure 3-4, appears.

   As you select different options, a preview of the selected layout option appears along the left side of the dialog box. The preview is a generalized preview, not an exact representation of how your form will actually appear.

6. **Choose the layout you want to use for your form and click Next (clicking on the radio buttons shows how each option will appear).**

   The style section of the Form Wizard appears, as shown in Figure 3-5.

   Once again, the preview shows a generalized view that changes as you select different options.

7. **Choose the style option that you want to use for your form and click Next.**

   The final section of the Form Wizard appears, as shown in Figure 3-6.

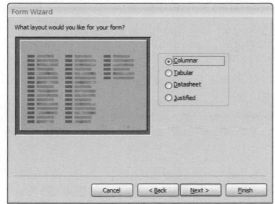

**Figure 3-4:**
Select the
layout for
your form.

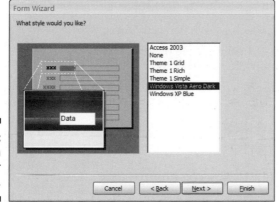

**Figure 3-5:**
Choose a
style for
your form.

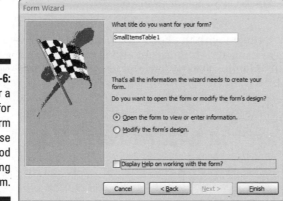

**Figure 3-6:**
Enter a
name for
your form
and choose
the method
of opening
the form.

8. **Enter a descriptive name for your form.**

    It's a good idea to use a name that is easy to remember and is related to the purpose of the form. For example, I used *SmallItemsTable1* to indicate that the form is linked to a specific table.

9. **Leave the default method for opening the form selected and click Finish.**

    The default option is Open Form to View or Enter Information. Your saved form looks a little something like the one shown in Figure 3-7.

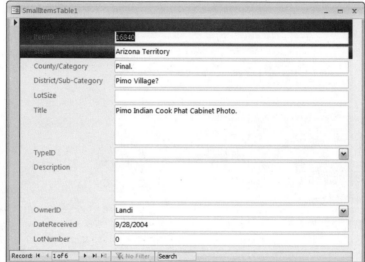

**Figure 3-7:**
The completed form is now ready to use.

Your form may look significantly different than the one shown in Figure 3-7, of course.

You might want to experiment with the Form Wizard by creating several variations of the same form using different layout and style options. The layout options can have quite an impact on how useful your form is for different purposes.

## *Knowing what the wizard can't do*

The Access Form Wizard is easy to use, but it doesn't offer all the options you might find useful. Here are a few of the things you simply can't do with the Form Wizard:

- ✔ The Form Wizard always adds labels to every field on the form; there's no option to leave off the labels you don't want or need.

- ✔ Speaking of labels, the Form Wizard always uses the field names from the tables or queries as labels. There's no option to change the staid Last_ Name to Put Yer Name Here (or whatever else suits your fancy).

- ✔ Although the Form Wizard gives you limited control over the form layout, it doesn't allow you to have absolute control. The Address field may *not* sit directly under the Name field, even though that's how you envisioned it in your mind's eye.

- ✔ If you want to create a hot pink form with fluorescent green labels, don't look to the Form Wizard. Come to think of it, don't look to me for help with that one, either!

Even though the Form Wizard won't handle these tasks on its own, Access does give you the opportunity to customize the form in Design View after the wizard finishes its work.

# Building Forms the Hard Way: Using Design View

Creating your first Access form from scratch in Design View can seem a bit daunting. When you select this option, you're faced with a blank grid, a Ribbon full of strange-looking icons above it, and no clue about what to do next. Figure 3-8 shows you what I mean.

## Introducing Design View tools

Before you begin using the Form Design View, have a quick look at the various icons that you'll encounter on the Ribbon, shown in Figure 3-9, and compare them to the yellow Cheat Sheet inside the front cover.

Here's a brief description of the tools:

- ✔ **Select Objects:** Click this button to use the mouse pointer to select objects that you've added to a form.

- ✔ **Control Wizards:** Click this button to enable wizards that help you add certain types of objects such as combo boxes and command buttons to your forms. Both combo boxes and command buttons are explained elsewhere in this list.

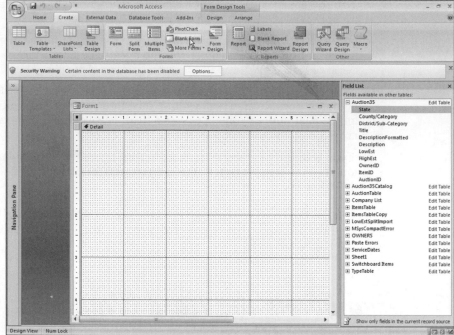

**Figure 3-8:**
Starting a
new form in
Design View
presents
you with a
whole
bunch of
unfamiliar
tools.

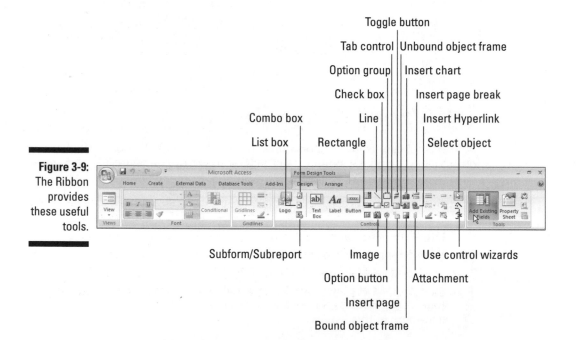

**Figure 3-9:**
The Ribbon
provides
these useful
tools.

✔ **Label:** Click this button to add a simple text label anywhere on your form.

✔ **Text Box:** Click this button to add a text box to the form. Unlike a label, a text box can be set to change the information it displays when the form is used. Text boxes actually have two parts — a label and the box where a user can enter information.

✔ **Option Group:** Click this button to create a set of related option buttons (such as Taxable and Tax Exempt). The buttons function as a group, and you can select only one option at a time. For example, you can choose Taxable or Tax Exempt for an order, but not both.

✔ **Toggle Button:** Click this button to add a button that has two states — up for off and down for on. For example, up for Taxable and down for Non-Taxable.

✔ **Option Button:** Click this button to add option buttons that work like a toggle button or a check box. Generally, you use option buttons in an option group to restrict a user from selecting more than one item in a group.

✔ **Check Box:** Click this button to add an item that can be selected or deselected independent of any other options.

✔ **Combo Box:** Click this button to add a box in which the user can select from a list of options or enter a new value. For example, you might have a list of books by your favorite author as items to suggest but also allow the user to enter the name of a book that isn't on the list.

✔ **List Box:** Click this button to create a list box from which a user can select a set of pre-existing values. A list box looks something like a combo box but doesn't allow the user to enter new values.

✔ **Command Button (or just plain Button):** Click this button to add a button that executes a macro or a VBA (Visual Basic for Applications) procedure.

✔ **Image:** Click this button to add a digital image (such as a company logo) to the form.

✔ **Unbound Object Frame:** Click this button to add objects such as text or images that don't change when moving between records.

✔ **Bound Object Frame:** Click this button to add objects that change when the information in the database changes — such as images that are stored in fields in the table.

✔ **Page Break:** Click this button to create multipage forms when you have too many objects to display on a single page.

✔ **Tab Control:** Click this button to create a form with two or more tabs that group related objects.

- ✓ **Subform/Subreport:** Click this button to add a subform so that the user can see records from a related table — such as the individual line items on an order.

- ✓ **Line:** Click this button to add lines to the form to differentiate between different groups of objects on the form.

- ✓ **Rectangle:** Click this button to draw a rectangle on the form so that users can see how objects are related.

- ✓ **And more:** Linger over each tool on the Ribbon to get a quick definition.

Okay, so you're probably scratching your head and wondering if you really have to know how to use all these tools before you can start creating your own forms in Design View. The short-and-sweet answer is no. Chapter 9 gives you a lot more information about using controls on your forms.

## Starting a form in Design View

Before you begin your first form in Design View, you have to understand the two different ways to open the Form Design View. When you look at the Forms list in the Create tab on the Ribbon, you are given a Form Design option. Clicking this item opens the Form Design View, but using this method presents you with a blank form that is not connected to any of your tables or queries. When you're starting out designing forms, you may prefer to open Design View by using a method that actually connects your form to a table or query. To use this second, easier method, follow these steps:

1. **Open the Access database to which you want to add a new form.**

2. **Click the Create tab on the Ribbon.**

   A list of forms appears.

3. **Select the Form Design icon.**

4. **Select the table or query you want to use as the source for the form from the list box on the left side of the screen.**

5. **Click the Add Existing Fields button in the Design Ribbon to produce the Field List (see Figure 3-10).**

 If the Field List is in your way, you can drag it to the right or click it off while you work. You can't dock the Field List, but unless your screen resolution is set quite small or your form is very large, you'll probably be able to find an out-of-the-way place for it.

**Figure 3-10:**
The field list
includes all
the fields
from the
source table
or query.

Field List ✕

Fields available in other tables:

⊟ AuctionTable
    AuctionID
    AuctionName
    AuctionDate
⊟ ItemsTable
    ItemID
    State
    County/Category
    District/Sub-Category
    LotSize
    Title
    TypeID
    Description
    OwnerID
    DateReceived
    LowEst
    HighEst
    AuctionID
    DescriptionFormatted
    LotNumber
    NeedsPhoto
    Reserve
    NeedsDescription
⊞ LIVEWINBID
⊞ OWNERS
⊞ Owners of valuable items
⊞ SmallItemsTable
⊞ Switchboard Items
⊞ TypeTable

Click to show only fields in the current record source

# Associating a table to your form in Design View

As I mention earlier, if you choose the Form Design option in the Forms section, you start out with a blank form that isn't connected to any table or query. In order for your new form to be of much use, you need to make that connection yourself; otherwise, you won't be able to add any fields to the forms.

To manually connect a form with a table or a query, follow these steps:

1. **Right-click the blank form when it is displayed in Design View to display the pop-up menu shown in Figure 3-11.**

2. **Select the Properties option.**

    The Form Properties dialog box for the form appears. Alternatively, you can just click the Properties Sheet button on the Ribbon to display this dialog box.

3. **Click the Data tab or the All tab.**

    Either option enables you to choose a table or query to associate with the form.

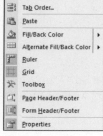

**Figure 3-11:**
Right-click
the form to
display this
context
menu.

4. **Click the down arrow to the right of the Record Source box to display the list of tables and queries.**

5. **Select the table or query that you want to use as the source for the form, as shown in Figure 3-12.**

**Figure 3-12:**
Choose the
record
source for
the form
from the
Form
Properties
dialog box.

6. **Close the Property Sheet.**

The Form Properties dialog box closes, but the Field List remains visible.

Although forms typically aren't very useful unless they're connected to a table or query, you can use forms that aren't connected to a table or query to display command buttons that run macros or VBA procedures. Chapter 17 provides additional information on these options.

If the Field List seems to be missing in action, click the Add Existing Fields button on the Design section of the Ribbon. Figure 3-13 identifies some of the items on the Form Design Ribbon in case you need a bit of review.

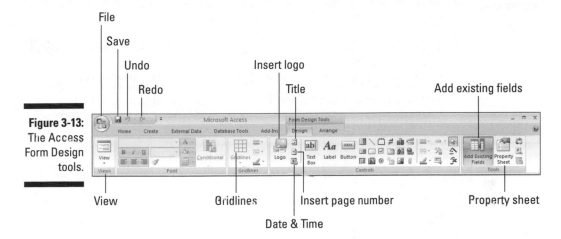

**Figure 3-13:** The Access Form Design tools.

## Adding fields to the form

After your form is connected to a table or a query, you can add fields from the table or query to the form. This is where can let your inner artist out (but it's also where you'll probably find that laying out forms so that they look good is a bit harder than you thought).

Access provides two options to help you lay out your forms. First, make certain that the grid is visible. It should be if you selected Form Design, but you can add a grid by clicking Gridlines on the Design Ribbon. Then make certain that the Snap to Grid option is checked on the Arrange Ribbon. To add a field to your form, follow these steps:

1. **Drag the field in the Field List into place on the form (see Figure 3-14).**

   Keep your fields some distance from the left edge of the form to leave room for the field labels. If you drop a field too close to the left edge, the label will be all scrunched together and will probably be unreadable.

If you get too close to the edge, delete the field from the form and try again instead of trying to fix the label. Trust me; I know from experience that this is the easier option (you can move the label while it still has a handle, but that disappears when you move to the next field).

Don't get too hung up on trying to precisely align the fields as you're adding them to the form. See "Aligning objects on a form," later in this chapter, for more information about making Access straighten things up a bit for you.

2. **To preview how your form will look when it's in use, click the View button on the top left side of the Access Form Design Ribbon.**

3. **To close the preview and return to Design View, click the button again and choose Design View.**

4. **Click the Save button or choose File⇨Save to save your work.**

   The first time you save a new form, you'll be asked to name the form (use a descriptive name). You can also press Ctrl+S to save the form.

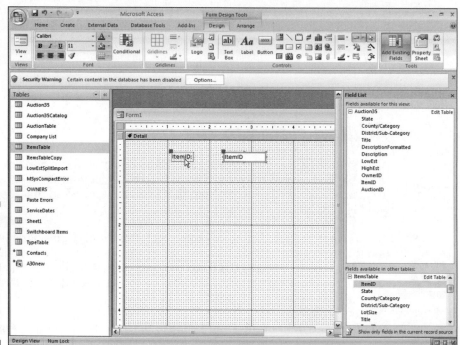

**Figure 3-14:** Add fields to the form by dragging and dropping them onto the form.

# Modifying Forms You've Created

You'll probably find that your first efforts at creating forms in Design View leave a bit to be desired. It can be somewhat difficult to get the fields to line up evenly even if you have the grid displayed and the Snap to Grid option active. In the following sections, you see how to make your forms look like they were designed by a pro.

If you've been previewing your work as described in the previous section, "Adding fields to the form," don't forget to switch back to Design View to make any further modifications.

Figure 3-15 shows a sample form that could definitely use some improvement. The fields don't line up with each other, the sizes of the fields are inconsistent, the vertical spacing varies considerably, and the form is much larger than it really needs to be. Despite all these problems, the form is still usable, but I don't think I'd want anyone to know that I created it.

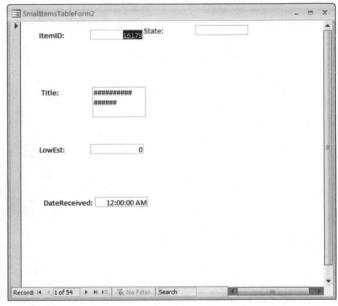

**Figure 3-15:** This form could really use some help in the appearance department!

You can do a number of things to improve a form like the one shown in Figure 3-15. You won't need to do all of them to every form you create, but you eventually need to know how to use all the various options that are available.

Access provides several commands to help you improve the appearance of your forms. Each of the commands is conveniently located in the Format section of the Property Sheet, as shown in Figure 3-16. In the following sections we look at each of these commands in turn.

## *Aligning objects on a form*

The Format list (see Figure 3-17) enables you to precisely align selected objects to each other or to the grid. No matter how sloppy you might have been when dropping fields onto your form, the alignment commands can make quite a difference.

Even though you may think you're aligning objects, Access really aligns labels. In other words, adjusting alignment alone may not perfect an unflattering form.

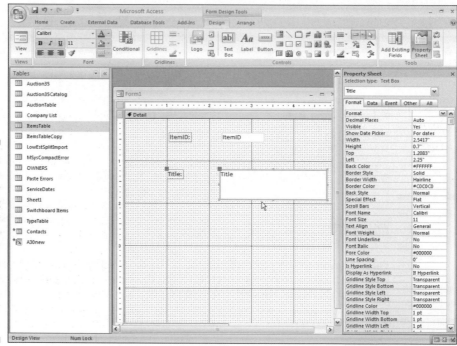

**Figure 3-16:** The Property Sheet provides you with the options you need to improve the appearance of your forms.

| Property Sheet | ✕ |
| --- | --- |
| Selection type: Text Box | |

Title ▾

| Format | Data | Event | Other | All |

| Format | |
| --- | --- |
| Decimal Places | Auto |
| Visible | Yes |
| Display When | Always |
| Scroll Bars | Vertical |
| Can Grow | No |
| Can Shrink | No |
| Left | 2.375" |
| Top | 1.25" |
| Width | 2.5833" |
| Height | 0.7" |
| Back Style | Normal |
| Back Color | #FFFFFF |
| Special Effect | Flat |
| Border Style | Solid |
| Border Color | #C0C0C0 |
| Border Width | Hairline |
| Fore Color | #000000 |
| Font Name | Calibri |
| Font Size | 11 |
| Font Weight | Normal |
| Font Italic | No |
| Font Underline | No |
| Text Align | General |
| Reading Order | Context |
| Keyboard Language | System |
| Scroll Bar Align | System |
| Numeral Shapes | System |
| Left Margin | 0" |
| Top Margin | 0" |
| Right Margin | 0" |
| Bottom Margin | 0" |
| Line Spacing | 0" |

**Figure 3-17:**
The Format list helps you to make objects line up with each other.

Before you use any of the alignment commands, be sure to select the objects that you want to align. You can drag a selection box around the objects to select them or you can hold down the Shift key while you click each object that you want to select. If you continue to hold down Shift and click a selected object, you deselect it. If you have the rulers visible, you can also click in a ruler to select all objects in a path going straight out from the ruler.

Things can get a bit tricky when you're working on cleaning up a poor form layout. For example, Figure 3-18 shows the result of selecting the four fields on the left side of the form and then right-clicking and choosing Align⇨Left.

One solution to the poor alignment of the data entry boxes might be to Shift-click each of those boxes and then align the boxes independently of the field labels. In this case, though, the real answer is to adjust the size of the fields and of the data entry boxes first, and then worry about alignment after the sizes are consistent. (See the following section, "Setting consistent sizes.")

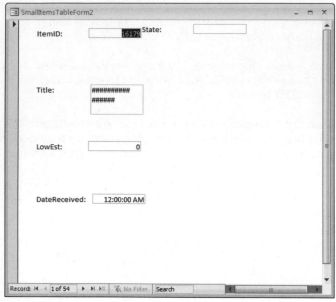

**Figure 3-18:**
The Align⇨
Left
command
aligned the
labels but
didn't really
help the
appearance
very much.

## Setting consistent sizes

The Align⇨Size submenu shown in Figure 3-19 helps you set consistent sizes for a group of selected objects. As mentioned in the previous section, "Aligning objects on a form," it's often best to set the sizes of the field objects before you attempt to align them — even though the Align menu appears before the Size menu.

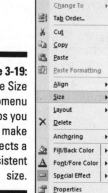

**Figure 3-19:**
The Size
submenu
helps you
make
objects a
consistent
size.

In the example form (refer to Figure 3-18), the different widths for the data entry boxes give the form a pretty inconsistent look. No amount of alignment can disguise the fact that the boxes are different sizes.

To repair this type of inconsistency in your own forms, select all the desired objects and choose Size⇨To Widest. Voilà! Each of the boxes is now the same width as the widest box.

You also have the option of making the boxes the same height, but you may want to resist that urge. One field (`Title`, for example) may need additional room for a user to type. (At least that's the case in Figure 3-18.)

After adjusting the size of the boxes, you can align the right side of the data entry boxes and align the two top fields along their top edge. Figure 3-20 shows the results.

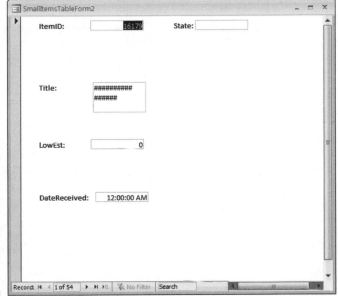

**Figure 3-20:**
A combination of consistent sizing and alignment greatly improves this form.

# Spacing horizontally and vertically

This is where you bring back the Property Sheet. When you select the fields on your form, the Property Sheet gives you a Format List. The Arrange Ribbon also gives you some options you might want to explore.

## Using the Align and Size commands together

The Align and Size commands really go together, which means that you may have to go back and forth a few times between the commands before you get the results you really want. Be patient and you'll soon develop a workflow that gives you the results you want with the least amount of effort. And then you'll be ready for even more complicated layout issues, like fixing spacing between objects. See "Spacing horizontally and vertically," elsewhere in this chapter.

Generally speaking, the best technique when dealing with spacing is to start out with all the fields equally spaced both vertically and horizontally before you do anything else.

Figure 3-21 shows the results of using the Property Sheet; I think the form looks much better. Keep in mind that you can also use Anchoring (linking controls and sections) from the Arrange Ribbon or simply right-clicking a selected object or objects to receive the Anchoring option.

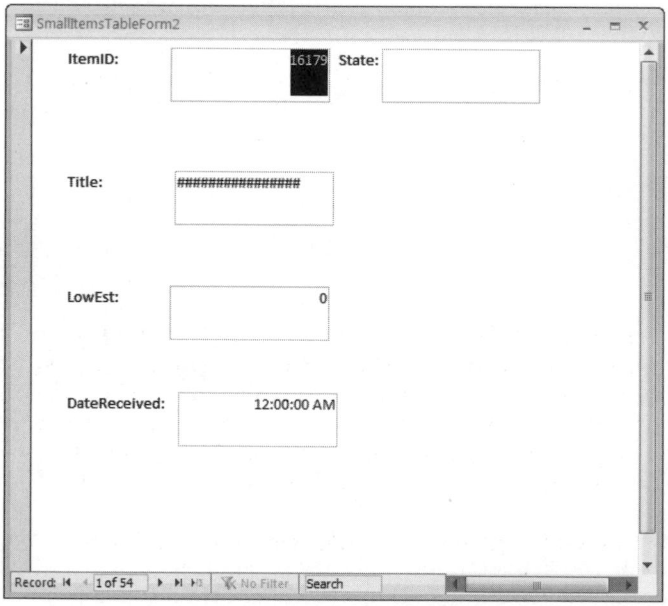

**Figure 3-21:**
Adjusting the spacing of the fields gives the form a consistent and professional look.

## Shrinking a big form down to size

Adjusting the spacing and size of a form's fields makes a much better-looking form, but there may still be some — ahem — *room* for improvement. Currently the form takes up more room on the screen than necessary, but you can easily fix this ailment by shrinking the form to a size that just accommodates the fields that appear on the form. Doing so is a two-step process because two different things control the size of the finished form.

To begin shrinking your form, switch to Design View by right-clicking the title bar and then drag the lower-right corner of the gray box (inside the Form window) that appears behind the fields, as shown in Figure 3-22. You want to make this area as small as possible without cutting off any part of any of the fields on the form.

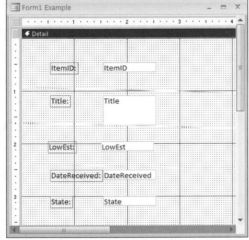

**Figure 3-22:**
Resize the
gray box
inside
the Form
window to
just fit the
fields on
the form.

After you resize the gray box, drag the lower-right corner of the Form window up and to the left until you've reduced the size as much as you can without cutting off the fields. (The Form window is the entire window where the form appears and has the title bar that says Form 1: Example in Figure 3-22.) You'll have to switch between Form view and Design View several times to check your results.

Figure 3-23 shows the final result of shrinking the form.

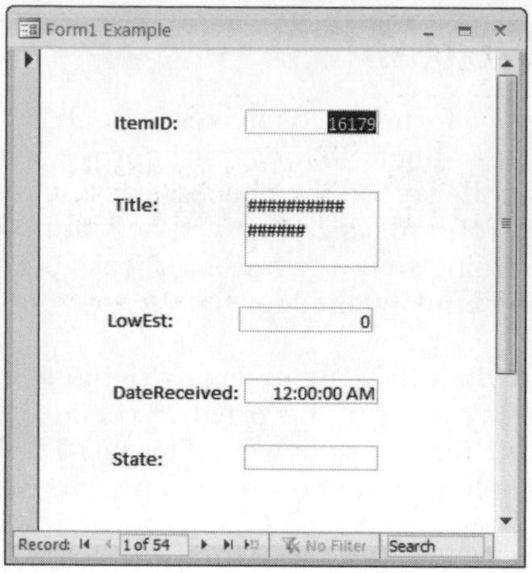

Form1 Example                                    _ □ X

ItemID:                                    16179

Title:              ##########
                    ######

LowEst:                              0

DateReceived:       12:00:00 AM

State:

Record: I◄  ◄  1 of 54  ►  ►I ►⊡   No Filter   Search

**Figure 3-23:**
The final
form is
much tighter
and takes
up less
room on the
screen.

You could, of course, make two shorter columns of fields. Even so, the finished form certainly looks a lot better than the form I started out with.

Don't hesitate to switch between Form view, Layout view, and Design View and explore the possibilities.

# Chapter 4

# Building Basic Reports

*R*eports are the real icing on the cake when it comes to getting useful information from a database. They provide information in a format that almost anyone can understand, and because most reports are designed for printing, reports also give your data an element of portability. By using Access reports, you can present a membership summary at your organization's board meeting, or you can show your banker that your business really is making money.

Building reports is certainly a more complex project than creating either queries or forms (see Chapters 2 and 3). Reports typically include page numbers, the date and time the report was printed, record grouping, and summaries, all of which make creating a report a task that requires a bit more planning. In this chapter, I show you how to build basic reports so that you have a good foundation on which to build in the upcoming chapters.

## Getting to Know the Types of Access Reports

You probably don't need me to tell you that there are many different uses for Access reports. Fortunately, all these different purposes can be fulfilled by a relatively small number of report types. As a result, you really need to master only a few types of reports in order to create virtually any report that Access can produce.

Even though Access lets you create only a few different basic types of reports, that doesn't mean that they all look the same. Indeed, you can create a huge number of variations by making very minor changes. The important point to remember is that your reports should fulfill your needs; feel free to customize them.

## Introducing simple reports

The simplest type of Access report just shows basic information as it appears in a table. Figure 4-1 shows an example of this type of simple report.

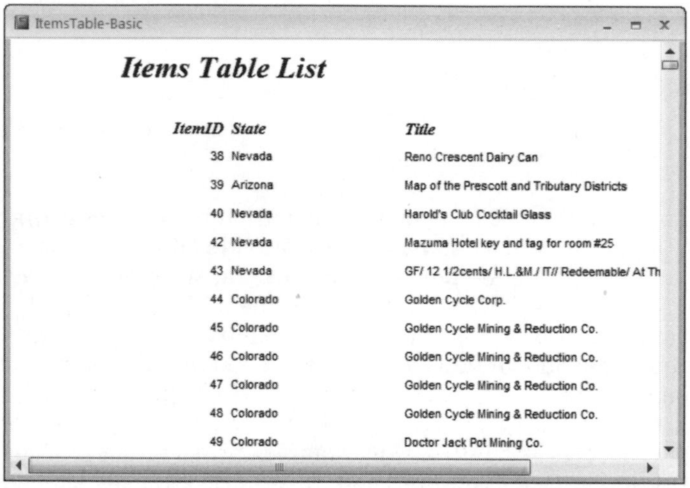

**Figure 4-1:** A simple Access report shows a list of items in a table.

In this case, the report shows three of the fields that are contained within a table instead of displaying the entire set of fields. That's actually one of the advantages even a simple report has over just printing a copy of the table: You don't have to print the entire table.

If you print a copy of a table, all the fields print in the order that they appear in the Datasheet view. If you have several fields and a lot of data, the printout will be very hard to follow because there are often too many fields to fit the width of a page. When you're building a report, however, you can create a layout that allows your data to print in a more readable format. And, of course, you can leave out the irrelevant fields. In Figure 4-1, for example, the report shows only the information that is needed for a specific purpose (taking inventory, perhaps).

## Using reports that group data

Reports that group related records are still relatively simple — just a small step up from the very simple report shown in Figure 4-1. By grouping the records as shown in Figure 4-2, the report enables users to find related items. In this case, the report groups the records by using the values in the `StateArea` field to make viewing items much easier.

**Figure 4-2:** This report groups the items according to the values in the `State Area` field.

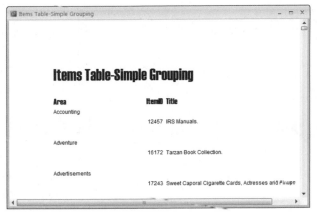

**Items Table-Simple Grouping**

| Area | ItemID | Title |
|------|--------|-------|
| Accounting | | |
| | 12457 | IRS Manuals. |
| Adventure | | |
| | 16172 | Tarzan Book Collection. |
| Advertisements | | |
| | 17243 | Sweet Caporal Cigarette Cards, Actresses and Pinups |

In addition to grouping records by using the entire value in each record in a specific field, you can use the grouping options to group records by using the first one to five characters in the field. This option is especially handy if your database contains typos that you haven't quite gotten around to correcting yet. Weed out the misspelled words into one report and make your changes. For example, suppose you know that someone misspelled California a number of times when entering data. If you group the report on `State` but only match the first two characters, you can probably still get the results you want.

## Using reports to summarize information

Sometimes you may need a report that summarizes the information in your database. For example, Figure 4-3 shows a report that lists the total, average, minimum, and maximum values of items in an auction, with records broken down by state.

Summary reports can include detailed records or they can simply show the summaries — the choice is yours and completely depends on your needs.

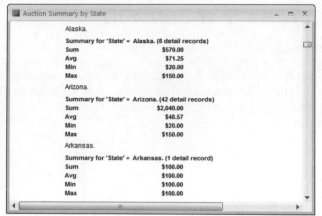

**Figure 4-3:**
This report
provides a
summary
of the items
in the
database.

# Creating Reports by Using a Wizard

You ought to get to know the Access Report Wizards before you spend a lot of time and effort trying to create reports in Design View. This is probably even truer for reports than it is for forms and queries, if for no better reason than to have some good examples you can look at when you decide to give Design View a try.

Access is loaded with wizards to help you with various tasks. In fact, depending on the choices you made while installing Access, you can find between 35 and 55 wizards if you look hard enough. Maybe they should have named this application Microsoft Merlin!

In the following sections, I show you how to use just one more wizard, the Report Wizard. This particular wizard is probably the handiest of all the wizards for most Access users.

## Using the Report Wizard

The Access Report Wizard works very much like the Query and Form Wizards I discuss in the previous two chapters. The Report Wizard takes you through a few extra steps that aren't necessary in those other wizards, but as long as you take your time and consider each of the options, you'll find this wizard is also quite easy to master.

Follow these steps to create a report with the Report Wizard:

1. **Open the Access database for which you want to create the new report.**

2. **Select the Reports option in the Objects list to display the list of reports.**

3. **Click Report Wizard in the Insert section of the Ribbon.**

   The Report Wizard, shown in Figure 4-4, magically appears.

**Figure 4-4:**
Choose the
table or
query and
then the
fields for
your report.

4. **Select the table or query that you want to use as the source of the report data from the drop-down Tables/Queries list.**

5. **Select the fields you want in the Available Fields list and then click the > button to move those fields to the Selected Fields list.**

   You can choose all the fields by clicking the >> button and you can remove fields by using the < and << buttons.

6. **Click the Next button to display the Grouping Levels section of the Report Wizard, shown in Figure 4-5.**

**Figure 4-5:**
Choose a
field to use
to group the
records in
the report.

7. **If you want to group the records, choose the field (or fields) and click the > button.**

   You can't group records based on certain types of fields, such as memo fields or OLE object fields.

   If you select a field to use for grouping, you can click the Grouping Options button and choose to group the records by exact match or by the first one-to-five characters in the field.

8. **Click Next to display the sorting options, as shown in Figure 4-6.**

   You can use these options to make sure that the report is sorted for improved readability.

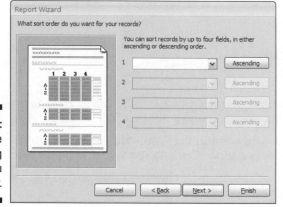

**Figure 4-6:** Select the sorting options you prefer.

9. **The Summary Options screen no longer exists (Sum, Avg, Min, Max), so you need to sort your records by fields and then move on as shown in Figure 4-7.**

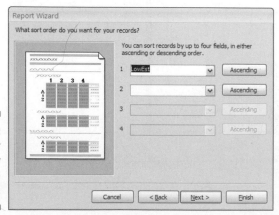

**Figure 4-7:** Sort your records by using these options.

10. **Click Next to display the report layout options, as shown in Figure 4-8.**

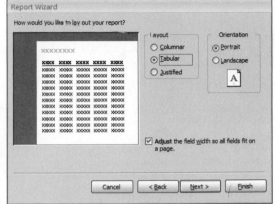

**Figure 4-8:**
Choose the layout options for your report.

11. **Select the report layout that you prefer.**

As you choose different options, the selected option is previewed in the left side of the dialog box.

Choosing Landscape orientation makes fitting reports that contain a number of fields onto a single page much easier.

12. **Click Next to display the report style options (see Figure 4-9).**

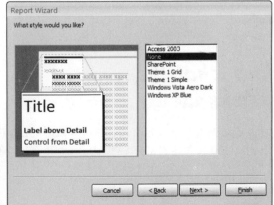

**Figure 4-9:**
Choose a style for your report.

13. **Select the style you want to use for your report.**

14. **Click Next to display the final Report Wizard section, as shown in Figure 4-10.**

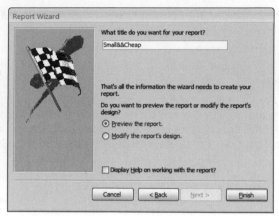

**Figure 4-10:**
Enter a
descriptive
name for
your report
so that it will
be easy to
identify.

**15. Enter a name for your report.**

This is both the name that you want to identify the report as in the Reports list and also the title that will appear at the top of the report, so you probably won't want to use the default name (the name of the table or query on which the report is based).

To show an ampersand (&) in the title (like `Nuts & Bolts`), use two of them (`&&`). A single ampersand is converted to an underline.

**16. Click the Finish button to build the report and then view it.**

When your new report appears on-screen, you can use the navigation buttons at the bottom of the report to view each of the pages in your masterpiece. You can also use the arrow keys and the Page Up and Page Down keys to navigate.

# Understanding what the wizard doesn't know

The Report Wizard does a pretty good job of creating reports, but like all the Access wizards, this wizard is more of a generalist than a detail freak. As a result, you'll almost certainly want to tweak your reports after the wizard is finished. Here are some of the things the Report Wizard really doesn't know about:

✔ **Formatting variations:** The wizard applies the same bland formatting to every field even if you would like to make certain fields stand out by using a different font, type size, or formatting (such as bold or italics).

✔ **Adding divisions:** The wizard doesn't add record separators, so sometimes people find discerning where one record ends and another begins a little difficult.

✔ **Adding external data:** The wizard doesn't know how to use data from external tables.

✔ **Conserving space:** The wizard has no clue about how much money you spend on paper, so it's perfectly happy to create reports that have excessive margins, wasted space for fields that could be condensed, and group summarizations that take up several rows when one would do just fine.

If you would like to do any of these things, you have to create reports on your own in Design View (or modify ones you created with the Report Wizard), which is the subject of the next section.

# Designing Reports from Scratch

Even though the Report Wizard does a pretty good job of creating a basic report, I have no doubt that eventually you'll end up using Design View to create or at least fine-tune most of the reports that you create in Access. Reports are simply too important and visible for you to accept something that's just *okay* — especially if the report is something you're going to show to other people. Sure, building a report in Design View is a bit of work, but the results can be worth the extra effort.

Take a brief look at the following section that tells you about some basic building blocks of Access reports. It's vital to understand the report bands if you want to successfully build an Access report.

## Understanding the report bands

Access uses separate sections called *bands* to control the layout and grouping in reports. These report bands are always nested in a specific order that's similar to an outline in many ways. In some cases, a particular band might be empty — for example, you might not care to use the report footer if you don't have anything that you want to appear at the end of the report. It doesn't matter if you use the Report Wizard or create the report from scratch — the report bands appear in both cases (right-click on the report while in Design View; your options will depend on where you click and what objects are selected).

The bands that might appear in a report (see Figure 4-11) include:

- **Report Header:** The header appears once at the beginning of a report and often includes things like a report title and the date the report was produced.

- **Page Header:** As you might guess, the page header appears at the top of each page of the report. You might use this for column headings, page numbers, or the date.

- **Group Header:** When you group records in a report, the group header is used to show where each group begins. Typically, this band includes the value of the field that is used for grouping. If you have multiple grouping levels, each level has its own group header.

- **Detail:** The innermost nested band is always the detail band that is used to show the details of each record.

- **Group Footer:** Each group header can have a corresponding group footer. This footer is typically used to add separators or summaries (such as group totals).

- **Page Footer:** This footer is used to specify information that you want to appear at the bottom of each report page, such as page numbers or dates. Even though the group bands and details bands are nested within the page bands, groups and details may take up several pages. Page footers help readers know where they are so that they don't lose their place.

- **Report Footer:** This appears at the end of a report. Often, the report footer band is left blank.

The report header, report footer, page header, and page footer are optional report elements. You can add blank copies of these elements by right-clicking on the report when it is in Design View. Both options are toggles, so if you want to view a page header, you also see the page footer. Likewise, if you hide the report footer, the report header goes away, as well. Page headers and footers are selected by default in new reports.

If you don't want one of the four elements to appear, move the mouse pointer to the bottom of the element's band, click it, and then drag the band up until the element is hidden (the title bar for the element remains visible). So, if you want a report header but not a report footer, display both the report header and the report footer and then drag the bottom edge of the report footer up until it disappears (you can always drag it down again if you change your mind).

You can resize any report band by dragging the bottom edge of the band up or down, or by dragging the right edge left or right.

Group Header

Page Header

Report Header

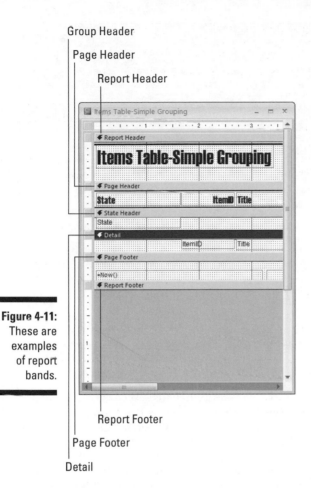

**Figure 4-11:**
These are
examples
of report
bands.

Report Footer

Page Footer

Detail

Understanding the different report bands is important because you use those bands to create reports that group and summarize the records the way you want. Knowing what each type of band does is vital to building reports that function the way you intend them to. And the report bands also help users keep track of their place in a long report.

## Setting up the report page

You may begin creating a report in Design View by clicking Report Design in the Insert section of the Ribbon. When you select this option, Access displays a blank report, as shown in Figure 4-12.

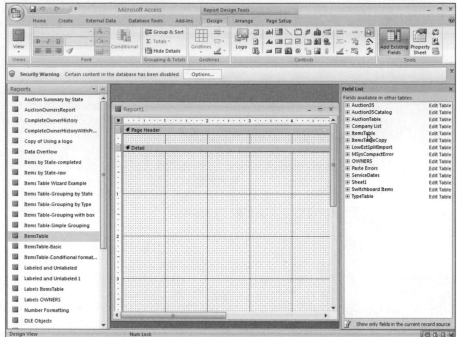

The field list (to the right) initially is empty because Access can populate the list only after you select a table or a query to use as the source for the report. The Ribbon above contains the same set of tools used for creating forms in Design View (see Chapter 3).

However, if you right-click in the report, you find options that you really should become familiar with because you will definitely need them when you create reports in Design View:

- ✔ **Sorting and Grouping:** Click this option to display the Sorting and Grouping dialog box so that you can sort your report or group the records. You can also find Grouping and Totals on the Ribbon.

- ✔ **Properties:** Click this option to display the Properties dialog box for a selected object so that you can control its properties. For example, you can modify the table or query that is the source of data for the report by using the Properties dialog box. You can also click the Property Sheet on the Ribbon.

The basic report that appears when you first start a new report in Design View is completely empty. You need to select a data source (a table or a query) before you can add any fields, set up any sorting, or apply any grouping. You can, however, add a report header or footer and you can add things like page numbers or dates to the page header or footer. These objects don't depend on data from a table or query. See the previous section, "Understanding the report bands," for more information about these elements.

### Adding page numbers

If you want page numbers on your report, you always add them to either the page header or the page footer because these report elements show up on every page of the report.

To add page numbers, follow these steps:

1. **With your report open in Design View, choose the Insert Page Number option on the Ribbon (the icon with a # sign in the middle of the Design section).**

   The Page Numbers dialog box, shown in Figure 4-13, appears.

**Figure 4-13:**
Use the Page Numbers dialog box to quickly add page numbering to your report.

2. **Choose the page number format you prefer from the Format section of the dialog box.**

   The first option simply shows the page number, while the second option displays the page number and the total number of pages.

3. **Choose whether you want the page numbering to appear in the page header or the page footer in the Position section of the dialog box.**

4. **Select the alignment you prefer from the drop-down Alignment list box.**

5. **If you want to show the page number on the first page of the report, make certain that the Show Number on First Page option is selected.**

6. **Click OK to apply your selections to the report design and close the Page Numbers dialog box.**

### Adding dates and times

You may want to add date and time markers to your report. These markers give readers of your report a sense of the newness of the data, which may be important if you are dealing with a database that is constantly being updated.

The date and time is updated whenever a report is previewed or printed, making it easier to make sure that you're looking at the most recent copy of a report.

To add the date or time to your report, follow these steps:

1. **With your report open in Design View, choose the Date & Time option from the Ribbon (the icon with a 5 and clock in the Design section).**

   The Date and Time dialog box, shown in Figure 4-14, appears.

**Figure 4-14:**
Use the Date and Time dialog box to add the printing date and time to your report.

2. **To add the date, make certain that the Include Date check box is selected, and then choose the date format you prefer.**

3. **To add the time, make sure the Include Time check box is selected and then choose the time format you prefer.**

4. **Click OK to apply your selections and to close the Date and Time dialog box.**

You no doubt notice that the Date and Time dialog box doesn't give you the option of choosing where in the document you want the date and the time to appear. That's because when you use this dialog box, Access always places the date and time fields in the report header if it is displayed. If the report header is not displayed, Access places these fields in the Detail band. Fortunately, you can drag and drop these fields wherever you want them to appear in the report layout. For example, you might want to place the date and time fields in the page header or footer. No problem.

### *Adding titles and other objects*

You'll probably want to add a report title and some other objects (such as a company logo or contact information) to your reports. Adding these types of objects is a bit more art than science because you're free to let your imagination take over in the area of content, placement, and even format.

Generally speaking, you'll likely find that the Ribbon provides the tools you need to add titles and graphics to a report.

To add a title to your report, follow these steps:

1. **Select the Label option in the Ribbon and then drag out a box in your report design where you want the title to appear.**

   The title typically appears in the report header. You can also just click where you want the label to begin, but dragging out the box for the label gives you more control over the size of the box.

2. **Enter the text you want for the title, click outside the label box, and then click the label box again to select it.**

3. **Use the Font section of the Ribbon to modify the appearance by choosing a font, a size, and any other formatting you prefer.**

To add an image, such as a logo, follow these steps:

1. **Select the Image option on the Ribbon.**

2. **Drag out a box in your report design.**

   After you've drawn the box, Access automatically displays the Insert Picture dialog box so that you can choose an image file to place in the box.

3. **Select the image you want to use and click OK to add it to the report.**

## *Choosing your tables*

Reports need to be associated with a table or a query in order to include any data. You could, of course, create a blank report with just a title, page numbers, and dates, but without any real data, your report would have little value beyond serving as lining for the bottom of a bird cage.

The table or query that provides the data for an Access report is called the *record source.* You choose the record source for a report by using the Property Sheet on the Ribbon. You can also go into Design View, right-click the report body, and choose Properties from the pop-up menu. In either case, the Property Sheet appears, as shown in Figure 4-15.

If the Data tab isn't already selected, click this tab to bring it to the front.

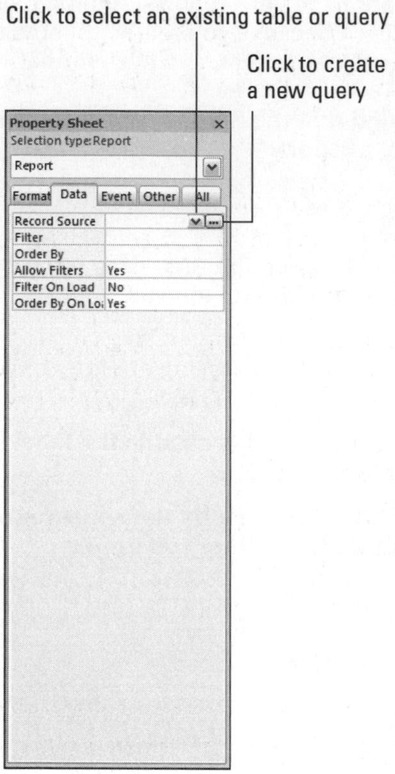

Click to select an existing table or query

Click to create
a new query

**Property Sheet**                          ×
Selection type:Report

Report                                   ⌄

Format  **Data**  Event  Other   All

Record Source                    ⌄ ┈
Filter
Order By
Allow Filters        Yes
Filter On Load       No
Order By On Lo: Yes

**Figure 4-15:**
Specify the
table or
query by
using the
Record
Source list
box.

You can select an existing table or query by clicking the down arrow on the right side of the Record Source list box and choosing from the list. Alternatively, you can click the button with the three dots to build a new query from scratch. After you select a table or query, you can add the fields to your report.

Although the Data tab of the Property Sheet includes both a Filter and Order By (sort) option, using these options can be a little confusing and prone to errors because you have to enter the filtering and sorting parameters manually. To avoid the possibility of typing errors, it's usually a better idea to select an existing query or create a new query as the record source instead of trying to create a filter or sort order in the Property Sheet.

## A little information about the Property Sheet

No doubt, you've come across the Property Sheet in your forays into the world of Access databases. When you create forms and reports, this box is indispensable. The Property Sheet offers tabs to help you change aspects of just about every part of your forms and reports:

✔ **Format:** As you might guess, this tab lets you change the format of a form or report.

✔ **Data:** This tab helps you pick the records and information that you want to put into the form or report. Use this tab to exclude irrelevant data and sort relevant data.

✔ **Event:** Here you can add VBA code to control what happens when an *event* such

as moving off a record, clicking a control, or changing a value occurs.

✔ **Other:** This tab is sort of the dumping ground for things that the Access programmers couldn't find a better place for, like Fast Laser Printing, Record Locks, and custom help file links.

✔ **All:** If you can't find a property, look on the All tab. Sure, you'll have to scroll through every property that applies to the selected object, but if it exists, the property will be listed here.

## Selecting the fields

As soon as you've selected a record source, you can begin adding fields to your report because the field list automatically includes all the available fields. Adding the fields can be a bit frustrating — especially if you're trying to be neat about it.

You typically add fields to the detail band in a report, although you can also add a field to a group band to show how the records are grouped. For example, you can add the State field to the group header if you want to group records by state. That way, your report lists the name of the state above each group of related records.

You add fields to the report design by dragging and dropping fields from the Field list onto the report layout. When you're dragging and dropping, remember that the mouse pointer indicates the position of the *field* and that the field *label* is farther to the left. If you intend to leave the labels in front of each field, be sure to leave enough room for those labels. I show you another alternative for aligning the labels in the next section.

Figure 4-16 shows an example (in Design View) of a report that includes all the report bands, uses grouping on the State field, and has a number of fields added to the report design. This report is a good starting point, but it still needs some work to make it into something you'd want to show to someone.

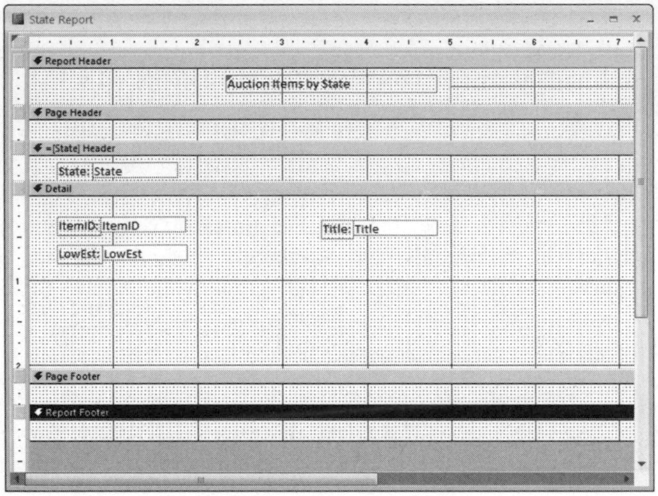

**Figure 4-16:** This report was created in Design View and groups records by state.

# Modifying Report Layouts

The basic report design shown in Figure 4-16 illustrates an important point about creating your own reports — you'll probably want to do a bunch of cleanup work before you call the design finished. A few simple modifications can really improve the final result.

## Deciding what needs to be done

Before you barge in and try to fix a report's layout, consider just what needs to be done. Here's a checklist of common layout issues that you'll want to evaluate and fix:

✔ **Problem: You want to change the location of the date and time fields:** By default, Access puts the date and time fields along the right edge of the report header. They probably should be moved to another location. Reserve the report header for the most important details — the page footer might be a good place for the date and time information.

**Solution:** Drag and drop the date and time fields wherever you want them to go.

➤ **Problem: You want to change the location and position of the title of the report:** Access is pretty sloppy about where things go. Centering the title improves the overall appearance.

**Solution:** You can drag and drop the title or you can align it by selecting it, right-clicking, and choosing Align.

➤ **Problem: You want to make the layout efficient:** An occupational hazard of dragging and dropping fields into a report is that the fields *look* as though they have been dragged and dropped into the report. You need to fix this if you want the report to look like anything other than a rough draft. In Figure 4-16, the detail band has both field labels and the field boxes laid out in a fairly inefficient way. The field labels could be moved to the page header, and the field boxes could be tightened up underneath the labels. In addition, the bottom of the detail band should be moved up so less space is wasted between records.

**Solution:** Align and resize the field boxes with the Align and Size submenus. These tools work the same with forms as they do with reports. See Chapter 3 for more details.

You can resize a report band by dragging its bottom edge. However, moving the field labels can be a bit trickier. I discuss this topic in "Moving and formatting those pesky labels," later in the chapter.

➤ **Problem: You want to hide unused bands:** In Figure 4-16, the report footer is empty (which is fine — don't feel compelled to use every field available to you), but because the white grid in it is showing, the report footer will still take up room in the final report.

**Solution:** Drag the bottom of the report footer all the way up to eliminate this problem.

➤ **Problem: You want to add visual cues to help users navigate the report:** Unless you add them, your report layout gives few visual cues about where records and groups begin and end. Adding some simple horizontal divider lines can make a complicated report much easier to understand by visually delineating the records and groups.

**Solution:** Drawing lines is simple; use the Line tool on the Ribbon.

## *Moving and formatting those pesky labels*

The fields that you add to a report consist of two parts. The label identifies the field, and the box that follows the label displays the values. That seems pretty simple and straightforward, but there's just one little problem with this arrangement — it's a bit difficult to move the label without also moving the data box. Go ahead and try it and you'll see what I mean. When you try to select and drag the label, the whole field moves. It's almost like the two are joined at the hip!

Actually, there is a simple trick for moving the label separately from the data box, but you'd probably have little success discovering the trick on your own, and even if you did, you'd find that it doesn't work quite the way you might expect.

When you click a field to select it, you select both the label and the data box. But if you carefully move the mouse pointer to the upper-left corner of the label, the pointer changes into a hand with the index finger pointing upward (see Figure 4-17). This is your chance! As long as the mouse pointer looks like that, you can drag and drop the label without moving the data box.

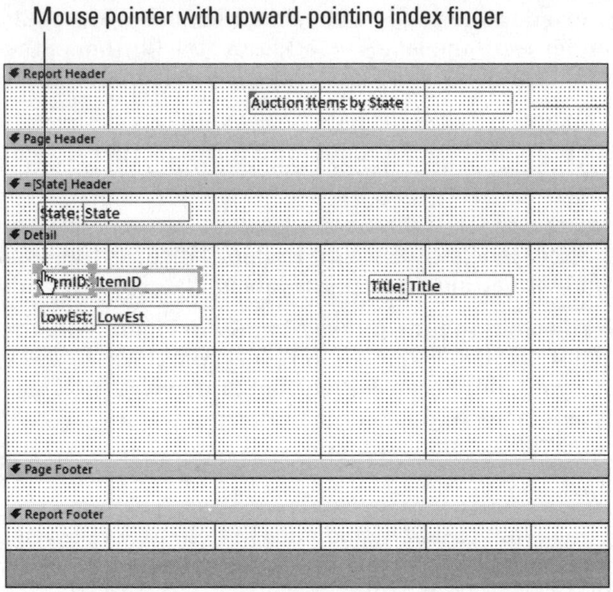

Mouse pointer with upward-pointing index finger

**Figure 4-17:**
Look for this mouse pointer if you want to move the field label but keep the data box where it is.

As promising as this trick seems to be, there's a catch to it (isn't there always?). The catch is that you can't use it to move the field label into a different report band than the data box. As a result, this trick doesn't help you move field labels into the page header in order to save space by having a single field label above each column on a page. Likewise, you can't save a little space (and make the report easier to read) by moving labels to the group header.

So, how can you move the field labels to a different report band? The answer is that you have to separate the labels from the data boxes by using cut-and-paste techniques. There simply isn't any drag-and-drop method for moving the labels to one report band while leaving the data boxes in another.

Here's how to move those pesky labels:

**1. Click the label to select it.**

2. **Right-click and choose Cut.**

   The data box won't move when you cut the label.

3. **Click the band where you want to place the label.**

4. **Right-click and choose Paste.**

5. **Repeat Steps 1 through 4 for each of the labels you want to move.**

6. **Use the Align commands to line up each of the label and data box pairs.**

   You may need to do some moving and resizing of the data boxes in the detail band before aligning the labels with the data boxes. If the pasted labels insist on sitting on each other, remember that the label in "selection" (the last-selected one) can be shifted by changing values on the Property Sheet. Remember that you can select two or more objects by holding down Shift as you click each object.

To make the text in each field align with the left side of the field labels, follow these instructions:

1. **Select the data boxes that you want to align.**

2. **Right-click the selection and choose Properties from the pop-up menu to display the Property Sheet.**

   You can also click the Property Sheet.

3. **Click the Format tab.**

4. **Select Left from the Text Align drop-down list box, as shown in Figure 4-18.**

5. **Click Close the list if you wish.**

   Of course, you may prefer different alignment options for numeric or currency fields, but that's just a matter of choosing what you want.

## Pulling the layout together to save paper

After you move your labels and otherwise clean up the mess you started with (as described in the previous sections), be sure to drag the bottom of each report band up to prevent your printer from spitting out a bunch of blank paper when you print your report. When you drag the bottom of a band up, Access won't allow you to shrink the band to less than the height necessary to show whatever fields are in the band. Even if you drag the bottom of the band up higher than the bottom of a field, the band won't shrink that far because the bottom of the lowest field in a band limits the amount you can shrink the band.

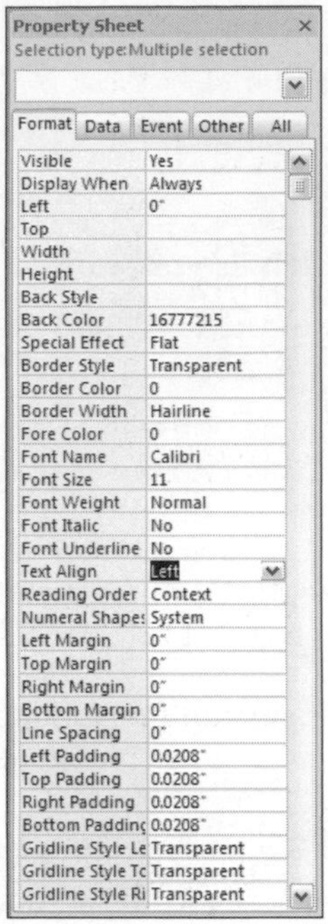

**Figure 4-18:** Make the data align with the labels by setting the text alignment for the field.

Figure 4-19 shows a completed report in Design View. Of course, this isn't how the report will look when it's printed.

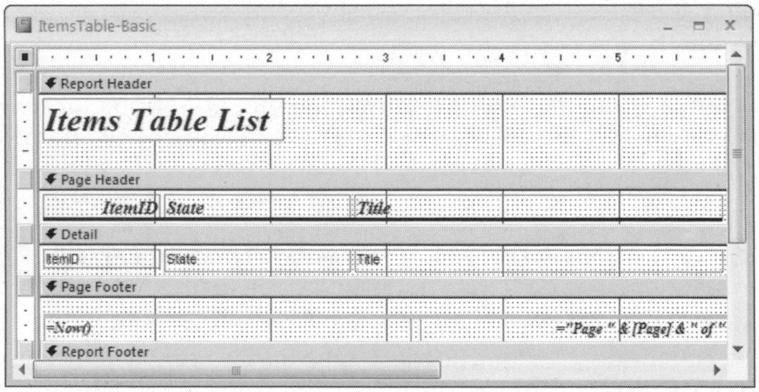

**Figure 4-19:** The completed report design is much cleaner than the original.

Figure 4-20 shows how the completed report looks in its printable version. To preview the report, click the View button. The finished report is compact, but it clearly displays the data in an understandable format. What more could you ask for? Well, perhaps a little more tweaking.

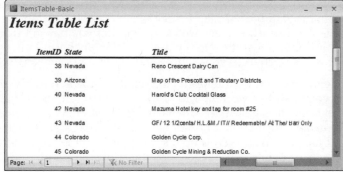

**Figure 4-20:**
The
completed
report in
Print
Preview
mode.

# Adding Data from External Linked Tables

Creating your reports within the same Access database that holds the records you need for the report is not always possible — or even desirable. Perhaps you need to use data from an Access database that is maintained by Mr. Smith in Accounting, who doesn't want you messing around with his creation. (Mr. Smith doesn't get out much.) Or maybe you're dealing with a situation in which you don't want to add anything to the primary database file because you've split the database into *front end* and *back end* applications — basically a database where the tables are in one file and all the forms, reports, and queries are in another file. Or perhaps you simply want to know how to add data from external linked tables to your report so that you'll have another fancy Access trick up your sleeve. Regardless of the reason, you *can* base Access reports on tables that exist in another Access database.

## Choosing a method for accessing external data

To use data from an *external* table, you must first establish a connection between your current database and the database file that holds the table you want to use. There are two ways you can create this connection:

✔ **You can *import* the table from the other database file into your current database file.** This method places a *static* copy of the table into your database file. That is, after you import the table, there's no remaining connection between that imported copy of the table and the external database file. If Mr. Smith in Accounting changes the information in his database after you import the table, those changes won't be reflected in the imported table. Likewise, if you change the table after you import it, Mr. Smith's database won't be affected. Obviously, this option has some merits. Mr. Smith can sleep well knowing that you haven't turned his database into a disaster. On the downside, if Mr. Smith's changes to the table are important to your report, you don't have access to them.

✔ **You can *link* to the table in the external database file.** The link ensures that you're always working with current data, but it also requires that the external database file remains available whenever you need to access the information. Another issue that's near and dear to Mr. Smith's heart is that you can screw up his tables. Of course, in the interest of maintaining peace in the office, you may not want to point out to Mr. Smith that his changes to the tables can monkey with your report. Rather, just be careful.

If you know that the external database file will always be available, you probably want to link to the external table instead of importing the table. That way you can be sure that whenever you run your report, it is accurate and up to date. If, on the other hand, the external database file might not always be available (or it might be moved and break the link) and you can live with a snapshot of the data as it existed when you imported it, importing the table may be your best choice. Only you can choose the best option for your situation.

## *Importing or linking external data*

After you decide which method you want to use to connect external data to your report, creating that connection is easy. You need access to the external database file, but you don't have to open that file.

The process is pretty much the same whether you decide to import the data or link to it. To create a connection to an external table in a different Access database file so that you can use the data in a new report, follow these steps:

1. **Open the database file in which you want to create your report.**

2. **Choose Access Database from the External Data section of the Ribbon.**

3. **Select the external database file that contains the table you want to import or link to.**

   If you need to browse to another server or folder in the network, you can do that, just as you would when looking for any file in Microsoft Office.

   In my example, I chose to link with my data source (shown in Figure 4-21).

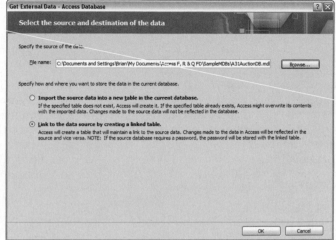

**Figure 4-21:**
Locate and
select the
external
database
file.

4. **Click OK to display the dialog box showing the list of tables in the database you selected in Step 3.**

   Figure 4-22 shows a list of tables. The two dialog boxes are quite similar. If you're importing, not linking, the dialog box shows tabs for all database objects — not just the tables.

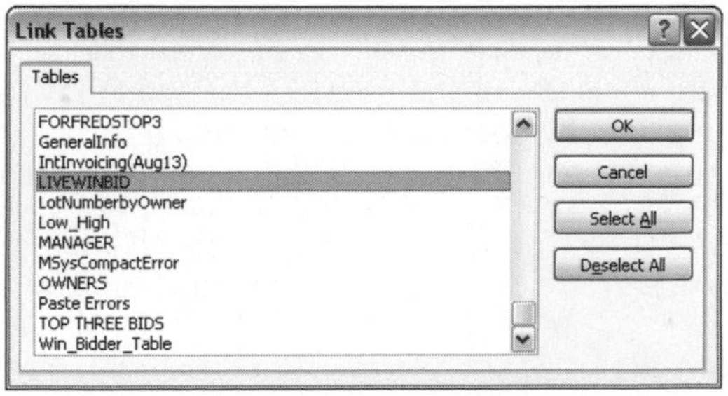

**Figure 4-22:**
Choose the
tables you
want to
import or
link to.

5. **Select the tables you want to use and click OK.**

   You can select multiple tables by holding down Shift or Ctrl as you click each table. You can select all the tables by clicking the Select All button.

   After you click OK, the dialog box closes, and the connection is created. Figure 4-23 shows the Tables list with a linked table, LIVEWINBID1. The arrow indicates an active link between the table and your report.

**Figure 4-23:**
The table is
linked.

After you import or link the external tables, you can use them exactly as you would any table you created within the current database. Being able to use external tables in your Access reports gives you many additional possibilities for creating reports (as well as forms and queries) that you may not have considered before. There's really no difference between internal and external tables. Whether you import the table or create a link to it, the table acts the same way.

# Part II
# Creating Effective Queries

The 5th Wave                    By Rich Tennant

"Our customer survey indicates 30% of our customers think our service is inconsistent, 40% would like a change in procedures, and 50% think it would be real cute if we all wore matching colored vests."

## In this part . . .

Queries enable you to choose which information is included in your forms and reports. You don't have to include everything in a form or report when applying a little focus can make you so much more efficient. This part shows you how to create very effective queries that improve your forms and reports. You also get an introduction to the language that is at the heart of all Access queries, SQL — *Structured Query Language* — so that you can soup up your queries for even better results.

# Chapter 5

# Creating Multi-Table Queries

*In This Chapter*

▶ Adding more than one table to your queries

▶ Linking an external database to a query

▶ Getting to know how query relationships work

*I*n Part I, I get you up to speed on the basics of queries, forms, and reports. In Part II, you get to tackle some really meaty topics. In this chapter, you see how to effectively use multiple tables in a query so that you can get even more useful information from your Access databases. Multi-table queries enable you to use information from two or more tables as if you had a single table containing a combination of the data from those multiple tables.

Using information from two or more tables requires the existence of a *relationship* between the tables so that Access can determine how to combine the data. Table relationships are fundamental and extremely important for making your Access databases powerful and efficient. This chapter shows you how to create these relationships.

## Understanding Multi-Table Queries

Queries act almost as surrogates for tables. That is, you can use a query in place of a table in nearly any place where you would ordinarily use a table. For example, you can just as easily use a query as the basis for a report as you can use a table for that purpose. You can't, of course, use a query as a place to store data — that's a job that can be handled by a table. But if what you need is a data source, a query can easily fill the bill.

 A query must ultimately have a table as the source of its data, but one query can build on the results from another query as long as the lowest level of the chain is a table.

A query typically extracts a group of information from one or more tables by using criteria you specify. That's why queries are so useful. Instead of showing every record in a report or in a form, you can choose to include a *subset* of the records in order to bring some focus to the report or form. You can also choose to include only the fields you want.

## Understanding the benefits of multiple tables

You may be asking yourself why you'd ever want to use multiple tables in a single query. Simply stated, using multiple tables in your queries gives you more flexibility, just as using multiple tables in a database gives you many benefits. The following list gives you a few of the many good reasons to use multiple tables to hold your data:

- **Efficient data storage:** Multiple tables can actually be a more efficient means of storing related data because they enable you to enter certain information once and then reuse that information in the future without re-entering it. For example, if you have a contact database, you can enter basic information about a company, such as the address, when you add your first contact at that company. After that, you can then simply refer to the same information when you enter additional contacts from the same company.

- **Easy updating:** Multiple tables are also far more convenient when you need to update information because you can make a single change and have it apply to all related records; you don't have to go in and change every single one of the records. A good example of this efficiency is when telephone area codes change and you can update the records for everyone in the old area code in a single step.

- **Easy data access:** Using multiple tables makes setting up lookup lists in forms much easier so that you can give users limited choices in specific fields and prevent keying errors. This also makes it easier for users to find the data they need.

- **Keeping remote relationships intact:** Many databases contain information that is only remotely related. Multiple tables provide a means of keeping that information together so that it's easier to exploit the few, distant relationships.

These are all great reasons to use multiple tables in a database, of course, but how do they relate to using multiple tables in a query? Using multiple tables in a query enables you to perform the following tasks:

- **To bring information together in one place:** Multiple tables are efficient for storing related information, but sometimes you simply need to bring that information together in one place — such as in a report. A multiple-table query often provides the best way to bring that information together.

✔ **To update information in a table based on its links to another table:** You guessed it — a multiple-table query provides the solution for this, too.

✔ **To create a table that combines specific fields and records from several tables:** A multiple-table query is really the only way to go for a situation like this. For example, you might want to provide your customers with a year-end summary of the business they've done over the year, and this could require you to pull information from your orders table in addition to your items list table.

You can probably think of a number of other examples of how using multiple tables in a query can help you accomplish your specific goals. Just as Access databases have thousands of functions, there are countless ways to use the information they contain.

## *Establishing relationships between multiple tables*

Storing various pieces of information in different tables is easy. The hard part is linking the information that's in one table to the information in another table so that you can create *relationships* between the tables. When information in two tables is related through linking, you can find records in each of the tables that are connected. For example, Figure 5-1 shows two related tables in an auction database. The two tables share a common piece of information that makes finding related records in the two tables much easier.

If you study Figure 5-1, you notice that there are no common fields between the two tables. That's because table relationships can be created between fields with different names as long as the two fields contain the same type of information. The USERBIDID and BIDID fields in this example both identify the bidder.

Figure 5-1 demonstrates one of the important points about using data from multiple, linked tables — that you can combine information in useful ways very easily. Suppose, for example, that you have a table named CURRENTA, which holds information about an auction's bidders, and that you have a table named LIVEWINBID, which contains information about the items that are sold in an auction. When you combine the two, you can create a list of the items that were won by each of the bidders. In this case, a single bidder might be the winner of a number of items, so the number in the BIDID field could show up multiple times in the LIVEWINBID table. That's why the line indicating the relationship between the tables has a 1 on the CURRENTA table side and an infinity symbol on the LIVEWINBID table side — a single record in the LIVEWINBID table can match any number of records in the CURRENTA table. This is called a *one-to-many* relationship between the tables.

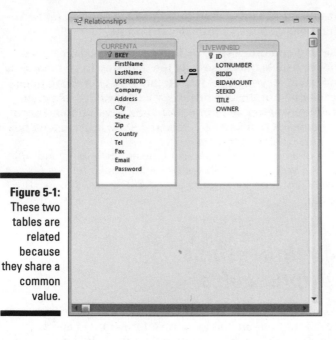

**Figure 5-1:**
These two
tables are
related
because
they share a
common
value.

See the section, "Understanding Relationships in Queries," later in this chapter, for more information on creating relationships if they don't already exist in your database.

# Adding Multiple Tables to Queries

In Chapter 2, I show you how to use both a Query Wizard and the Query Design View to create simple queries with a single table as the source of the data. Now I give you the lowdown on building queries that include fields from more than one table. (Using fields from another query works exactly the same way except that you choose a query instead of a table as the record source.)

## Selecting multiple tables up front

The method you use to select the tables for your query depends on the option you select to begin the query. Here's a brief review of the two methods:

✔ **Query Wizard:** If you decide to use the Query Wizard, you choose the wizard from the Query Wizard/Query Design option in the Create section of the Ribbon and then add the fields you want to use from a table in the Tables/Queries list box. Then you select the next table that you want to use and add its fields to the query. You continue this process until you've added all the tables and their fields to the query.

✔ **Design View:** If you create your query in Design View, you select the tables for the query by using the Show Table dialog box. You can add more than one table at a time by selecting all the tables you want to use before you click the Add button (see Figure 5-2). Ctrl-click to add each table you click to the selection, or Shift-click to add a contiguous range of tables to the selection. Click Close to close the Show Table dialog box after you've added the tables to the query.

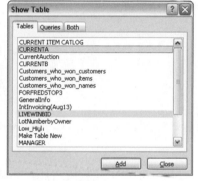

**Figure 5-2:** Select all the tables you want to add to the query and click Add.

You can use whichever method you prefer to add the tables to the query. Adding the tables in Design View means that you still need to add the fields you want to the query (see Figure 5-3); on the other hand, you may prefer doing the Design View method because you can more easily control the order in which the fields appear in the query.

Notice that in Figure 5-3, the links between the tables in the query automatically appear when you add those tables to the query design. In this case, the selected tables are the same ones shown in Figure 5-1, so the tables are linked the same way as they were in the earlier figure.

Sometimes you may see the link but won't be able to see the fields that are related because not enough space is allocated to display all the fields in a table. You can display the linked fields by scrolling the field list with the scroll bar along the right side of the list of fields, or you can drag the edges of the list to expand the list so more fields are visible.

If you add multiple tables to a query and no links appear in Design View, you have to create the links before you can run the query. Access won't allow you to save your work or run the query if the links don't exist before you begin creating the query. One way to add the links is to drag the field name from one table to the other, making sure, of course, that you drop the field onto the field that it is supposed to link to in the second table.

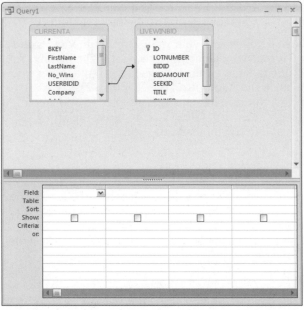

**Figure 5-3:**
When you
add the
tables to
the query
in Design
View, none
of the fields
are auto-
matically
added to the
design grid.

Each table in a query must be linked to at least one other table in the query. It's not necessary for every table to be linked directly to every other table, though. In fact, if you have three or more tables in a query and every table is linked to every other table directly, your database design is probably pretty messed up! (I show you a tool in Chapter 20 that may help you deal with this type of problem.)

## Adding the tables you forgot about to your query

Inevitably, as you start to create more complex multiple-table queries, you'll discover that you need to add a bit more information, but that the information you need is stored in a table that you forgot to add to your query. This isn't quite the disaster that it might seem because it's pretty easy to add tables to a query that you've already started working on.

If the new table that you want to add already has an established table relationship with at least one of the tables in your query, you simply need to open the Show Table dialog box and add the new table. Follow these steps:

1. **Choose Show Table from the Query Setup Group in the Design section of the Ribbon, or right-click on the top pane of the query grid and select Show Table.**

   The Show Table dialog box appears.

2. **Add the new table by selecting it and clicking Add.**

If the new table you want to add doesn't have an established table relationship with one of the existing tables in the query (or if you're not sure whether it does), things are a bit trickier. You need to establish that relationship (as discussed in the section, "Understanding Relationships in Queries," later in this chapter) before adding the new table.

How can you tell whether the new table is related to one of the existing tables in the query? First, save your query design by choosing File⇨Save, by clicking the Save button, or by pressing Ctrl+S. By saving your query design first, you avoid the dreaded possibility of losing the query if something goes wrong and you can't save it later.

After you save the query design, add the new table to the query and look for a link to an existing table. If the link is there, you're home free. If there's no link, right-click on the new table and choose Remove Table from the pop-up menu. Then create the link (see "Understanding Relationships in Queries," later in this chapter) before trying to add the table again.

## Choosing the fields to use

You can add fields from the query tables to the design grid in several ways:

- ✔ Drag and drop fields from the tables at the top of the Query editor onto the columns in the lower section of the Query editor window.
- ✔ Double-click fields in the tables at the top of the Query editor window.
- ✔ Click in the Field row of the design grid to display a list of the available fields and then choose a field from the list.
- ✔ Double-click the asterisk (*) at the top of either the field list in each table or in the Field row of the design grid to add all the fields from the specified table to the grid.

  You will not be able to specify criteria for all those fields.

Adding the fields to the grid is the easy part. Choosing the fields that should be included and the order in which they appear is just a touch more complicated.

There are no hard-and-fast rules about which fields you should include or their order in the design grid, but the following guidelines may help you decide what will work best in your queries:

- **List the most important fields first.** That is, if you intend to do any grouping, add the grouping fields first in the order that you plan to use them to group the records — with the least selective grouping (such as `State`) coming before more selective grouping (such as `City`).

- **Follow grouped fields with non-grouped fields that you want to use for sorting the records.** Once again, place the most important sorting fields to the left of fields that aren't so important.

- **Finally, include fields that you want to use to select which records to include in the results.** You don't have to include these criteria fields in the results if you don't want them there. You can deselect the Show check box for any fields you don't want included in the results.

- **Be sure to include every field that you want to show in the results.** The results can be a simple Datasheet view, a form, or a report.

- **Exclude any fields that aren't important to your results.** The idea here is to keep the results just a bit cleaner and easier to use. For example, you might not need to include fields like automatically generated indexes that Access uses to create unique records. Typically, these types of values aren't very useful in a report.

You can delete fields by clicking the column header to select the field in the query design and then pressing the Delete button on your keyboard.

You can use and adapt these guidelines to best suit your needs. If you're more comfortable throwing in every available field just to make sure they're all there, feel free to include them all. Just be aware that it's really easy to add an extra field later if you've left one out of your original query design.

## Making Access use the correct table

The second row of the query design grid shows the table that is the source for the field in that column. If all of your query designs in the past have been single-table queries, you might not have given the table entry much thought. But when you begin creating multiple-table queries, the table entry can be very important.

You might have fields with the same name in different tables. For example, you might use `State` as a field name in several different tables in a single database. Generally, these duplicated field names aren't a problem, but consider the following scenario in which the problem is very real:

Imagine for a moment that you have two tables in your database that use `State` as a field name. The first table lists the names and addresses of your customers. The second table lists the items that were won by bidders in a recent auction. Now, suppose that you're required to file a report with the tax department showing all the items sold to buyers in your state. If your query uses the State field from your customer list, there's no problem. But suppose you accidentally used the State field from the items table and that table showed the state where the item originated instead of the state where the buyers live. Clearly, in the second case, your report isn't going to satisfy the tax collector. (And when have you known a tax collector who had a sense of humor?)

Access allows you to choose a table and field name that don't match. That is, if you have already selected a field and then change the source table by making a different selection in the Table cell, the field name remains the same even if no field by that name exists in the new table. If you change the source table, be sure that the field exists because otherwise the query results will be meaningless.

# Linking to External Databases in Your Queries

Chapter 4 briefly touches on the idea of using information from external databases in your reports. Here I expand on that idea and consider some additional ways that you can use external data with your queries.

## Understanding the types of external data you can use

If you read Chapter 4, you already know that you can use data that exists in another Access database. But Access isn't the only application that produces databases. Fortunately, Access can work with information from many different types of databases without a whole lot of fuss and bother.

Access uses *drivers* — small helper applications — to import or link to external data. You won't usually notice when Access is using a driver because quite a few of them are built in to Access. Depending on the version of Access you're using, different drivers may be built in. For example, Access 2007 has built-in drivers that provide the ability to import or link to the following types of files:

- ✔ Access databases and projects
- ✔ dBASE databases
- ✔ Excel spreadsheets

- Fixed-width and delimited text files
- HTML and XML files
- Lotus 1-2-3 spreadsheets
- Microsoft Exchange databases
- Microsoft Outlook databases
- Paradox databases
- Windows SharePoint services

In addition, Access can use *ODBC* (open database connectivity) drivers to connect to quite a few other types of database files, such as SQL Server, FoxPro, and Oracle. Some of these ODBC drivers are installed automatically when you install Access, but Access can also use ODBC drivers that are supplied by other manufacturers.

Every driver provides a different level of support for features that are native to other file types. In some cases, you may not be able to use every type of data that a foreign file can contain. This problem is usually the result of ancient ODBC drivers that came with an old database application and can sometimes be corrected by searching the manufacturer's Web site for newer drivers that you can install.

Even after you successfully import or link to external data, keep in mind that some types of information make no sense in an Access database. For example, if you link to an Excel worksheet that is laid out as a database but that contains formulas in the database range, those formulas mean nothing in Access. You can create the link, but you'll probably see a cryptic message that says something like `Method 'Columns' of object 'IImexGrid' failed`. If you see a message like this, be sure to have a look at the linked (or imported) data to see whether it makes sense before you try to use the information in Access (the message in this example is simply a strange way of telling you that Access couldn't import everything from the Excel worksheet).

## Importing versus linking external data

The Get External Data section of the Ribbon offers two options. You can choose to *import* data or to *link* to the data. Access is perfectly content to use the information either way, but you should be aware of the important differences between the two options. If you import data, the copy of the data that you import exists only within your Access database. Any changes that are made to the external data after you import the information won't be included in your version of the table. If you want to maintain an active link so that you're always working with current information, you must choose to link to the external data instead of importing it.

## Linking to tables in another foreign database format

It's just a fact of life that different people like to do things different ways. That's one reason why, from time to time, you may need to use data that was created in a format other than Access. In order to use that information, you need to bring it into Access. To link to data in another database format, follow these steps:

1. **Open the Access database where you want to use the external data.**

2. **Choose Get External Data⇨Select the source and destination of the data.**

   The Get External Data dialog box appears (see Figure 5-4).

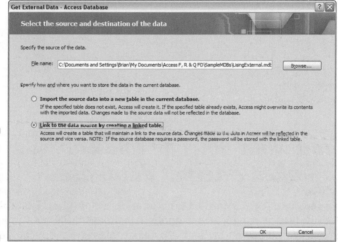

**Figure 5-4:** Use this dialog box to link to external data.

3. **Click the Browse button to select the file you want to use as the data source.**

4. **Select the Link radio button.**

5. **Click OK.**

   The linked table appears (Figure 5-5) in the Tables list with an arrow in front of the table name to indicate that it is a linked table. If you linked to a non-Access table, the table's icon shows the type of the file.

*REMEMBER*

Depending on the type of file you're linking to, you may encounter different steps and prompts during the linking process. For example, if you link to an Excel worksheet, you're asked to indicate whether the top row of the data includes the field labels.

**Figure 5-5:**
Access
informs
you that the
link was
successfully
created.

# Knowing what you can and can't do with a linked external database

After you've successfully created a link to an external database table or spreadsheet database range, you can use that linked table just about the same way you would use an ordinary Access table that is contained within your database file. There are some things you *can't* do to a linked table, however. As Figure 5-6 shows, if you attempt to open a linked table in Design View, Access informs you that you can't modify some of the properties in a linked table. In most cases, the only property you can modify in a linked table is the table's name.

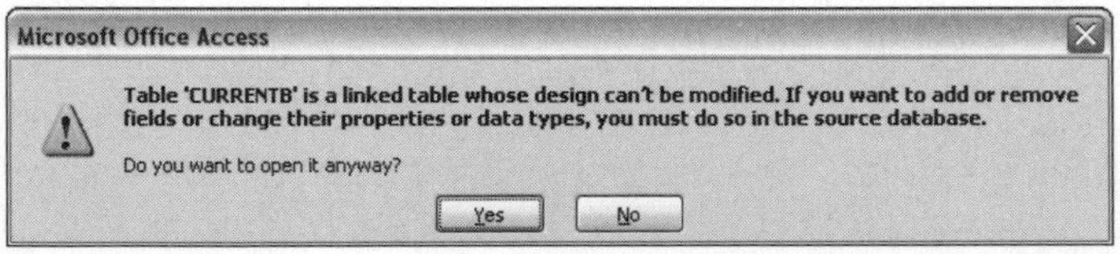

**Figure 5-6:**
You cannot
modify most
of the prop-
erties in
linked tables.

> **Microsoft Office Access**
>
> ⚠ Table 'CURRENTB' is a linked table whose design can't be modified. If you want to add or remove fields or change their properties or data types, you must do so in the source database.
>
> Do you want to open it anyway?
>
> [ Yes ]    [ No ]

See Chapter 6 for information on how to use a query to create a new table. Creating a new table is an easy way to get around the fact that you typically can't modify the properties of a linked table.

# Understanding Relationships in Queries

In order to use multiple tables in a query, the tables have to be related. In the following sections, I give you a closer glimpse at those relationships; you find out how to create the relationships necessary for adding extra tables to a query.

## Getting to know how tables are related

When you add related tables to a query, Access shows you that the tables are related by drawing lines between the tables in the Query editor. You must make sure that the table relationships are established before you begin creating your queries. If you begin creating a query and attempt to use tables that aren't already related, you have to create the table relationships and then continue building your query.

Except in unusual circumstances, all the tables in a typical Access database are generally related in some way. The relationships may be distant and travel through several intermediate tables, but tables that are unrelated to any other tables usually signify that either the relationships have not yet been established or that the unrelated table may not actually belong in the database.

Although you can view table relationships in the Query editor, Access provides a better option for working with table relationships. The Relationships window (accessed in the Advanced Tools section of the Ribbon), shown in Figure 5-7, not only displays any existing relationships, but it also enables you to create and edit relationships.

In Figure 5-7, two relationships are displayed. The `TypeID` field is shared by both the TypeTable and ItemsTable tables, and those fields were used to create one relationship. The ItemsTable and OWNERS tables are similarly related, using a common field.

If you choose to enforce referential integrity for a link, Access includes the symbols that show the type of relationship between the tables. *Referential integrity* is a method of ensuring that your related data is protected; it's covered in the "Setting up table relationships" section, later in this chapter.

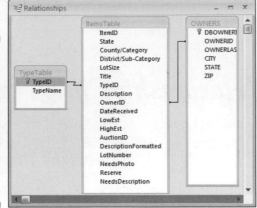

**Figure 5-7:**
The Rela-
tionships
window
enables you
to view,
create, and
edit table
relation-
ships.

You can create relationships between fields in two different tables as long as those fields contain related information and are of the same type (you can link an AutoNumber field to a Number field if the Number field has its FieldSize property set to Long Integer or Replication ID). It isn't necessary for the fields to have the same name, although using the same name for the field in the two tables does give you a good clue when you're creating the links. You can't, however, create links to memo or OLE Object fields.

## *Making sure that you choose the right relationships*

You need to choose the right relationships. No, I'm not talking about family matters or dating here. Tables can be related to each other in several different ways:

- **One-to-many** relationships have a single value in one table that is matched up with more than one value in the other table. This is the most common type of relationship. For example, in the typical relationship between a customer table and an orders table, each customer is usually assigned a unique ID in the customer table. That ID can appear in the orders table many times — once for each order placed by the customer.

- **One-to-one** relationships have unique values that can appear only once in each table. This type of relationship is far less common because one-to-one relationships aren't very useful in most instances.

- **Many-to-many** relationships are actually just two one-to-many relationships with an intermediary table that is used to create the link.

Don't worry too much if the types of table relationships seem a little confusing right now. Usually, Access automatically creates the correct type of relationship (usually a one-to-many relationship). In Chapter 15, you can find out how to make Access use a different type of relationship if necessary.

## Setting up table relationships

The relationships between the tables in your database are what make it a *relational* database that is far more efficient and useful than a *flat-file* database like one you might create in an Excel worksheet. Although this book isn't intended to cover basic database design issues, such as creating table relationships, you should know the process in case you somehow missed that step in designing your databases.

If you need more basic information, check out *Access 2007 For Dummies* published by Wiley.

Setting up table relationships requires some initial planning. When you're creating the tables for your database, you need to think about how those tables will be related. This means that you have to include fields that are common to two or more tables and that contain information that is shared between the tables. Say you have a Customer ID field and a Catalog Number field; these are but two examples of the types of fields that are likely to occur in multiple tables — you use the same customer ID in both a customer table and an orders table. Likewise, you use a catalog number in both an inventory table and an order detail table. To add table relationships in your database, follow these steps:

1. **Open the Access database in which you want to create the table relationships.**

2. **Choose Advanced Tools⇨Relationships to display the Relationships window, shown in Figure 5-8.**

3. **Click the field in the first table that you will use to link to the second table, hold down the left mouse button, and drag the pointer onto the related field in the second table.**

   You may need to first scroll the field display in the two lists to make the two fields visible.

4. **Release the mouse button.**

   The Edit Relationships dialog box appears, as shown in Figure 5-9.

**Figure 5-8:**
Open the
Relation-
ships
window
to create
new table
relation-
ships.

5. **Select the Enforce Referential Integrity check box if you want Access to make sure that certain rules are applied when you make changes to the records in the tables.**

   If you don't want to enforce referential integrity, skip to Step 8.

   Referential integrity ensures that you cannot delete or otherwise change data under specific circumstances. For example, you can't delete a customer's record in your customer table if there are still active order records under the customer's ID.

**Figure 5-9:**
Use the Edit
Relation-
ships dialog
box to
specify the
parameters
for the
relationship.

6. **If you chose to enforce referential integrity, choose the Cascade Update Related Fields check box if you want Access to automatically update the related tables when the primary table is modified.**

   For example, if you assign new customer ID numbers in the customer table, you want the orders table to reflect those new ID numbers, right?

7. **If you chose to enforce referential integrity, choose the Cascade Delete Related Fields check box if you want Access to automatically delete the associated records in the related tables when the primary table is modified by deleting a record.**

   For example, if you remove a customer from the customer table, you should also delete any remaining records for that customer in the orders table.

8. **Click the Join Type button.**

   The Join Properties dialog box appears, as shown in Figure 5-10.

   What Access calls a *join* is what I call a *relationship.* A join simply brings records from various tables together.

---

**Figure 5-10:**
Use the Join
Properties
dialog box
to specify
which
records
to use.

---

9. **Choose the type of join that's most appropriate for your database from the three choices.**

   In most cases the first choice is the correct one because you want to match the records between the two joined tables. The other two choices create what is called an *outer join,* where records from either the left or the right table are included even if the other table does not have matching records.

10. **Click OK to close the Join Properties dialog box.**

11. **Click Create to create the link (or *join*) between the two tables.**

12. **Repeat Steps 3 through 11 for each of the table pairs for which you want to create a relationship.**

After you finish creating the table relationships, those relationships appear in the Relationships window. You can drag the tables and resize them as necessary to make the links between the tables easier to visualize.

While viewing the relationships in the Relationships window, you can see a copy of the relationships by using the File⇨Print Relationships command. This command displays an on-screen report showing the relationships, and clicking the Print button gives you a printed report. You might need to move the tables to fit it all on one printed page.

# Chapter 6

# Modifying Data with Queries

. . . . . . . . . . . . . . . . . . . . . . . . . . . . . . . . . . . . . . . . . . . .

### *In This Chapter*

▶ Knowing what you can and can't modify

▶ Introducing data-modifying query types

▶ Creating tables from scratch with queries

▶ Using queries to update data

▶ Using queries to delete old and add new data

. . . . . . . . . . . . . . . . . . . . . . . . . . . . . . . . . . . . . . . . . . . .

*Y*ou can do a lot more with queries than simply selecting data to show in a Datasheet view, form, or report. You can also use queries to actually change the information that's contained in your database. This capability opens up whole new worlds of tasks that you can accomplish with Access because you can easily make either mass changes or very selective ones simply by creating the proper query.

In this chapter, you find out what you can do with a data-modifying query. The topics include using a query to create new tables, to update existing information, to remove specific data, and to add new records. Armed with these techniques, you'll become more efficient at manipulating your Access databases so that you can get more done in less time and maybe even find time to do some things that are a bit more fun with the spare time that you'll gain.

## *Understanding What You Can Modify with a Query*

Queries are very powerful tools. They give you the ability to automate a broad range of actions in your Access databases without requiring you to master some strange-looking and difficult-to-understand computer programming language.

## *Knowing what you can modify*

One of the most frustrating things about using queries to modify your databases is simply getting a handle on just what you can do with a query. Oh sure, you already know that you can use a query to select specific records and specific fields, but what else can you do with a query? Just what kinds of modifications are possible by using queries?

Here are some of the things you can do with a query:

- ✔ **Modify field values in a table.** You can change the prices of items you want to put on sale, change the name of a customer's company if another company buys it out, update telephone area codes for customers who live in a specific city, or modify the descriptions of a series of products based on some new requirement from your attorney that says you have to warn customers that the kites you sell aren't intended for flying in winds of over 2 miles per hour.

- ✔ **Remove specific records from a table.** With this type of query, you can remove all of your old flames from your address list when you get engaged, get rid of all of your cousin Larry's vegetable-flavored ice cream varieties (you knew they were a dumb idea in the first place, didn't you?), or delete any one-of-a-kind products from your inventory table after they're sold.

- ✔ **Add new records to an existing table.** You can quickly add a new series of products that you've just begun selling, add the latest members to your club's local membership list by using the list e-mailed to you from the national office, or add shipping and handling charges for each customer based on the amount of stuff they bought at your most recent auction.

- ✔ **Create a new table using a specified group of records from a single table or records that you generate from several tables.** You can create a table to send to your bookkeeper that lists the customers who purchased items so that the bills can be prepared, you can create a table for your newsletter editor that lists the members' birthdays for the upcoming month, or you can create a table of customers who bought your canned lizard meat spread so that you can send them a mailing announcing your new line of pickled banana products (are you sure it was cousin Larry who thought up that line of ice cream?).

I'm the first to admit that this list barely scratches the surface, but it does give you at least a few ideas about how queries can do so much more than simply select a set of records.

## *Knowing what you can't modify*

As powerful as queries are, they can't do everything. It's important that you get a feel for the limitations of queries. Here are some things that you can't modify with a query:

- ✔ **You can't use a query to modify the basic structure of an existing table.** For example, you can't use a query to change the data type or size of a field in a table.

- ✔ **You can't directly change the values used in AutoNumber fields.** However, you can use an *append query* to add enough records to indirectly change the next value used.

- ✔ **You can't use a query to change the names of objects in your database.** You can work around this limitation by using a *make-table query* to create a new table, but this solution doesn't really help if you have already created queries, forms, or reports based on the existing table.

  Append and make-table queries are different kinds of *action* queries. Action queries are designed for the specific purpose of modifying data in a table. If you want to make changes to data by using queries, become familiar with these queries. Lucky for you, I discuss action queries in the following section, "Called to Action: Data-Modifying Queries."

- ✔ **You can't change the sort order of a table so that an OLE Object field is used as the sort key.** Even if you use a make-table query, you're stuck because OLE Object fields simply can't be used for sorting.

- ✔ **You can't create a whole new database file with a query.** Queries can exist only within an existing database.

These limitations aren't so bad when you get right down to it. After all, a query is really intended to manipulate data, as opposed to modifying the basic building blocks of your database. You can easily make those types of changes yourself and use queries for what they do best.

# Called to Action: Data-Modifying Queries

When you begin creating a new query, Access automatically sets the query type as a select query. But if you want to modify data in a table, a select query just won't cut it. In Access, queries that modify data are called *action* queries. If you want to create an action query, you must select the query type when the query is open in Design View.

## Making sure you don't do any damage

Because all action queries modify your data in some way, you need to be careful that you don't make changes to your database that you later regret. That's one of the primary reasons that all new queries start out as select queries. You can always safely run a select query without worrying about changing your tables because select queries simply don't make any changes. After you've verified that your select query returns the results you want, you still have to be sure that you choose the proper type of action query and that you specify the correct tables to modify, but at least you know that your query is using the right records.

You must keep the differences between the types of action queries in mind as you create your own action queries. A simple mistake, like choosing to create a make-table query when you actually should have used an append query or an update query, can have some pretty extreme consequences — especially if you ignore the warnings that Access provides when you try to run one of these queries! If you're not sure what you're doing, it's okay to experiment. Just back up the work you don't want to lose.

Action queries include the following types:

- **Append queries** add new records to an existing table. Those new records can come from a single table, or they can be built up from records in two or more tables. The only fields append queries deal with are the ones that are already in the existing table, so if you create an append query that includes fields that aren't already in the target table, Access simply discards those extra fields when the records are appended.

- **Delete queries** remove records from a table. Any records that match the specified criteria are completely deleted, even if you specify only some of the existing fields in the query.

  If you want to remove only certain field values from a table without deleting the complete records, use an update query instead of a delete query.

- **Make-table queries** create a new table that includes all the fields specified in the query.

  Make-table queries always delete any existing table that has the same name as the specified target table, so you need to use some caution to make sure you don't accidentally overwrite a table that you really need.

- **Update queries** modify values in an existing table. Only the fields specified in the query are changed, so any fields that you don't specify are left untouched. When you want to delete only some fields (but not all the records), this is your action query of choice.

*SQL queries* can also modify data. Although many people consider SQL queries to be a separate type of Access query, in reality, all Access queries are SQL queries. I discuss SQL — Structured Query Language — in Chapter 7.

I often find that I need to create a couple of different types of queries and then run those queries in the proper sequence in order to accomplish a particular goal. For example, to create a table that contains the billing information for an auction, you might first create a make-table query that builds a new table containing information about the prices of the items that were sold at the auction. Then you would create an append query to add the buyer's premium and one that adds shipping and handling charges to that new table. This combination of different query types enables you to produce results that wouldn't be possible with a single query.

The Design section of the Ribbon produces a large and loud warning if you take an inappropriate action.

# Creating New Tables with Queries

Okay, you may find this a little strange, but I happen to think that make-table queries are actually kind of fun to create and use. After all, can you think of another way that you can so quickly create a new table and fill it with selected data from a couple of different tables? It almost seems magical the way a make-table query allows you to be both creative and extremely productive at the same time.

## Why you would want to create new tables

There are often several different ways to accomplish the same goal. That's certainly true in Access. For example, if you consider the example of selecting and gathering data for a report from a set of tables, one method to meet your objectives would be to create a complex select query and then base your report on that query. If you need to summarize the data in the report and perform calculations based on various subtotals, your report design could become quite intricate and difficult to troubleshoot or even to verify.

As an alternative to that option, you may want to consider using a make-table query to first bring together the basic data for your report. After you set up the new table, you can continue to use the same complex report design, or you can use another query to perform the calculations and then base your report on the already summarized data. This second method offers a couple of advantages:

✔ You have an actual table where you can examine and verify your data.

✔ Your report is easier to design.

✔ You don't need to deal with so many troubleshooting issues.

In addition, having the data in a new table makes exporting that data to another application such as Excel, Word, or even QuickBooks a snap.

## Creating your first table with a make-table query

A make-table query enables you to create a new table by using records from one or more existing tables. For example, you can convert an existing select query into a make-table query that creates a table that shows the winning bidder for each item in an auction.

To create a make-table query, follow these steps:

1. **Create the select query that you want to use as the basis for your make-table query.**

   Figure 6-1 shows an example query. Be sure that you save the query before continuing.

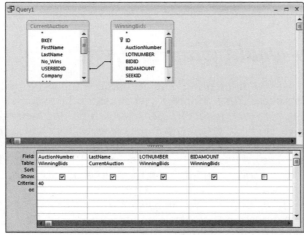

**Figure 6-1:** Begin by creating your select query.

2. **Test your query by clicking Run (the large exclamation mark) in the Design section of the Ribbon.**

TIP

You want to make sure that your query returns the expected results before you convert the query into a make-table query (you may also choose View from the top-left side of the Ribbon or right-click and choose Datasheet view). If your query didn't return the results you expected, correct the errors and test it again. When you're satisfied with the results, continue to Step 3. Figure 6-2 shows a sample query that returned the expected results.

**Figure 6-2:**
Run your
select query
to ensure
that it
actually
produces
the results
you
intended.

3. **In the Design section of the Ribbon, click Make-Table Query.**

The Make Table dialog box appears, as shown in Figure 6-3.

**Figure 6-3:**
Enter the
name for the
new table
that you
want to
create.

4. **Enter a name for your new table in the Table Name text box.**

REMEMBER

Be careful not to use the name of an existing table unless you really do want to completely replace the existing table with the new table.

5. **If you want to create the new table in a different Access database file, select the Another Database option and then specify the name of the database file in the File Name text box.**

   You can click the Browse button if you prefer to browse for the file and avoid the possibility of typing the filename incorrectly.

6. **Click OK.**

   The Make Table dialog box closes, and you return to Design View. The only visual clues to show that your query is now a make-table query (and not a select query) are the description in the Design View title bar and the icon that is displayed on the Query Type icon on the Ribbon.

7. **Save the query before continuing.**

   Choose File⇨Save, press Ctrl+S, or click the Save button on the Ribbon.

8. **Click the Run button to run your query.**

   A warning message similar to the one in Figure 6-4 appears. The warning message indicates the number of records that will be added to your new table. You can't undo the action you're about to agree to, so be careful (see Step 8).

**Figure 6-4:**
This warning tells you what will happen next and gives you a chance to change your mind.

Microsoft Office Access

You are about to paste 1437 row(s) into a new table.

Once you click Yes, you can't use the Undo command to reverse the changes. Are you sure you want to create a new table with the selected records?

[ Yes ]   [ No ]

9. **Click Yes to continue and create your new table.**

If, instead of displaying a message similar to the one shown in Figure 6-4, Access displays a message telling you that an existing table will be deleted before you run the query, be sure that the correct table name is shown before you click the Yes button. Otherwise, you could destroy an existing table that you actually want to keep.

# Updating Data by Using Queries

There's no doubt that creating new tables by using a query (as described in the previous section) is both useful and interesting, but you may have even more call for updating existing data with a query. With update queries, you can make changes throughout a database quickly and efficiently.

Imagine for a moment how bored you would be to search through a table containing several thousand records to find and manually change a specific value. For example, suppose you have a database that contains, among other things, a customer list of several thousand people and businesses. You've just found out that the telephone area code for a city where a hundred or so of your customers live has just been changed from 702 to 775. Sure, you can spend a whole bunch of time looking for all the affected customers and then manually change their area codes, but an update query can do the job in moments (and you wouldn't have to wonder whether you missed anyone when you nodded off somewhere at about the 83rd on-screen page of the Datasheet view).

You might be tempted to use the Editing option to change the value 702 to 775 in the table, and, indeed, that option would work if you wanted to change *all* occurrences of the values to something else. But in a case in which you want to change only certain instances of that specific value based on the contents of another field, Find⇨Replace won't do the job because you'd still have to manually verify each change. (What if several people paid $702 for an item?) For this more complex situation, you really need to use an update query to make the changes easily and efficiently.

## Creating an update query example

You can use an update query to modify a series of records. In the following steps, I use the example mentioned in the previous section: The telephone area code needs to be changed for a group of clients. It's always a good idea to have more than one criterion to cross-check your queries. For example, if you want to change a current area code, you should also make sure that the city and state match. Each of these items is important to check before making any changes because if any of them don't match, you don't want to make any changes.

To create an update query, follow these steps:

1. **Create the select query that you want to use as the basis for your update query.**

Figure 6-5 shows an example query in which the state must be NV, the city must be Reno, and the phone area code must be 702. (In this case, the field contains only the area code, not the whole telephone number.)

2. **Test your query by clicking the Run button.**

   Figure 6-6 shows the results of running the query.

**Figure 6-5:**
Create a select query that selects the records you want to update.

3. **Right-click in the title bar or click the View button to return to Design View.**

4. **Right-click in the body of the query and select Query Type; then choose Update from the pop-up menu.**

   Query Type⇨Update will light up in the Design section of the Ribbon.

5. **In the Update To row of the affected field, enter the new value you want to apply to the selected set of records.**

   In this case, you enter **"775"** as the new value. (Access automatically adds quotation marks when you enter values in a text field, but you can include them yourself, too.)

   Figure 6-7 shows how the query looks after being changed to an update query and having the update value added.

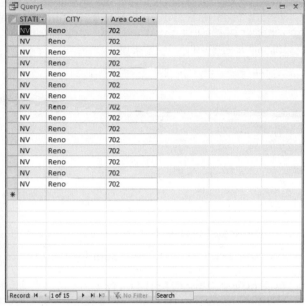

**Figure 6-6:**
Verify the
query
results
before you
update the
records.

**Figure 6-7:**
The update
query is
now ready
to run.

6. **Click the Run button to run your query.**

Access displays a message, similar to the one shown in Figure 6-8, that tells you how many records will be updated. This number should be the same as the number of records that the select query selected. If it isn't, click No in Step 7 and review your actions.

**Figure 6-8:**
Access tells
you how
many
records will
be updated.

**7. Click Yes to continue and update the records.**

Figure 6-9 shows the result to the table of running the update query.

If Figure 6-9 has you a little confused, that's okay. I specifically set up this example so that it would produce results that you might not expect. It's very important that you take an analytical eye to every change you make to your database; otherwise, you'll have real problems down the road. Read the following section, "Understanding the update query results," for information about interpreting your results.

**Figure 6-9:**
This is a
sampling of
the records
after the
update
query was
run.

| O\ | CITY | STATI | ZIP | Area Code |
|---|---|---|---|---|
| | Carrizozo | NM | 88301 | |
| | Reno | NV | 89503 | 775 |
| | Reno | NV | 89511 | 775 |
| | Highlands Ranch | CO | 80163-0222 | |
| | Weimar | CA | 95736 | |
| | Washoe Valley | NV | 89704 | |
| | Sherman Oaks | CA | 91401-5722 | |
| | Dayton | NV | 89403 | |
| | Los Alamos | CA | 93440 | |
| | Pasadena | CA | 91102 | |
| | Carson City | NV | 89704 | 702 |
| | Hermiston | OR | 94838 | |
| | Washoe Valley | NV | 89511 | |
| | San Jose | CA | 95125 | |
| E. | Reno | NV | 89503 | |
| | Lake Monroe | FL | 32747 | |
| | Encino | CA | 91316 | |
| | Bishop | CA | 93514 | |
| | Riverbank | CA | 95367 | |
| | Fernley | NV | 89408 | |
| | Mt. Vernon | WA | 98273 | |
| | Yucaipa | CA | 92399 | |
| | Bandon | OR | 97411 | |
| | Mentone | CA | 92359-9569 | |

Record: |◄ ◄ 7 of 241 ► ►| ►❑ No Filter  Search

## *Understanding the update query results*

If you refer to Figure 6-9, you might be scratching your head. That's a good thing. In my example, the area code for any cities other than Reno remained as 702, and *most* of the Reno records were changed to 775. But why is there a record for Reno without an entry in the Area Code field? Why wasn't that record updated to show 775?

The answer is simple. The select query I set up had three criteria. To be selected (and therefore updated), each record had to match *all* the criteria. One of the criteria was that the existing value in the Area Code field had to be 702. In this case, the last Reno record that is visible in Figure 6-9 didn't meet that criterion because there was no value in the Area Code field for that record.

The original value may have been a different area code — not an uncommon occurrence in some large cities where several area codes are used — and you wouldn't want to change that value incorrectly. Or for some other reason (pilot error?), the field might have been empty. The update query actually does work exactly as it's supposed to because the nonmatching record was left untouched.

# *Deleting Data with Queries*

Any action query has the potential for being destructive, but delete queries seem the scariest. After all, with just a couple of clicks, a delete query can permanently wipe out years of data entry work. If the potential damage a delete query can do doesn't scare you into backing up your database files, you may be one of those people who keep rattlesnakes as house pets.

Delete queries remove all trace of the selected records from your database. Because of this simple fact, it's even more important to first create your query as a select query and test it to see what results it returns before you change the query type to a delete query. Did I mention that you should be careful?

As an alternative to permanently deleting records by using a delete query, you may want to consider adding an Active field to your table and marking the records you were thinking of deleting as inactive. That way, you can retain those records for possible future use but exclude them from any reports by only including active records.

Creating a delete query is virtually identical to creating an update query. Here's how to proceed:

1. **Create a select query, as shown in Figure 6-10.**

   In this case, I specified that the state must be NV, and the phone area code field should be empty (Access refers to this as a *null* value).

**Figure 6-10:** Create the select query that selects the records you want to delete.

2. **Test your query by clicking the Run button.**

   When you change the query type, all the selected records are slated for deletion, so make sure the results are correct before moving on.

3. **Right-click and choose Design View or click the View button to return to Design View.**

4. **Right-click and choose Query Type⇨Delete Query.**

   The Delete Query option lights up in the Design section of the Ribbon.

   Performing this step changes the query design slightly, as you can see in Figure 6-11.

5. **Click the Run button to display a warning message similar to the one shown in Figure 6-12.**

   If something doesn't seem right, you should click No and go back over your work.

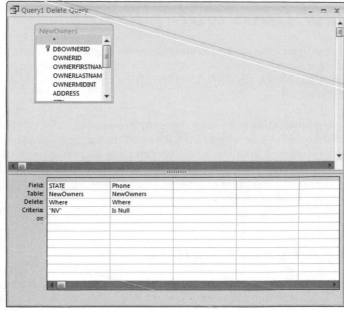

**Figure 6-11:**
The delete
query is
ready to
delete
records
from your
database.

**Figure 6-12:**
This dialog
box is your
last chance
to save the
records
before
they're gone
for good.

6. **Click Yes to continue and delete the records.**

Access doesn't allow you to delete records from a table if doing so would violate referential integrity rules. For example, if you have a customers table and an orders table that are linked with referential integrity enforced, you can't delete customers who still have open orders. See Chapter 5 for more information on referential integrity.

# Adding New Data with Queries

Compared with delete queries, append queries seem almost tame. Instead of permanently removing records from your database, an append query adds new records to a table. Any existing records remain untouched, and you can sleep a little easier.

Even though append queries seem benign, you should still exercise caution with append queries just as you do with any other action query. After all, you're still modifying the data, and that can have its consequences — if you aren't careful, an append query can add a whole bunch of bogus information to your database in the blink of an eye. The old saying, "garbage in, garbage out," certainly applies here!

## Using an append query

If you've been following along in this chapter, by now you've had some practice creating action queries from a select query. The process is pretty much the same no matter which type of action query you want to create. First, you create your select query and make certain that it actually produces the set of records that you expect. After you're sure that the select query is functioning properly, you change the query into an action query, supply any additional parameters, and run the query to perform the action. You can read more about parameters in Chapter 15.

Creating an append query generally follows the same path as any of those other types of action queries. However, some additional options may make an append query even more useful to you.

The purpose of an append query is to add new records to a table. That's nothing new, of course, but stop for a moment and think about the implications of that statement. Notice that I didn't say where the new records were coming from. The source of the new records doesn't have to be a table in your current database file. This simple fact opens up a whole bunch of possibilities:

- You can use a table in another Access database on your PC as the source of the new records.

- If you are on a network, you can use an append query to add records to your database from a database file on your server or on another PC.

- If several people are using copies of the same database file on their laptop PCs, you can use an append query to consolidate the information from each of them when they stop into the office.

- You can import or link to files from other applications such as Excel, so the source of the new records doesn't even have to be an Access database.

You can also use something called *database replication* to synchronize differ-ent copies of a database, but the process can be pretty complex to set up and administer. Database replication is a topic that's beyond the scope of this book, but if you're really inclined to give it a try, the Access help files sketch out how to do it.

The following steps show you how to use an append query to add records to a table. In my example, the basis of these new records is some data in an Excel worksheet that needs to be added to an existing Access database table. Here are the steps you need to follow:

1. **Click External Data from the Ribbon. Choose Microsoft Excel (or the appropriate file type if your data is in another format).**

   Get External Data⇨Import will work if you don't want to create a live link to the data. In this case, you use the link option, but you need to con-sider how you want to add records on an ongoing basis before making a choice. The import option might be a better choice if you intend to con-tinue adding new records to the external file rather than starting with a clean set of records the next time you run the append query.

2. **Choose Link to the data source by creating a linked table (radio/ option button).**

3. **Select the file, as shown in Figure 6-13.**

   In my example, I selected an Excel worksheet file.

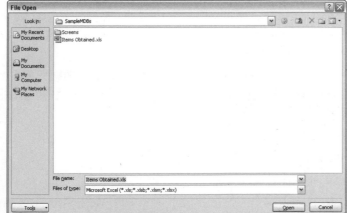

**Figure 6-13:**
Choose the external file you want to use as your data source.

4. **Click the Open button to display the Link Spreadsheet Wizard, as shown in Figure 6-14.**

A second, nearly identical screen may follow (click Next), asking for more details. Select or deselect the First Row Contains Column Headings check box as appropriate for your data. It's much easier to use data from an Excel worksheet that has column headings that match the field names in your Access table than to use data from a worksheet with different names or none at all.

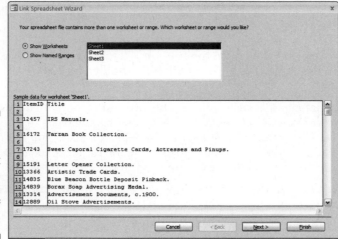

**Figure 6-14:** Select the worksheet or range that is the source of your data.

5. **Select the worksheet or the range that you want to use in Access.**

   The sample data area shows how the selected worksheet or range appears.

6. **Click Next to continue.**

7. **Specify a name for your linked table and click Finish.**

8. **When Access displays the warning message, click Yes (as shown in Figure 6-15).**

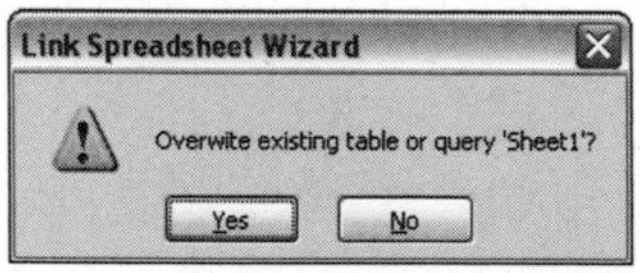

**Figure 6-15:** You are given a warning.

9. **Create your new select query by using the linked table (it will be in the Navigation Pane) as the data source.**

    You can click the asterisk at the top of the list to add all the fields to the table.

10. **Choose Query⇨Append Query to display the Append dialog box, as shown in Figure 6-16.**

11. **Click the down arrow at the right side of the Table Name list box and then choose the table where you want to append the new records.**

12. **Click OK to continue.**

13. **Choose Query⇨Run or click the Run button.**

    A message appears, telling you how many new records will be added to the table.

**Figure 6-16:**
Access is
ready to
append your
new
records.

14. **Click Yes to add the new records to your table.**

As this example demonstrates, you can easily add records from sources other than tables that already exist in your database, greatly expanding your database possibilities.

## Combining make-table and append queries

I've found that neither a make-table query nor an append query can always fit the bill, but sometimes a combination of the two is exactly what I need. In the auction database, I regularly need to generate a table that the bookkeeper can import into QuickBooks. Here's a quick-and-dirty description of how it works:

1. **Create a table by using a make-table query.**

   This query generates the initial table with, say, the winning bids. Of course, your make-table query could generate a table with final sales, lowest temperatures, or any other data.

2. **Use an append query to add records.**

   In my example, of course, these additional records are for shipping and handling and the buyer's premium.

You could create a table with one extremely complex query, but if a couple of simple (and easy-to-troubleshoot) queries can do the job, why not go for the easier solution?

Action queries certainly give you a much higher level of automation and control than the simpler select queries that I discuss in the beginning chapters of this book. As long as you respect the power of action queries, as well as their capability to really mess up your database if you're not careful, you can find many uses for action queries in the future.

# Chapter 7

# Expanding Queries with SQL

*Y*ou've been using Access for a while, and if you've been reading the book from the beginning, you probably have a pretty good handle on the various types of Access queries — with one big exception, that is. I haven't really talked much about *SQL* queries. Well, now it's time to acknowledge the elephant over in the corner. This chapter sheds some light on what SQL is and how it affects your Access databases.

If you're completely happy writing queries with a Query Wizard or in Design View, you can just skip this chapter and avoid being exposed to another programming language. But if you want to supercharge your queries (or you want to find out something about Access that you can use to impress your computer-geek friends when they start spouting off a bunch of incomprehensible jargon), this is the chapter for you. After all, how cool will it be to drop something like, "Oh, I use a SQL union query to merge results in my Access database all the time"? Well, okay, maybe it's not all that cool, but it might impress your boss. And don't you want to discover just a bit more?

## Getting the Scoop on SQL

*SQL* (usually pronounced like "sequel") stands for *Structured Query Language,* and it's a computer programming language that is used in most modern database applications.

Yes, that's right! SQL is actually a pretty common language that is used to create queries in most of the popular general database applications on the market today. For example, IBM DB2, Microsoft SQL Server, MySQL, Oracle, and Sybase are all SQL databases. Although it's not as obvious, Access fits right into that crowd, too. (Don't worry if you've never heard of those other types of databases, you can stick with Access and forget about them without really missing anything.)

## Understanding the "S" in SQL

The S in SQL stands for *structured,* which means that SQL commands always follow a defined *syntax.* This syntax is pretty basic:

```
COMMAND object OPTIONS;
```

SQL statements include a command; they specify the object, such as a database, a table, or a field on which to execute the command; and they specify any options that are needed to alter how the command functions. Also, SQL statements always end with a semicolon (;) to tell the SQL application that the end of the command has been reached and it's time to execute the command. For example, the following snippet demonstrates a SQL select query that shows records for customers from Nevada:

```
SELECT CustomerName FROM Customers WHERE State = "Nevada"
```

So, there's your SQL lesson, now let's move on. Okay, just kidding, but that's really SQL in a nutshell. To use SQL effectively, you need to know a bit more — such as some of the commands you can use.

By convention, SQL documentation always shows all the SQL commands and options in uppercase. In fact, some SQL database applications may not understand commands that aren't in uppercase; fortunately, Access isn't one of them. You can use any capitalization (or lack thereof) that you want, and Access will still understand. However, if you think you may eventually advance to using SQL with other database programs, get into the habit of using the "correct" capitalization. In all the commands you see in this chapter (and throughout the book), I follow standard SQL conventions.

To put the idea of a structured language into a bit clearer focus, consider the difference between human languages and computer programming languages. Humans are typically quite adaptable and can usually understand statements that don't follow normal sentence structure. Computer programs, on the other hand, are easily confused and need to have commands structured in a very precise way so that the program can understand what to do. To further understand what I mean, consider something my father told me about what happened when he was young and working in a local butcher shop. An elderly immigrant came in and said, "Give you to me a chicken." Although that wasn't the normal syntax he was used to hearing, my father clearly understood what was being requested. Imagine what a hard time a computer would have trying to figure out a statement that was so different from what it expected. The lady would probably still be waiting for her chicken!

## Putting SQL in its place (at the heart of all Access queries)

Maybe you're surprised to discover that every Access query is actually a SQL query. No matter what method you use to create a query in Access, that query is converted to SQL and stored in your Access database as SQL. For example, Figure 7-1 shows a simple append query in Design View.

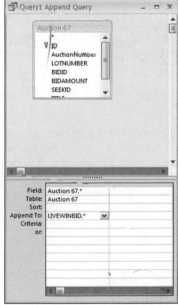

**Figure 7-1:**
This simple append query is actually stored as a SQL query.

The query shown in Figure 7-1 looks like this in SQL:

```
INSERT INTO LIVEWINBID
SELECT [Auction 67].*
FROM [Auction 67];
```

Here's a quick look at what this all means:

```
INSERT INTO LIVEWINBID
```

says to insert records into the LIVEWINBID table.

```
SELECT [Auction 67].*
```

tells Access to select all the fields in the table named Auction 67 (the asterisk is a *wildcard* for all the fields in a table).

```
FROM [Auction 67];
```

tells Access to get the records from the table named Auction 67.

Okay, so I agree that this isn't quite normal human language, but you probably didn't have any real trouble understanding the gist of it even before the explanation.

# Understanding How SQL Can Help

By now you're probably wondering what the big deal is and why you should even care about SQL. After all, can't you simply go on using the Query Wizard or creating your queries in Design View?

Actually, you can just ignore SQL — if you're willing to give up some of the power that's packed into Access, that is. However, there are some powerful reasons for expanding your knowledge of SQL. Put simply, SQL can help you improve your forms and reports in ways you might not imagine right now. For example, you might discover that using a SQL *data-definition query* enables you to change the type of existing data so that it can be more accurately displayed in a report.

## Going beyond the automated query functions

Even though the Query Wizard and Design View enable you to do an awful lot, you simply can't create some types of queries without resorting to SQL. These are what Access calls *SQL-specific queries* and include the following types of queries:

- ✔ **Data-definition:** These queries allow you to create or alter objects in the database by using *Data Definition Language* (DDL) statements.

- ✔ **Pass-through:** These queries allow you to send commands directly to an ODBC database server so that you work directly with tables on the server. Usually, the Microsoft Jet database engine that Access uses processes the data.

- ✔ **Subquery:** With this type of query, you use a SQL SELECT statement in a select or action query to retrieve "selected" records.

- ✔ **Union:** You use this type of query to combine the results of two or more select queries into a single query.

Access doesn't actually support all the SQL statements that are available in some other SQL databases, but it does allow you to use the most common and useful statements. Access 2002 and later versions support a few additional SQL statements that aren't supported in older Access versions, but only if you use the latest Access 2002, Access 2003, or Access 2007 file format for your database.

## Creating an indexed table with SQL

SQL-specific queries can't be created with a Query Wizard or in Design View. Even though you have to do some manual work, SQL queries *do* enable you to do some things you can't do with an ordinary query.

Chapter 6 shows an example of how you can use a make-table query to create a new table in your database by using fields from one or more existing tables. When you use a make-table query in this way, the fields in the new table have the same data types as the existing fields. This limits you in creating tables because you can't specify the data type, and you also have no way to specify a *primary key* (or index) for the table.

The following SQL data-definition query demonstrates a totally different way to create a new table. Working from scratch, you can

- ✔ Specify the data type for each field.

- ✔ Set a specific size for several of the fields (in my example, the fields are Lastname and Firstname, but you probably have different names for your own).

- ✔ Set those fields as required fields.

- ✔ Define a field (in my example, the ContactID field) as a primary key for the table.

Here's how the SQL query looks:

```
CREATE TABLE Contacts
([ContactID] integer,
[Lastname] text (25) NOT NULL,
[Firstname] text (25) NOT NULL,
[Phone] text,
[City] text,
[State] text,
[ZIP] text,
CONSTRAINT [Index] PRIMARY KEY ([ContactID]));
```

To enter the SQL code into Access 2007, follow these steps:

1. **Click Query Design in the Create section of the Ribbon.**

2. **Close Show Table by clicking the Close button.**

3. **Right-click to bring up SQL View.**

4. **Type the SQL code on the blank query sheet, also known as Query Editor.**

Figure 7-2 shows how my Contacts table appears in Design View after the SQL query is run.

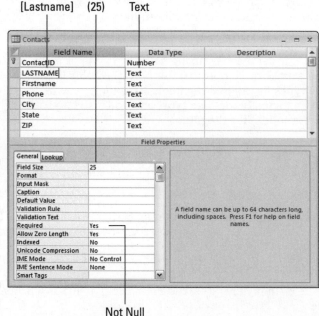

**Figure 7-2:** What you see after running the CREATE TABLE SQL query.

## Modifying a table with SQL

You can use a SQL query to modify the structure of an existing table. Such modifications might include

- Adding a key to a table
- Changing the data type of a field
- Changing the size of a field
- Making a field a required field

Any of these functions might be especially handy if you use a make-table query to create a new table by using records from one or more other tables.

The following SQL query example adds a primary key to an existing table (such as one you might create with a make-table query):

```
CREATE INDEX Lot
ON [Auction40] (Lotnumber)
WITH PRIMARY;
```

In this example, the table is named Auction40, and the field on which the primary key is based is named Lotnumber. The new index is named Lot. By creating a primary key, you can use the table in a relationship in which referential integrity is enforced, and you can ensure that the values in the Lotnumber field are unique.

Do you need to change the next number that will appear in an Autonumber field? If so, a little bit of SQL can help. Here's what you need:

```
ALTER TABLE Tablename ALTER COLUMN Fieldname Counter
        (StartingValue, Increment);
```

Just replace the *Tablename*, *Fieldname*, *StartingValue*, and *Increment* arguments with the appropriate values. Unfortunately, this trick won't work if the table has joins. You can, however, remove the joins and then add them back later.

After you become comfortable with creating SQL queries, you can use the same SQL statements for the query as the RecordSource or RowSource property in a form or a report. You usually use a query or a table as the RecordSource or RowSource, but an SQL statement works just as well.

These examples barely scratch the surface of what you can do with SQL in Access, but they do show you the possibilities that await you when you move beyond an ordinary query.

# Viewing the SQL You've Already Created and Didn't Know About

Every query that you create in Access is actually defined by a set of SQL statements that Access automatically generates from your query design. It simply isn't possible to create a query without generating the corresponding SQL statements — even if you didn't know they were there.

## Switching to Design View

If you're still stuck on using the Query Wizard to create all of your queries, it's time to bite the bullet and switch to Design View. You have to open the query in Design View before you can have a look at the SQL statements that are behind your queries.

If you want to create a SQL query from scratch, it's unnecessary to add any tables to the query by using the Show Table dialog box — even though Access automatically shows the Show Table dialog box when you click the Query Design option in the Insert section of the Ribbon.

To have a look at the SQL statements in a query you've already created, open the query in Design View, as shown in Figure 7-3. To open a query in Design View, select the query in the Queries list (left column) and right-click in the title bar, or click View in the upper-left corner of the Ribbon.

## Changing to SQL View

To see the SQL statements underlying your queries, you need to switch the query from Design View to SQL View. To change to SQL View, choose View⇨SQL View or right-click the title bar and choose SQL View from the pop-up menu.

Figure 7-4 shows the same query from Figure 7-3, but this time it is shown in SQL View.

**Figure 7-3:**
Open a
query in
Design View
so that you
can later
switch to
SQL View.

**Figure 7-4:**
In SQL View,
you can
view the
SQL
statements
that define
your query.

Figure 7-4 illustrates an important point about SQL statements. You don't have to worry about line breaks in the code because line breaks are simply ignored when the statement is executed (the semicolon ends the statement). On the other hand, line breaks do make it a bit easier for humans to understand the statements. Here I've added some line breaks (by pressing Enter) to break down the SQL statements into more understandable pieces:

```
UPDATE NewOwners
SET NewOwners.PHONE = "775"
WHERE (((NewOwners.PHONE)="702")
AND ((NewOwners.STATE)="NV")
AND ((NewOwners.CITY)="Reno"));
```

Even without any previous knowledge of SQL, this set of SQL statements is pretty easy to understand (Access is not case-sensitive). It tells Access to update the NewOwners table by setting the value of the PHONE field to 775 only when three criteria are met: The existing value in the PHONE field must be 702, the value in the STATE field must be NV, and the value in the CITY field must be Reno. You might even say that the SQL statement is easier to understand than trying to understand the same query in Design View!

## Seeing the results in Datasheet View

Before you actually run your query, you can check the Datasheet View to get an idea of what the query will do. Figure 7-5 shows how the query shown in Figures 7-3 and 7-4 appears when you switch to Datasheet View. (Since this is a real-world example, I hid many columns in Figure 7-5 for customer privacy.)

To switch to Datasheet View, choose View⇨Datasheet View or right-click the query title bar and select Datasheet View from the pop-up menu. You'll probably want to switch back to SQL View after you've checked the results in Datasheet View.

Datasheet View doesn't actually show the results of running the query. Rather, it shows the set of records that will be selected and processed when you run the query. In other words, the Datasheet view of your query shows you which records will be selected or changed by running the query, but it shows you how those records appear before any modifications occur. That makes the Datasheet view a good way to verify that your query is going to choose the correct records before you commit to any changes to those records.

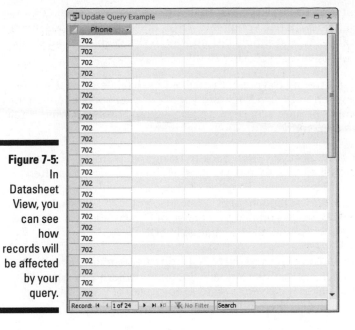

**Figure 7-5:**
In Datasheet View, you can see how records will be affected by your query.

## Going back to Design View

Usually, you can switch back to Design View by choosing View⇨Design View or by right-clicking the query title bar and choosing Design View from the pop-up menu. But Figure 7-6 shows that sometimes you simply don't have this option available.

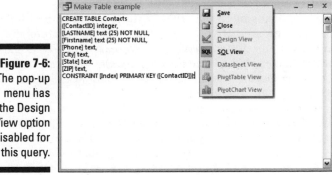

**Figure 7-6:**
The pop-up menu has the Design View option disabled for this query.

Figure 7-6 illustrates all too well the fact that you can't create certain types of queries in Design View. When you create a SQL query that isn't possible to create in Design View, Access simply has no way to represent that query in Design View, so it disables Design View in the pop-up menu.

This might seem frustrating to you, but imagine how exasperating it would be if Access did switch to Design View and your SQL query was changed into something that could be shown in Design View — you'd probably have a few choice words to say to someone at about that point.

Even though you can't always switch back to Design View from SQL View, in most instances, you'll be able to make the switch back and forth as often as you like. Switching between the two types of views is actually an excellent way to gain a better understanding of SQL because you can see what happens to the SQL statements when you make a change in Design View (or what happens in Design View when you make a change in SQL View).

Don't forget that you can copy and paste SQL statements to and from the SQL View in the Query editor (that blank query document where you typed SQL instructions). This makes it easy for you to keep copies of your SQL queries in a text document for documentation purposes, for example.

# Getting Your Feet Wet with Simple SQL Statements

Although this book doesn't have the space for anything resembling a full course on SQL programming, I can at least get you headed in the right direction with some good tips and best practices.

Earlier in this chapter, in "Changing to SQL View," I show you how to switch from Design View to SQL View so that you can examine the SQL statements that Access automatically generates whenever you create a query. Although you can use SQL statements as either `RecordSource` or `RowSource` properties in a form or report, the more common use for SQL statements is to enter them in the SQL View of the Query editor.

When you start playing with the powerful tools, Access treats you like a pro, assuming that you're a database expert. In many cases, it doesn't display the warning messages you typically see when you run a query. Just to be safe, use a copy of your database rather than the real, working copy you depend on.

You'll likely want to begin working with SQL by making small changes to existing queries so that you can switch back to Design View to see the results of your changes. That way, you can build your experience and confidence at the same time.

Before you make any modifications, though, make certain to follow some important do's and don'ts:

✓ **Don't put a semicolon (;) anywhere but at the end of a command.** The only place that a semicolon (;) can appear in a statement is at the very end of the statement. The semicolon tells Access that the statement is complete and ready to execute.

If you happen to forget the semicolon, the world might end tomorrow, but Access ignores your little error and runs the query anyway.

✓ **Do get in the habit of using uppercase for SQL keywords, even though you don't have to.** SQL *keywords* (such as commands and options) are always shown in uppercase by programming convention, but you aren't required to follow this convention if you are preparing SQL statements for use only in Access.

Even though using uppercase for SQL keywords isn't required, it's not a difficult convention to follow, and it can help you to find problems later. Most SQL examples you'll find online or in books follow the convention, and this will make it easier for you to compare what you've entered to the examples.

✓ **Don't forget brackets.** If a table name or a field includes spaces, such as `Auction 40 Results`, enclose the name in square brackets, as in `[Auction 40 Results]`.

Actually, it's always safe to enclose names in square brackets, so using them is a good habit to develop — that way you won't forget to add the brackets when they're important.

✓ **Do specify the table name.** You can get away with not specifying the table name when you specify a field name if there's only one table in the query, but it's safest to always specify the table name in square brackets just before the field name. Use a period after the closing square bracket just before the first character of the field name. For example, type `[Customers].State` to specify the `State` field in the Customers table.

✓ **Do use wildcards, but don't be fooled.** To use wildcards in SQL statements in Access, you use a question mark (?) to match a single character and an asterisk (*) to match any number of characters (including none).

In *ANSI* (American National Standards Institute) SQL, the version of SQL used by some other SQL database software programs, an underscore (_) is the wildcard for a single character, and a percent sign (%) is the wild-card for any number of characters. If you want to experiment with SQL examples you find on the Web or in other sources, be sure to look for these differences because they can cause your statements to fail (and the error message you see probably won't provide a lot of help, either).

✔ **Do consult the Help files when you need to.** The actual application that processes the SQL statements you create in Access is called Microsoft Jet. As a result, you'll find Help file information that lists various language elements you can use in the Help file section called Microsoft Jet SQL Reference.

✔ **Do consult the Help files when you need to, Part II.** If I haven't stressed this point already, let me tell you that there are some important differences between the ANSI data types and those that are supported in Access. You probably won't encounter any problems unless you try to copy an example of a SQL data definition query from the Internet, but if you do, check the Help file to see how to modify the query to use Access data types.

✔ **Don't forget that you're using a nonstandard form of SQL.** Access supports some nonstandard SQL features, such as the `TRANSFORM` command for creating crosstab queries, the `PARAMETERS` declaration for creating parameter queries, and a few extra built-in functions for analyzing data. You can't use these commands and functions with other SQL programs.

✔ **Don't forget that you're using a nonstandard form of SQL, Part II.** Access doesn't support all the keywords that are defined in the ANSI standards. If you attempt to copy an example from another source (say from an online resource) and you find that it doesn't work, you'll probably want to check the Microsoft Jet SQL Reference in the Help file to see whether you're using unsupported keywords.

You don't have to use SQL in order to make awesome forms and reports. But as you expand your knowledge of Access, a little SQL here and there can only help you. Although some of the points I mention here may seem a bit heavy, you can certainly create SQL queries without fully understanding all the SQL features.

# *Making Useful SQL Statements*

SQL queries can be useful and surprisingly simple. You don't have to write a best-selling novel in SQL in order for SQL statements to be effective.

If you've created an especially useful query, use it as a template for future queries. You can quickly and easily create a variation of that query by copying, pasting, and editing the SQL statements as necessary. This technique certainly beats going through the whole process of building a new query in Design View or the Query Wizard.

## Updating records with SQL

Updating records is one of the more common uses for queries, and it's also a good place to start if you're just starting out making SQL statements. SQL update queries are pretty easy to understand because they're simple and straightforward.

Consider the following example:

```
UPDATE [AuctionResults]
SET [AuctionResults].[AuctionNumber] = 87
WHERE [AuctionResults].[AuctionNumber] = 85;
```

This query changes the value in the AuctionNumber field of the AuctionResults table from 85 to 87. Another, shorter way to create this query is:

```
UPDATE AuctionResults
SET AuctionNumber = 87
WHERE AuctionNumber = 85;
```

You can, of course, create the entire SQL statement on a single line. In addition, if you don't need to specify any criteria, you can leave off the line that begins with WHERE and simply place the semicolon at the end of the second line.

If you need to update more than one field, simply add a comma after each field and then specify the additional field updates, as in this example:

```
UPDATE AuctionResults
SET AuctionNumber = 87,
Status = "Sold",
WHERE AuctionNumber = 85;
```

## Creating and filling tables using SQL

A make-table query both creates a new table and fills the new table with data from an existing table. In SQL, this type of query is known as a *select into* query because the query first selects records and then places them into the new table.

One very handy use for this type of query is to create a backup of an important table, as in the following example:

```
SELECT AuctionResults.*
INTO AuctionBackup
FROM AuctionResults;
```

In my example, I've created a simple backup of the entire AuctionResults table (remember that the asterisk is a wildcard, so it includes all fields) into a new table named AuctionBackup. In a real-world example, you might want to add the auction number to the end of the new table's name, as in AuctionBackup85, so that you can keep a running history of each sale in a new table.

To modify this query to make it into an append query rather than a make-table query, you need to use INSERT INTO, as in the following example:

```
INSERT INTO AuctionBackup
SELECT *
FROM AuctionResults;
```

This example adds all the records from the AuctionResults table into the AuctionBackup table. To be useful, you would probably want to empty the AuctionResults table between sales so that only new records would be added to the AuctionBackup table when you run the query.

If you want to add a single record to the table and specify the field values in the query, you use a slightly different syntax:

```
INSERT INTO AuctionBackup (AuctionNumber, AuctionTotal)
VALUES (87, 300);
```

Notice that both the field names and the values must be enclosed in parentheses. If you forget to add parentheses, Access displays an error message when you attempt to run the query.

## Summarizing values using SQL

You can also do a number of different calculations using *SQL aggregate functions*. These are built-in functions that are similar to the functions you've probably used in formulas in Excel worksheets hundreds of times. For example, the following query returns the sum of the winning bids from Auction 87:

```
SELECT Sum(WinningBid)
AS Total
FROM AuctionResults
WHERE AuctionNumber = 87;
```

## Making the most of SQL's flexibility

Each of the examples in this chapter is relatively simple to create and to understand, and using SQL View makes it very easy for you to quickly and easily modify an existing query to suit your needs. But don't be fooled. SQL is a powerful and complex language that takes practice to perfect. By understanding how these examples work, you can create new queries and change existing ones with speed and flexibility.

You may want to consider keeping a selection of your favorite SQL queries in a file for quick reuse in the future. One excellent way to do this is to create an Access table that contains two text fields. The first field could be used to hold a query type or description, and the second field could hold the text of each of your saved queries. Having a set of prebuilt query templates could make you into the real Access Query Wizard!

In addition to Sum, you can use Avg for the average value of the field, Count to return the number of records, First or Last to return the first or last value in the selected records, Min or Max to find the minimum or maximum value, StDev or StDevP for the population or population sample standard deviation, and Var or VarP for the population or population sample variance.

## Deleting records using SQL

Delete queries are the bad boys of queries because they have the potential for being so destructive. Even so, here's an example of a SQL query that deletes records that match a specified criteria:

```
DELETE FROM AuctionResults
WHERE AuctionNumber = 87;
```

# A Nod to VBA Programmers

As useful as SQL queries are to ordinary people who want a bit more control over their Access queries, those SQL queries become more valuable than gold when you start automating your Access applications with *VBA* (Visual Basic for Applications). VBA is the programming language that enables you to automate various operations in the Microsoft Office programs.

This book isn't the venue for a VBA tutorial, but I do want to touch on one aspect of VBA — using SQL queries as the basis for VBA programming code. When I create Access applications for my clients, I often use SQL queries in my VBA code. You can produce fully automated procedures that run much faster than manual queries when you do this. In addition, you can combine a number of operations in a single VBA procedure so that there's no chance that a user will forget to perform an important step that's necessary to successfully complete the task.

To a great extent, you can practically drop an SQL query into VBA code without changing a thing. For example, consider the following VBA statement that executes a delete query:

```
DoCmd.RunSQL "DELETE Customer.* FROM Customer"
```

Even without any background in VBA, you can probably recognize the SQL query portion of the statement:

```
DELETE Customer.* FROM Customer;
```

Although I can't give you a full VBA lesson, I can give you a set of guidelines about using SQL statements in VBA code. VBA is slightly less forgiving of creative syntax than SQL, so following some general rules is pretty important:

- To execute a SQL statement, the line of VBA code must begin with `DoCmd.RunSQL` followed by a space.

- Any double quotes within your existing SQL statement must be replaced by single quotes. You can very easily make this change by using the Edit⇨ Replace command in Notepad. Place all text strings within single quotes.

- Use the ampersand (&) to *concatenate* (link strings of) values within the statement. For example, the following adds the value in the LotNumber field from the LiveWinBid table to Lot: to produce a result such as Lot:101 to be placed in the LotNumber field of the new table:

```
'Lot:' & LiveWinBid.LotNumber AS LotNumber
```

- Your entire SQL statement must be enclosed within double quotes — this is the only place where double quotes should appear in the VBA statement unless you're building the SQL statement on the fly or if you are using the underscore (_) and continuing the statement on a second line (in that case, the first line must end with double quotes, and the second line must begin with them).

- Use the plus sign (+) to concatenate the values of VBA variables with your SQL statement and create a new SQL statement on the fly. For example, the following code creates a string by using the word *Auction* and the value of a VBA variable called `myNumber` to produce a string value based on the current value of the `myNumber` variable (this is the one place where you use double quotes other than at the beginning and end of the SQL statement):

```
'Auction" + myNumber +"' AS AuctionName
```

✔ The semicolon at the end of the SQL statement has to go. Just go ahead and delete it, and the world will be a happier place.

Even if you've done a bunch of VBA programming, the rules about concatenating values might require some experimentation before you'll fully grasp how they work. But other than those two rules, this set of rules is really just about all you need to take your SQL queries and throw them into some VBA code and dazzle the world.

The rules regarding single and double quotes are very important, and they're also frequently stated incorrectly in other texts. Using the two types of quotes improperly makes for runtime errors that can be awfully confusing to decipher.

# Chapter 8

# Dealing with Quarrelsome Queries

● ● ● ● ● ● ● ● ● ● ● ● ● ● ● ● ● ● ● ● ● ● ● ● ● ● ● ● ● ● ● ● ● ● ● ● ● ● ● ● ● ● ● ● ● ● ●

● ● ● ● ● ● ● ● ● ● ● ● ● ● ● ● ● ● ● ● ● ● ● ● ● ● ● ● ● ● ● ● ● ● ● ● ● ● ● ● ● ● ● ● ● ● ●

$O$ne of the most frustrating things about computers is that sometimes they just don't seem to work correctly. You think that you've done everything right, but the next thing you know, some cryptic error message that seems to have been translated through about six languages pops up. Or even worse, no messages appear, but the darn thing just produces really screwy results. Don't you just hate it when that happens?

A lot can go wrong with Access queries. It really doesn't take much to throw the whole process off base, and discovering the real problem is sometimes pretty difficult. In this chapter, you can see a number of things that commonly make queries act up. I also show you how you can send those problems packing.

## Troubleshooting Queries That Don't Quite Work

If you really want to see the cause of most problems with your Access queries, get up from your desk, walk to your bathroom, and look in the mirror. Yes, it's really true — *you* are the ultimate source of the issues that make your queries misbehave. Actually, you shouldn't feel too bad about your role in the problem; it's good news because it means that you can fix most query-related problems by getting a handle on what you did wrong. Rarely do you have to worry about some bug in Access, so you can concentrate specifically on what's in your query to figure out what isn't quite right.

## Understanding the clues Access gives you

Troubleshooting any type of problem requires a certain mindset if you want to find and fix the problem as quickly as possible. The first rule of troubleshooting is to be as methodical and logical as possible. Very few problems are ever solved by simply throwing up your hands and saying, "It just doesn't work."

The methodical approach to solving problems with Access queries can be summarized like this:

1. **Read the error message and click Help.**

    If an error message appears, read it carefully and click any help links that are included in the message. You may have trouble understanding what the message means, but it's the best clue you're likely to get.

2. **Think over every change you've made or identify the parts of your query that relate to the Help information.**

    If a query was working before you changed something, you have a pretty good clue about why the error occurred. Try to remember every little change you've made, not only in your query, but also in your database file.

    If the query runs but produces unexpected results, remember that Access is only doing what you told it to do and is not getting creative on its own.

3. **Modify the parts of the query related to the issue noted in the Help file for the error to see whether your actions make things better.**

4. **Finally, if you see nothing obviously wrong or your changes don't improve your results, you may need to just start over and create a new copy of the query from scratch.**

    Starting over and repeating what you think are the exact same actions often corrects a problem (and this solution is frequently faster than continuing to agonize over a query that won't give up its secrets).

## *Locating the problem*

Locating the specific cause of a problem you encounter when you attempt to run a query isn't always easy. After all, if you knew that something was going to be a problem, you would try not to put it in your query in the first place.

Each error you encounter will be a bit different, but here's a look at a typical Access query (containing deliberate errors) to see how you may go about locating the problem. In this example, I use an append query as it appears in SQL View (see Chapter 7 for information about using SQL to write queries):

```
INSERT INTO AuctionBackup
AuctionNumber, AuctionTotal
VALUES 87, 300;
```

You may not see anything wrong with the query, but Access sure does. When you attempt to run the query, Access displays the message shown in Figure 8-1.

**Figure 8-1:**
Access
encountered
an error
trying to run
the query.

To troubleshoot the problem, follow the steps in the previous section, "Understanding the clues Access gives you," to methodically identify, repair, and re-run the append query. Specifically,

1. **Click the Help button in the warning message box.**

   Figure 8-2 shows an example of the Help information you might see.

2. **Armed with the information you receive, close Help and then click OK in the warning message box.**

   At this point, Access does its best to pinpoint the first instance of the error by highlighting the item that triggered the error message, as shown in Figure 8-3.

   Now you're getting somewhere. With my example, you can say that the error seems to be caused by the highlighted item, the field name AuctionNumber.

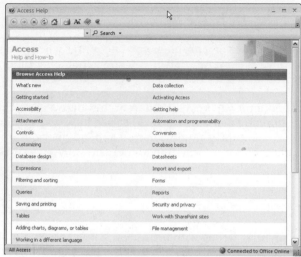

**Figure 8-2:**
Access 2007 offers a general Help screen.

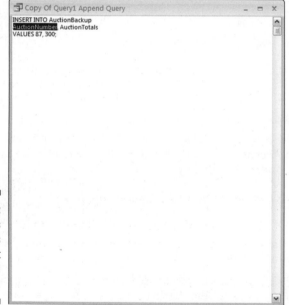

**Figure 8-3:**
Access highlights the item that triggered the error.

3. **Modify the parts of the query that seem to relate to the error message you received.**

In this case, you can quickly rule out a spelling error in any of the keywords because INSERT, INTO, and VALUES all appear to be correct. This leaves you with a punctuation error as the probable cause, and AuctionNumber as the location of that punctuation error.

If you're baffled, choose Help➪Access Help and look for terms in the Help file that can make things clearer.

For example, if you look up INSERT INTO in the Help file, you discover that the field names belong in parentheses — your punctuation error is that the field names should be surrounded by parentheses. So, armed with this information, you should modify the query like this:

```
INSERT INTO AuctionBackup
(AuctionNumber, AuctionTotal)
VALUES 87, 300;
```

Unfortunately, my example has more than one problem in it, so even with this change, if you try to run the query again, Access greets you with the same error message that you received before. But this time, when you click OK, Access highlights 87 in the third row because values also have to be enclosed in parentheses. You have to change the query one more time so that it looks like this:

```
INSERT INTO AuctionBackup
(AuctionNumber, AuctionTotal)
VALUES (87, 300);
```

4. **Continue the process until no error messages appear and you get the results you expect; alternatively, if you can't make the error messages go away, scrap the query and start from scratch.**

   After making the changes prescribed in my examples and running the query again, Access displays a message telling you that you're about to append one row to the table. That's more like it!

If an error prevents Access from executing a query, Access always tries to help you find the error, first by displaying an error message and then by highlighting the item that seems to be the cause. If you're working in Design View, try switching to SQL View to get more specific information about the error.

## Using Datasheet View as a troubleshooting tool

Often, the problem with a query isn't that the query won't run but rather that it doesn't produce the results that you expect. Access is more than happy to run a query that doesn't really do anything (or that does something other than what you intend), and because the query doesn't produce any errors, you can easily miss the fact that the query results are empty or incorrect — especially if you're in a hurry.

Always check your results! Don't assume that just because you see no error message that there's no error.

One quick way to check for record selection errors is to switch the query to Datasheet view before you run the query. Datasheet view shows you which records will be selected without actually performing any actions. Datasheet view is an excellent option for verifying that your query is correctly structured, especially if the query you want to run will delete records or update a table.

Figure 8-4 shows a select query that displays a list of city names and a count of the number of customers in each of those cities (in addition to the normal way of creating a select query, click the Totals option in the Design section of the Ribbon). The State field specifies which states are included in the results. The figure shows a subtle error in the query.

As Figure 8-5 shows, switching to Datasheet view displays an empty result. (Remember to choose View➪Datasheet View or right-click the query and choose Datasheet View from the pop-up menu to switch to Datasheet view.)

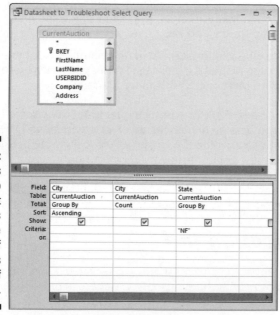

**Figure 8-4:**
This query is supposed to display a list of cities with the number of customers in each of the cities.

**Figure 8-5:**
Datasheet
view shows
that the
query isn't
returning
the
expected
results.

If you get into the habit of switching to Datasheet view just before you run your queries, you can train yourself to identify subtle errors before they muck up your forms and reports. When you see, for example, a Datasheet view like the one in Figure 8-5, your uh-oh detector is going to turn on automatically, and you'll immediately ask yourself what's wrong. Remember that typing error I mentioned? In this case, the selection criterion for the State field is mistyped as NF rather than NV. Switching back to Design view and correcting the typing error solves the problem, as Figure 8-6 shows.

The errors you're most likely to discover by using Datasheet view are record-selection errors. These types of errors can be directly traced to problems with any criteria you have specified, so if you don't see the expected results in Datasheet view, examine the criteria you have entered.

Empty results in Datasheet view aren't always the result of an error, of course. It's also possible that you've specified your criteria properly, but that your database simply doesn't contain any matching records.

### Correcting thorny problems

After you locate a problem with a query, the fix is usually pretty obvious. Sometimes, though, you may have a *really* messed-up query that leaves you at a loss as to the best way to fix it. For example, if you're working in Design View and you change the table that's associated with one of the fields in the design grid to a table that doesn't have the field, your query won't work until you correct the table association. The difficulty with this type of error is that you may not realize what's causing the problem.

If you encounter a really nasty situation in a query that seems to defy correction, step back for a moment and think about what's going on. If possible, delete a field or two from the query to simplify it, and then check the results in Datasheet view. When the simplified query starts producing the results you expect, add back one field at a time until you find the culprit.

**Figure 8-6:**
After you correct the typo, the query selects the correct records.

| City | CountOfCity | State |
|------|-------------|-------|
| Carson City | 1 | NV |
| Elko | 1 | NV |
| Ely | 1 | NV |
| Fallon | 1 | NV |
| Fernley | 1 | NV |
| Gardnerville | 1 | NV |
| Goldfield | 1 | NV |
| Henderson | 1 | NV |
| Incline Village | 1 | NV |
| Las Vegas | 1 | NV |
| Manhattan | 1 | NV |
| Midas | 1 | NV |
| Minden | 1 | NV |
| Reno | 1 | NV |

Datasheet to Troubleshoot Select Query

Record: 1 of 14   No Filter   Search

## *Troubleshooting Sassy SQL*

SQL-specific queries can present their own set of potential errors. Because you create these types of queries as text instead of by making selections in the Query editor, you really have to watch out for things like spelling and punctuation in addition to syntax errors.

## Figuring out what went wrong

Because so many different types of errors are possible in queries you create in SQL View, you really need to give yourself all the advantages you can. That way, you can concentrate on being productive.

One very important point to remember when you're creating SQL queries is that, as I mention in Chapter 7, you should always enter any SQL keywords in all-uppercase characters. Access won't protest if you don't capitalize, but it's still a good idea because the caps make spotting typing errors in keywords a bit easier in your finished query. For example, Figure 8-7 shows a SQL query with a common typing error and the error message that Access displays when you try to run the query.

**Figure 8-7:**
This SQL-specific query won't run because of a typing error.

In this case, the word Table is misspelled as Tabel, and Access highlights the misspelling when you click the OK button in the message box. But even if Access didn't highlight the misspelled word, the caps help make the error jump right out at you with even a quick glance at the SQL statement.

If your SQL query runs without any errors but produces unexpected results, you must dissect the query to figure out the source of the problem. It can be quite difficult to locate a logic error because, after all, you wouldn't have created the query like that if you didn't think you had the logic all worked out. Your best bet in such a situation is probably to put on your Sherlock Holmes hat and then carefully read through the query as if it were a story. When you find the place where the story doesn't seem to make any sense, you've found the problem!

## Trying Design View

Another method that you may find helpful when you're troubleshooting a SQL query is to switch to Design View. This option isn't available for SQL-specific queries that cannot be shown in Design View, of course. If the View⇨ Design View (upper-left section of the Ribbon) command is grayed out/dull (or Design View on the right-click on the pop-up query menu), you won't be able to switch to Design View. But if the option is available, your query is one of the types that can be shown in Design View.

Switching to Design View is a handy way to determine whether your SQL query has a language problem or a logic problem. If you have a language problem (also called a *syntax error*) such as a keyword spelling error, missing or incorrect punctuation, or items in the wrong place in the SQL statement, Access displays an error message when you try to switch to Design View. If Access can show the query in Design View, your problem is one of incorrect logic, not incorrect use of the SQL language elements.

## Things to watch out for in SQL queries

Frankly, a lot of things can go wrong with SQL queries. Here's a list of some common problems to watch out for:

- ✔ **Spelling errors:** Misspellings are easy to make and they can stop a query cold. Watch for not only misspelled SQL keywords, but also for table and field names that are misspelled.

- ✔ **Punctuation:** SQL often uses somewhat confusing punctuation, and the online help examples may not seem very, well, helpful. A handy thing to remember is that you should include any punctuation shown in the examples, with the exception of square brackets (but you should use square brackets around filenames and around field names if either of them includes any spaces) and ellipses (. . .).

✓ **Correct order:** The elements in a SQL statement have to appear in the correct order. If you have keywords, table names, or field names in the wrong place, it's even possible that the query will run but that it will do something (probably destructive) to the wrong table.

✓ **Correct dialect:** ANSI SQL and Access SQL are two dialects of the same language, and sometimes you need to modify examples you find on the Web or in books so that they work correctly in Access.

## Simplifying your SQL to find the problem

If you create a complex SQL query that runs without producing an error message but doesn't do what you expect it to, you may want to try simplifying the query to pin down the problem. This is where you find the cut-and-paste options awfully handy!

Many SQL queries look extremely complicated, but when you break a typical "scary" SQL query down to its components, it's basically a select query combined with an action query. It's reasonable, therefore, to begin your troubleshooting by first testing the select query. To test a select query, follow these steps:

1. **Copy your existing query, paste the SQL statement into a blank SQL View window, and then delete everything except the pieces that fit neatly into a select query.**

2. **Test your select query and then modify it as necessary.**

   You know you're done when the records you want to see appear when you switch to Datasheet view.

3. **When you're satisfied that the correct records are being selected, add back the fancy bits, such as the ORDER BY clause for sorting or the GROUP BY clause for grouping.**

4. **When the select query is functioning properly, save it with a new name.**

Remember that you can use a query as the data source for a query instead of using a table as the data source. After you debug your select query, you might want to consider using it as the source for the remainder of the action query.

# *Avoiding Improper Relationships*

It's the relationships between the various tables in your Access databases that make it possible for you to combine the data in those tables effectively. You really can't create a useful query involving multiple tables if you haven't specified the proper relationships between those tables.

## *Understanding how bad relationships can mess you up*

How you deal with your in-laws has nothing to do with this discussion, so you can stop making any wisecracks right now. No, what I'm talking about here are the kinds of problems you face when trying to create Access queries that produce reasonable results. If there are problems with the way the table relationships are defined in your databases, your queries will not produce good results.

Access uses *primary keys* and *unique indexes* to ensure that table relationships are properly defined. Both primary keys and unique indexes enable Access to ensure that each record in a table is unique. Some records may be similar, but each record must have at least one piece of information that ensures that no other record is an exact duplicate. Primary keys are unique indexes. A table can have only one primary key, but the same table can have more than one unique index. The primary key controls the sort order of the records.

When you create table relationships, you generally use a primary key or a unique index in at least one of the tables to define the relationship with the other table. For example, in Figure 8-8 the relationships between three tables are shown. Each of the tables is linked, using a field that is a primary key or a unique index in one of the tables. In this case, the DBOWNERID field is a primary key in the Owners table, and the BIDID field is a unique index in the LIVEWINBID table. You'd have to open the tables in Design View to examine the field properties (bottom of the page) to know that these fields are unique indexes.

Click Database Tools on the Ribbon and apply the Relationships option to view the joins. The result may be an overwhelming number of connected (joined) tables, but you can right-click and hide the ones that don't apply, moving the important tables across each other or up for clarity.

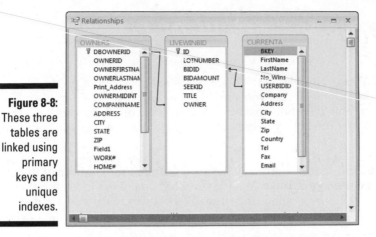

**Figure 8-8:**
These three
tables are
linked using
primary
keys and
unique
indexes.

Unfortunately, Access doesn't require you to use either primary keys or unique indexes to define table relationships. If you create a relationship between two tables by using fields that aren't defined as primary keys or unique indexes in either table, Access creates an *indeterminate* relationship, as shown in Figure 8-9.

**Figure 8-9:**
Indeter-
minate
relation-
ships result
from linking
fields that
aren't
primary
keys or
unique
indexes in
either table.

When there's an indeterminate relationship between tables, Access can't determine which records are actually related. In the case of the relationships shown in Figure 8-8, for example, you can't tell whether the winning bidder is Søren or Cole because they may both have the same BIDID. If you create a report that generates invoices for the winning bidders by using a query that included these tables, you could send an invoice to the wrong bidder.

## *Making sure your relationships make sense*

Even though Access allows you to create relationships that are pretty meaningless, that doesn't mean that you should do so. See Chapter 5 for more information on table relationships, but here are some quick do's and don'ts to consider so that the links you create between tables produce the results you want:

- ✔ **Do use a field that is a primary key or a unique index in one of the tables to create your links.** Making sure that one of the fields is either the primary key or a unique index enables you to create a one-to-many relationship, which is generally the most useful type of table relationship.

- ✔ **Don't create relationships in which fields are primary keys or unique indexes in both tables.** This action creates a one-to-one relationship. In most cases, the tables in one-to-one relationships should be combined into a single table (the exception to this rule is when you need to allow certain users access to some of the fields without allowing them access to other fields).

- ✔ **Do define the fields that you use for links so that the fields have the same data type in both tables.** You can create links between fields with different types, but you won't be able to enforce referential integrity if you do.

## *Correcting relationships that don't work*

The method you use to correct a problem with a relationship depends on the type of problem you need to fix. You can, for example, simply open a table in Design View, select a field, and change that field's Indexed property to Yes (No Duplicates) to make the field into a unique index. This type of change doesn't require you to delete the existing relationship before you make the change.

Often, however, you may need to right-click the relationship in the Relationships window and select Delete from the pop-up menu before you can make the necessary changes. For example, if you want to change the data type of a field that's part of a relationship, you need to delete the existing relationship before you can change the data type. After you save the modified table design, you can re-create the relationship.

# Junking Joins That Don't Join

A problem that you may encounter that is closely related to the table relationships are *joins* that don't produce the results that you want. Joins determine which records from the two tables are included in the results of the query.

## Understanding why default joins may not work

When you create a table relationship, Access automatically creates a default type of join that may not work for you.

You can create three basic types of joins:

- ✔ **Inner joins** are the default type of join. All records from both tables that match are selected.

- ✔ **Left outer joins** include all the records from the first (left) table in the relationship even if there are no matching records in the second (right) table.

- ✔ **Right outer joins** include all the records from the second (right) table in the relationship even if there are no matching records in the first (left) table.

The terms inner and outer are sometimes left out, so a left outer join is also simply called a *left join,* for example.

You typically want your queries to return only the records that have matching values in both tables, and for this purpose, the default inner join is the perfect choice. But in some cases, you want slightly different results. For example, if you have one table that lists all the items in an auction and another table that lists the bids that were received, you probably want to be able to produce a report that lists all the items — even those items for which there are no bids. If the table of items is on the left side of the join, you need to create a left outer join to produce this result. Choosing a default inner join would leave out the items that didn't receive bids.

## Correcting your joins

There are two primary ways to change the type of a join. Generally, the easiest way to modify a join is to edit the relationship by using the Relationships window. You can also modify the join in a query by changing the SQL statement in SQL View.

To modify the join type by using the Relationships window, follow these steps:

1. **Choose Relationships in the Database Tools section of the Ribbon.**

   You can also right-click the title bar of the query when it is in Design View and choose Relationships.

   The Design section of the Ribbon opens, and the Edit Relationships option appears.

2. **Choose the preferred Tables/Queries and click the Join Type button.**

   The Join Properties dialog box appears, as shown in Figure 8-10.

**Figure 8-10:** Choose the join type that fits your needs.

3. **Click to select the join type you want.**

   Option 1 produces an inner join, option 2 produces a left outer join, and option 3 produces a right outer join.

4. **Close the Join Properties dialog box by clicking OK.**

5. **Click OK to close the Edit Relationships dialog box.**

You can also modify your query directly in SQL View to create a different type of join. For example, a default inner join that selects only matching records from two tables may look like this:

```
SELECT ItemOwners.OWNERLASTNAME, WinningBids.LOTNUMBER
FROM ItemOwners
INNER JOIN WinningBids
ON ItemOwners.OWNERID = WinningBids.OWNERID;
```

To change this to a query that selects all the records from the left side table (ItemOwners in this example), modify the query to look like this to create a left outer join:

```
SELECT ItemOwners.OWNERLASTNAME, WinningBids.LOTNUMBER
FROM ItemOwners
LEFT JOIN WinningBids
ON ItemOwners.OWNERID = WinningBids.OWNERID;
```

# Steering Around Empty Query Results

One of the more frustrating things that can happen when you're creating queries is to have the results of the query turn up empty. And with no results, your forms or reports won't be very useful, either.

## Understanding some of the causes of empty query results

Sometimes a query produces empty results for a very good reason — none of the records match the criteria you've specified. Although this can happen when you've specified just one criterion, it's far more likely to happen if you've specified a larger number of them.

For example, suppose you set up a select query that has three fields, CustomerName, State, and NumberOfWinningBids. If you specify that the value in the NumberOfWinningBids field must be greater than zero and no other criteria, your query will probably return quite a few results. Now imagine that you also specify that the State field should contain RI. If you don't actually have any customers in Rhode Island, the query won't return any records when you run it.

Sometimes (more often than anyone wants to admit) a query returns an empty result because you've specified criteria that don't make any sense. For example, say you mistyped the selection value for California as CQ rather than CA. Access will return exactly the results it should — none!

## Correcting a query that doesn't return any data

It's pretty easy to correct a query that uses a single criterion and produces no results. You simply have to look at the query and correct whatever error you've made in entering the criterion (or, if there is no error, accept that returning no records is the correct result).

Correcting a query that uses multiple criteria is a bit harder because you have to locate the error before you can correct it. One method you can use is to remove the criteria one at a time until you start seeing results (use the Datasheet view for this). If you set up your query so that the most important fields are to the left of less important ones, then remove the criteria starting at the right and moving left. Eventually, you'll discover what's causing the problem, and then you can determine why the last criteria you removed was causing a problem.

# Preventing Data Destruction

Suppose you spend several thousands of dollars on a fancy new PC with all the bells and whistles. But just before you transfer all the files you've created over a number of years from your old clunker of a PC to the new one, you suddenly realize that your house is on fire and you only have time to grab one PC before you rush out the door. The question is which PC do you save?

If you said that you'd save the old PC and all of your data, give yourself an A. If you saved the new PC, you either have an off-site backup of all of your data or you don't understand the value of your data. A new PC is a lot easier to replace than the years of work that could be lost on your old PC.

## Beginning by backing up

If you don't keep an up-to-date copy of your really important files someplace off-site, you're asking for trouble. But you're not alone, because most people think that backups are something they'll do when they have time. Anything I say here probably isn't going to change your behavior in that regard.

Instead of trying to convince you to back up all your data, let me just suggest that you at least make a copy of your important Access databases so that they're safe from anything you do while practicing creating queries. Really, it isn't going to take you any time at all to make a copy, now is it?

Access even has a command, File⇨Manage Database⇨Back Up Database, that's designed specifically to make backing up database files much easier. Now you can't even use the "it's too complicated" argument.

## Avoiding destructive query results

Whenever you create an action query, you're creating a query that has the power to modify or destroy data. Access tries to warn you before committing any changes, but we all know how easy it can be to ignore those warning messages. "Sure, I want to delete 661 records; why else would I run this query?"

One of the surest ways to avoid destructive query results is, of course, to never create an action query. Simple select queries don't make any changes to your databases, so they're always safe to create and run. In the real world, though, action queries are a fact of life.

You can give yourself one extra chance to make sure you have things right by switching to Datasheet view to check the results before you run your query. That way, you can review the records your delete query is going to destroy.

## What to do if your database seems to be kaput

If you try to open your database and Access displays an error message that indicates that the file is corrupt, you'd better hope that your backup isn't too far out of date. But if you have no backup, you're stuck with what seems like your only copy of a bad file. Not the best situation. The following list shows you some things you can try.

Any repair attempt has the potential for causing even more problems, so be sure to make a copy of your kaput database file before trying to fix it.

- Choose the File⇨Manage Database⇨Compact and Repair Database command. In some cases, this command actually repairs minor errors, but it's actually more useful for removing the junk from your database file and making the resulting file smaller.

- Databases that have been converted from one Access file format to an older Access file format with the File⇨Convert Database Into command can sometimes act a little strange in some types of list views. If tables, forms, reports, or queries seem to have disappeared after a file format conversion, try clicking the Access Options button on the bottom of File and choose different view modes to see whether the objects reappear.

- If the tools built in to Access don't seem to be able to recover your database file, try one of the big-gun, third-party software options like the AccessFIX utility, discussed in Chapter 20. This tool can often correct problems just when you think all hope is lost.

# Part III
# Building Really Useful Forms

The 5th Wave                    By Rich Tennant

"Look-what if we just increase the size of the charts?"

## In this part . . .

Forms put a much friendlier face onto your database by making data entry and editing much easier tasks. This part shows you how to create forms that are really useful, and it tells you how to create forms that tackle data from more than one table at a time for even more efficiency.

# Chapter 9

# Building Better Forms by Using Controls

. . . . . . . . . . . . . . . . . . . . . . . . . . . . . . . . . . . . . . . . . . . . . . . . . . . . . . . .

## In This Chapter

▶ Introducing controls

▶ Using controls with forms

▶ Changing how controls operate

. . . . . . . . . . . . . . . . . . . . . . . . . . . . . . . . . . . . . . . . . . . . . . . . . . . . . . . .

**C**reating better, more usable forms is an art. This chapter introduces the various types of objects (known in Access-speak as *controls*) that you can add to your forms; it shows you how to make effective use of these controls.

Forms can have the most direct effect on how friendly your database application seems to users. The controls that you choose to use in your forms can make or break this impression. The right set of properly configured controls makes for a form that is logical and easy to use. A haphazard selection of controls that are simply thrown onto a form without some forethought about how users actually work with the form can make the form an odious tool that people hate using.

## Getting to Know the Controls

You build Access forms by using various controls. Even when you can use a Form Wizard (More Forms on the Create section of the Ribbon) or Design View to create a form, the objects that you use as building blocks for your forms are called controls. (See Chapter 3 for the basics of creating forms.)

There's nothing particularly meaningful behind the name *controls*. Programmers like to have names for the objects that they use, and it happens that they like to call the objects that appear on forms (and reports) controls. I guess that's better than calling them Ralphs (not that I have anything against the name Ralph, of course). You could probably make the argument that the name *control* fits because this object controls what you see when you view a form. Here's a brief explanation of the types of controls:

- ✔ **Bound controls:** Each of the fields that you add to a form is known as a *bound* control. This type of control is connected — bound — to some data in your database. Most of the controls that you add to your forms are bound controls.

- ✔ **Unbound controls:** The things that you add to a form that aren't connected to any data are called unbound controls. These unbound controls typically serve to make your form look fancier — a company logo — or to convey useful information — a label that explains the purpose of a bound control.

- ✔ **Calculated controls:** Objects that display data that is the result of an *expression* (or *formula* for you spreadsheet fans) are called calculated controls. You use these types of controls to show things like shipping charges, sales tax, or order totals.

You add most controls to a form in Design View by selecting the control you want (choose your form on the Insert section) and then dragging out the size you want for the control on the Form Design, or by dragging a field onto the form from the Field List (Add Existing Fields from the Design section).

## Common Controls You Can Use

The most common type of control that you're likely to add to a form is a labeled field box, a bound control. Figure 9-1 shows a very simple form that has the LastName field (a labeled field) added from the Field List (which will be on the right side of the form).

A field box is also called a text box, but a text box is not always associated with a particular field. Text boxes are also used for calculated controls.

 The Label control and the Text Box control appear next to each other on the Ribbon (Design), and they appear to be quite similar. But they're not the same type of control. You should always use a label instead of a text box when you want to display static, unchanging text in a form.

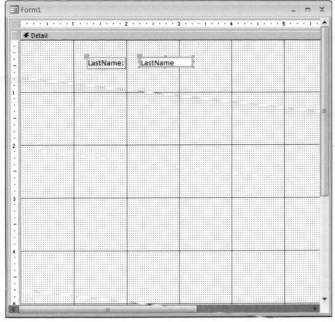

**Figure 9-1:**
Add a field
box for the
LastName
field by
dragging it
from the
Field List for
the Current-
Auction
table.

## List box controls

Another type of control you may find very useful is the list box. This type of control enables a user to select from a set of predefined choices (and sometimes to enter a new value). The two variations of list boxes you can use on your forms are:

- ✔ **Combo Box:** When you use combo boxes, the list isn't displayed until you open it by clicking the down arrow at the right of the combo box. You can set up a combo box to enable users to enter new values in addition to selecting an existing value.

- ✔ **List Box:** When you use an ordinary list box, the whole list of values is visible at the same time. Users can only select the values that are shown in the list — they can't add a value that's not in the list.

Figure 9-2 shows how a Combo Box (top) compares to a list box (bottom) when both are added to a form design. Both controls show the word Unbound because neither of them has been associated with a field yet.

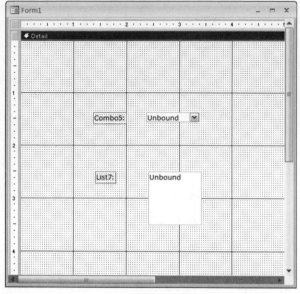

A third variation of the list box control that you're probably familiar with is the *drop-down list*. Drop-down lists are only used on *data access pages* — Web pages that ask users to input information. Drop-down list boxes look a lot like a combo boxes, but they don't allow users to add new values to the list.

## Option button controls

Option buttons used to be called radio buttons because they acted like the station selection buttons on old-time car radios — when you pushed in one button to select a station, all the other buttons popped out. But because radios no longer have buttons like that, what had been a useful and descriptive name for a particular type of form control became less intuitive, and, alas, anachronistic for many users. The name *option button* won out. My nostalgic lapse has helped define the key element that makes an option button an option button: When you choose one option, you elect not to choose any of the other options.

Option buttons (which appear on the Ribbon as buttons) usually present users with a fixed set of mutually exclusive choices. If they choose vanilla, they can't have chocolate or banana.

Option buttons are similar to list boxes (but not to combo boxes, from which users can enter a new value). Option buttons can be used individually to offer users a simple yes or no choice, but this is seldom a good idea because users don't expect it and can become confused.

## Check box controls

Check boxes give users two choices — true or false. Although forms seldom show the choice as true or false, that's really what a check box does. When a user selects a check box, the value is set to true. When the check box is deselected, the value is false. This type of choice is called *Boolean*, and it's associated with the Access Yes/No data type.

# Adding Controls to Your Forms

The controls may look interesting sitting in the Ribbon, but they don't serve any purpose in your database until you add them to a form. In Chapter 3, I show you how to create simple forms, but this section gives you a gander at how you can use some of the more advanced controls to create even more useful forms.

Earlier in this chapter in the section "Getting to Know the Controls," I show you that controls can be bound to a field, unbound (not associated with a field), or be associated with a calculated value. In most cases you can use bound controls so that the control actually selects or modifies values in the database. Bound controls require a record source — an associated table or query that stores the data.

- ✔ If you drag a field from the Field List onto a form, you create a bound control.
- ✔ If you simply select a control and click the form design without dragging a field from the Field List, you create an unbound text box control.

You can change an unbound control into a bound control by following these steps:

1. **Right-click the control and choose Properties from the pop-up menu.**

   The Properties dialog box appears.

2. **Click the Data tab.**

3. **Select the field you want to bind to the control from the Control Source list box.**

   Figure 9-3 shows an example of binding a list box control to a database field.

You can use the drop-down list box at the top of the Properties dialog box to select a different object if you want to view or modify the properties of another object.

**Figure 9-3:**
Selecting a
control
source
changes an
unbound
control into
a bound
control.

## Adding list boxes to your forms

List boxes (and their combo box variants) enable users to select a value from a list. The source of that list can be a table, a query, or a fixed list of values that you load into the control when you create the control. The selected value is stored in the table that is associated with the form.

The table that's associated with the form is *not* the source of the values that are displayed in the list box. This terminology can be a bit confusing until you realize that each field in a record can only hold a single value. So, in order for the list box to return a single value, the list box has to get its values from a source other than the table where the selected value is stored.

So how do you choose the type of source that will best serve your needs? Here are some guidelines that can help:

> ✔ **If the list of values is relatively short and won't be changing, you can use a value list that you enter into the control or a database table.** A list entered directly into the control is easy to create, but so is a small table. Database users are less likely to modify a list that is typed directly into the control, if for no better reason than that they don't know where the list resides.

✔ **If the list of values can change over time, you can use a table or a query as the source of the list.** In most cases it's easiest to simply use a table as the source.

✔ **If the list of available values must be conditional based on some other value, you must use a query as the source of the values.** For example, say you have a set of shipping options, but you want to restrict the methods depending on what the product is. (Who wants to send a piano FedEx Next Business Day?)

You can add a list box to a form with a wizard or you can use Design View and build the list box yourself. The following steps show you how to add a list box to a form without using a wizard. In my example, the list box uses an existing table as the source of the values for the list box.

To add a list box to a form, follow these steps:

1. **Open the Access database where you want to create the new form.**

2. **In the Objects list (column on left and also called Navigation Pane), click Forms.**

   A list of forms appears. Choose the one you will use.

3. **In the Create section of the Ribbon choose Form Design.**

   A new, blank form opens.

4. **Choose Add Existing Fields from the Design ribbon.**

5. **Choose the table to associate with the form from the drop-down Field List box.**

   In this example I selected a table called ItemsTable, which stores information about items that are consigned for auctions.

   You can leave the Field List dialog box open, but you can also move it if it is in your way.

6. **In the Design section of the Ribbon, click the List Box button to select it, but don't drag a list box onto the form design just yet.**

   Selecting the List Box button before dragging the associated field onto the form tells Access to create a list box when you later drag the field onto the form. Make certain that the Control Wizards icon is not selected (toggle until it is dull rather than vivid) so that you can complete these steps without using the wizard.

7. **Drag the field that you want to appear as a list box onto the form.**

   In this example I selected the TypeID field.

8. **With the list box you added to the form still selected (highlight just the box, not the label), choose the table that holds the values you want to appear in the list box from the Row Source drop-down list on the Data tab of the Properties dialog box (properties will cover the Field List).**

I selected the table named TypeTable. (See Figure 9-4.)

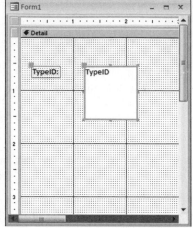

**Figure 9-4:**
The list box shows TypeID when in Design View.

9. **Right-click and choose Form View or click the View button on the tool-bar to see how your form and the new list box appear.**

Figure 9-5 shows the form I created in this example.

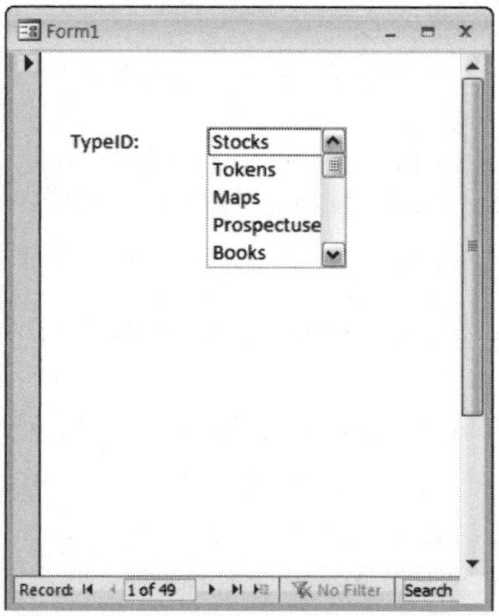

**Figure 9-5:**
The list box displays the list of values from the table that is the row source.

10. **Return to Design View and save your work.**

Although the list box displays the proper values, Figure 9-5 does demonstrate one area where the default setup for a list box leaves a little bit of room for improvement. When a list box displays values from a table, the values are shown in the order that they appear in the table. Often, this means that the values aren't sorted intuitively, which can make locating a specific value difficult — especially if the list of choices is quite long.

Chapter 17 shows you how to improve your forms by making sure that values that are shown in list boxes are sorted for easier selection.

The form used in this example also demonstrates something about form design that you may not have considered. In this case, the form allows users to select a value for one of the fields in the associated table, but it doesn't give users enough information to enable them to make an intelligent choice. To be of much use, the form needs to display additional fields so that users can tell which record they're modifying. The record counter at the bottom of the form simply doesn't do the job!

## Adding option groups

Option buttons enable a user to select one item from a list of choices, but unlike a list box, option buttons always use a fixed set of choices that all appear together on the form. Option buttons enable users to determine which of the choices is currently selected (the XYZ button on the Ribbon in the Design section).

Creating an *option group* (the structure that ties the option buttons together so that users' choices are properly recorded) can be a bit complicated, but Access provides a very handy wizard, the Option Group Wizard, that simplifies the task considerably. This wizard not only helps you create the various option buttons, but it also helps you create the option group. Option buttons are pretty useless without an option group.

To add an option group and option buttons to a form, follow these steps:

1. **Open the form you want to use in Design View.**

2. **Make sure that the form has a table associated with the form's Record Source property.**

3. **Click the Control Wizards icon (magic wand) in the Ribbon (Design section) to select it.**

   Toggle to highlight the wizard.

4. **Click the Option Group icon (XYZ) in the Ribbon.**

5. **Click inside the form design where you want the option group to appear.**

   The Option Group Wizard dialog box appears, as shown in Figure 9-6.

**Figure 9-6:**
The Option Group Wizard helps you create option buttons and an option group.

6. **Enter the labels that you want to appear next to each of the option buttons in the rows under the Label Names heading.**

   In this example, I'm using Control Source and Default Value as the two option button labels.

   Press the Tab key to move from one label to the next.

7. **Click Next to continue.**

8. **Choose either to have one of the option buttons selected by default or to not have a default selection. Then click Next.**

9. **Enter the values you want to save in the database for each choice.**

   You can either:

   - Enter numeric values.

   - Accept the default numeric values.

   - Enter Boolean values such as True/False or Yes/No.

      You can only use the Boolean values if you only have two option buttons in the group.

      If you enter Boolean values, Access changes the values to –1 for true and 0 for false.

10. **Click Next to continue.**

11. **Choose the option for storing the value.**

You can either

- Save the value in a *variable* for later use.
- Store the value in a field in the table.

12. **Click Next to continue.**

13. **Select the appearance options you prefer, as shown in Figure 9-7, and then click Next.**

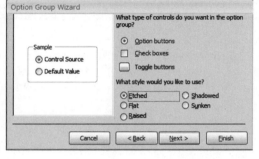

**Figure 9-7:**
Use these
options to
determine
how your
option
buttons will
appear.

14. **Enter the label that you want the option group box to display in the form.**

15. **Click the Finish button to complete the task.**

Figure 9-8 shows how the two option buttons from this example appear in Form View.

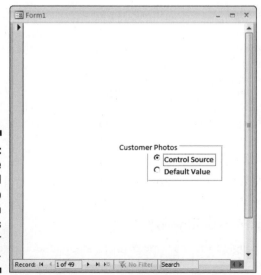

**Figure 9-8:**
The
completed
option group
and option
buttons as
they appear
on the form.

## Buttons, toggles, check boxes, and other options

Option buttons, toggle buttons, and check boxes do somewhat complicate your life as a database designer because of the way these controls store information in your database. This complication comes about because various controls don't store the values you see on the form. Instead, they store numerical values that you need to interpret before you can use these values effectively.

If you will only have two options that a user can select, you might want to consider using a toggle button control instead of option buttons. A toggle button typically takes up less space on a form than do option groups.

## *Using check boxes on forms*

Check boxes are very familiar elements you can use on forms. They, like the closely related toggle button, have two possible states:

- **Selected:** They return a value of Yes, True, or -1 (equivalent values as far as Access is concerned).
- **Deselected:** They return a value of No, False, or 0.

Although the Option Group Wizard (see "Adding option groups," earlier in this chapter) gives you the options of creating option groups containing check boxes or toggle buttons, these two types of controls are not usually used as mutually exclusive members of an option group. To avoid confusion, it's probably best to use controls in ways that are familiar to users — otherwise you greatly increase the possibility of errors.

It's usually best to associate check boxes or toggle buttons with a field whose Access data type is Yes/No because then you won't have to do any conversions to use the value returned by the control. You can also use these types of controls as unbound controls if you use their value in a VBA procedure or in an Access macro.

Adding a check box or a toggle button to a form as a bound control is very easy:

1. **Select the control from the Ribbon.**

   Check Boxes and Toggle Buttons appear in the Design section of the Ribbon, but the Toggle is *not* the large button.

2. **Drag the field from the field list onto the form.**

   Figure 9-9 shows how these two controls appear after they have been added to a Form Design separately.

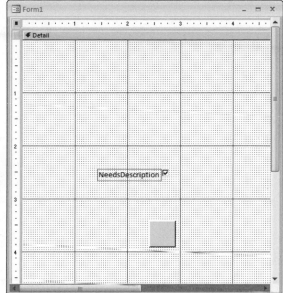

**Figure 9-9:**
A check box (upper) and a toggle button (lower) appear on this form design.

# Adding labels to toggle buttons

If you refer to Figure 9-9, you see an important difference between a check box control and a toggle button control. Even though both were added to the form as bound controls, Access added a label for the check box control but not for the toggle button control. Unlabeled buttons are an accident waiting to happen, so you may want to add some indicator that tells the user the purpose of the button. Three options you can consider are:

✔ **Use the label control:** You can use the Label button to add a label on the form. This may be the best choice if you need to use a lot of text to explain the purpose of the button.

✔ **Add a caption:** You can add a caption to the button by using the Caption text box on the Format tab of the button's Properties dialog box (see Figure 9-10). Captions have to fit onto the face of the button, so this option is best if you can create a one- or two-word description.

✔ **Use a picture:** If you have an image that clearly indicates the button's purpose, you can use that image by selecting it — using the Picture text box on the Format tab of the button's Properties dialog box. Access has a selection of images you can use, or you can browse for another image. Unless the image you choose is very easy to understand, however, you probably want to use a label, too.

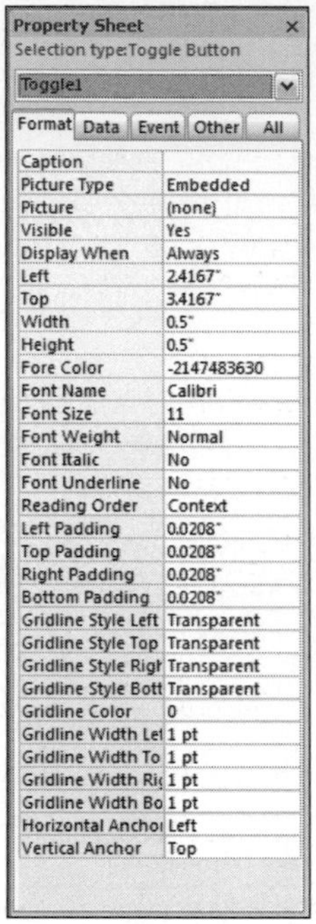

**Property Sheet** ✕

Selection type:Toggle Button

| Toggle1 | ⌄ |

| Format | Data | Event | Other | All |

| Caption | |
| --- | --- |
| Picture Type | Embedded |
| Picture | (none) |
| Visible | Yes |
| Display When | Always |
| Left | 2.4167" |
| Top | 3.4167" |
| Width | 0.5" |
| Height | 0.5" |
| Fore Color | -2147483630 |
| Font Name | Calibri |
| Font Size | 11 |
| Font Weight | Normal |
| Font Italic | No |
| Font Underline | No |
| Reading Order | Context |
| Left Padding | 0.0208" |
| Top Padding | 0.0208" |
| Right Padding | 0.0208" |
| Bottom Padding | 0.0208" |
| Gridline Style Left | Transparent |
| Gridline Style Top | Transparent |
| Gridline Style Righ | Transparent |
| Gridline Style Bott | Transparent |
| Gridline Color | 0 |
| Gridline Width Lei | 1 pt |
| Gridline Width To | 1 pt |
| Gridline Width Rig | 1 pt |
| Gridline Width Bo | 1 pt |
| Horizontal Ancho | Left |
| Vertical Anchor | Top |

**Figure 9-10:** You can use the Format tab of the button's Properties dialog box to specify a caption or a picture for the face of a toggle button.

# *Incorporating ActiveX Controls*

There's something fun about finding cool stuff that's hidden on your PC and playing around with what you've found. Okay, so I admit that this isn't on par with finding out that you've just won the grand prize in some contest you forgot about months ago. If you're a curious person who likes to tinker, however, trying out some of the extras that are stashed away on your hard drive is something you won't want to miss.

The programs you install on your PC are made up of a whole series of small components, including a bunch of pieces that are called *ActiveX* controls. When you install programs, those ActiveX controls are *registered* on your system to make them accessible to the programs. It turns out that any program — not just the program that installed the ActiveX controls — can access all those registered controls. Access just happens to be one of the programs that can use ActiveX controls, so you've got a whole bunch of new toys to play with!

You can add almost any ActiveX control that's registered on your system to an Access form, but that doesn't necessarily mean that you can do anything useful with it. Some ActiveX controls are pretty cool and some can do useful things; the only way to know for certain about a specific one is to give it a try.

Because the ActiveX controls that are available on your system depend completely on what programs you have installed, it's impossible for me to predict which ActiveX controls you may find. Your set of ActiveX controls will certainly be very different from the set that is on my test system.

I know that you've always wanted an Access database that has a form that plays music (humor me), so that's the example I use — a copy of the Windows Media Player ActiveX control. Of course, you may find something much more appropriate and business-y to add.

Here's how to amaze your friends by adding an ActiveX control to a form:

1. **Open a new form in Design View.**

2. **Choose the button with the small red "x" from the Design section.**

   The Insert ActiveX Control dialog box, shown in Figure 9-11, appears.

**Figure 9-11:**
Choose an ActiveX control to add to your form.

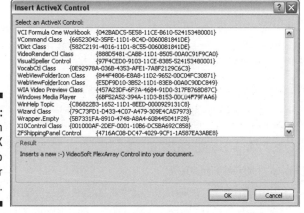

3. **Scroll down the list until you find the ActiveX control that suits your purpose (or fancy).**

   I chose the Windows Media Player ActiveX control, not just because I love cool music, but also because this control should be available on any Windows PC (antitrust laws be darned).

4. **Click OK to add the control to the form (you may also paste your favorite URL into the Property Sheet on the Other tab).**

5. **Right-click and choose Form View or click the View button to change the form to Form View.**

   Figure 9-12 shows the Windows Media Player ActiveX control in an Access form while it's playing the movie from a recent Antique Clinic in California. Gorgeous!

**Figure 9-12:** Access provides a bit of entertainment by way of an ActiveX control.

In order to make the Windows Media Player ActiveX control play something like an Internet radio station, you set the URL property on the Other tab of the control's Properties dialog box:

1. **Find the proper URL for your favorite Internet radio station:**

   a. Open the station's stream in Windows Media Player (not the ActiveX control).

   b. Choose the Property **Sheet** to display the Properties dialog box.

2. **Copy the URL shown in Location.**

3. **Paste the URL into the URL property of the ActiveX control.**

# Modifying the Characteristics of Controls

You can modify the characteristics of any control that you add to a form. Whether you're adding a button, a list box, or the Windows Media Player ActiveX control, you have access to many different properties that you can set and tweak to your heart's content.

## An example of setting default values

Often, setting up a form so that certain values are automatically entered in specific fields can be quite handy. For example, Figure 9-13 shows a simple form that is used to check in items as they're received. In most cases, items are checked in immediately, so the DateReceived field value will almost always be the current date. Why not make the form a bit easier to use by automatically entering the current date in this field? That's what I thought, too.

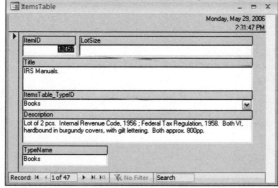

**Figure 9-13:** Make this simple form even better by setting a default value for the Date-Received field.

Here's how to set up a date field so that the current date is automatically entered (but can be overwritten if necessary):

1. **Create your basic form with a Date field on the form, or add a Date/Time to a pre-existing form in Design View.**

2. **Right-click the Date field and choose Properties from the pop-up menu.**

   The Properties dialog box for the Date field appears (it may be called Text something-or-other at this point, but you can change the Title).

3. **Click the Data tab, and then click the Default Value text box.**

4. **Click the Build button (the button with three periods) to the right of the text box.**

The Expression Builder dialog box appears. It contains three columns or list boxes.

5. **In the first list box (the one on the left), click the Common Expressions option.**

This option appears toward the bottom of the list.

6. **In the second list box (the one in the middle), click the Current Date option.**

Again, this option may appear toward the bottom of the list.

7. **Click the Paste button.**

The term Date() appears in the text box at the top of the Expression Builder dialog box. See Figure 9-14.

**Figure 9-14:**
The Expression Builder dialog box helps you create expressions for setting default values.

8. **Click OK to close the Expression Builder dialog box.**

9. **Switch to Form view to see the results.**

The date field shows the current date.

You can type expressions directly into the Default Value text box without bothering with the Expression Builder dialog box. To do this, you simply enter **=Date()** to indicate that you want today's date to be the default value.

# *Blocking access to certain controls*

In some cases, you may want to prevent users from changing the values that are entered in certain fields. For example, you may not want users to be able to change the value for a date field if you set a default of the current date as the date the record was created. Access makes it pretty darn easy to block users from making changes to values in specific fields.

To block access to a field, first open the Properties dialog box for the field. Figure 9-15 shows the Properties dialog box for the date field used in the last exercise.

**Figure 9-15:**
Use the Properties dialog box to block users from changing values.

To prevent a user from entering values in a field, you have two options:

✔ Set the `Enabled` property to No to prevent the user from moving the cursor into the field.

When this property is set to No, the field still appears on the form, but it is grayed out. Users expect this type of behavior, so this is the recommended option.

✔ Set the Locked property to Yes to allow users to move the cursor into
   the field, but also to prevent them from making any changes.

   Using this option can cause confusion, so I recommend avoiding it.

## Improving controls by using tab order

When you add controls to a form, Access sets up the *tab order* so that users
can press Tab to move to the next control or Shift+Tab to move to the previous control. But if you move controls around on a form, the tab order can get
a bit out of whack. Fortunately, there's an easy way to correct this problem.

Figure 9-16 shows the Other tab of the Properties dialog box for a control.
You use the Tab Index property on this tab to specify the tab order for your
form. When a user presses the Tab key, the cursor moves to the next highest
Tab Index, and Shift+Tab moves the cursor to the next lowest Tab Index.

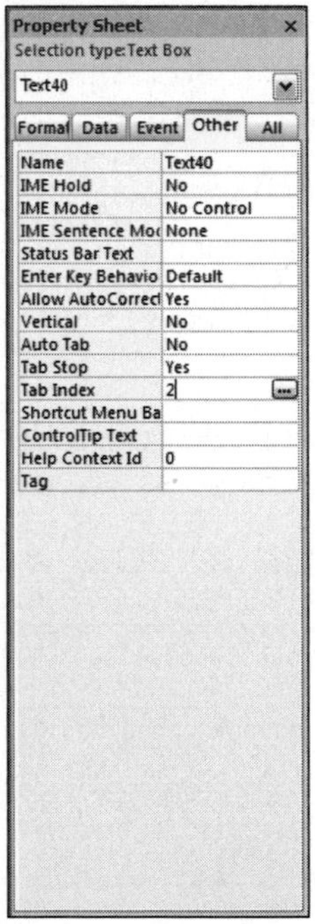

**Figure 9-16:**
Use the
Tab Index
property to
control the
tab order of
the controls
on a form.

# Chapter 10

# Using Multiple Tables in Forms

## In This Chapter

▶ Using subforms with forms

▶ Moving fields from tables to forms

▶ Connecting forms to other databases

▶ Selecting the right subform view

▶ Moving from record to record

*M*ultiple, related tables help you organize the information in Access databases efficiently. But to use that information effectively, you must often access data from more than one table at a time. You may, for example, want to see all the items that you have for sale (easy enough). What if, however, you want to see that information split into groups according to which of your clients owns which items? That's when using multiple tables in the same form comes in handy. With multiple tables feeding data to a form, you can easily access related groups of items.

This chapter shows you how to create and use forms that incorporate data from more than one table. It explores the sometimes confusing line between forms and subforms, and it shows you how to use different types of subform views to most effectively present the information. In addition, this chapter discusses the unique navigation challenges that are presented by multiple-table forms.

In many cases, using multiple tables in a form enables you to deal with your database in a more logical and intuitive manner. Tasks like navigating between records are slightly more complicated in multiple-table forms, but proper form design can help reduce any possible confusion.

# Understanding Forms and Subforms

The form examples that have been discussed so far in this book have all pretty much been ordinary forms. That is, the forms have enabled users to view and edit records from a single table. In the following sections, I turn your attention to forms that are made up of a main form and a *subform*.

Forms and subforms are most definitely *not* the same thing as the list boxes I discuss in Chapter 9.

 ✔ List boxes enable a user to make a selection from a list of values and store the selected value in the current table. The list of values can come from either

 • Values that are stored in another table

 • A set of values that is stored in the list box control itself

 ✔ Subforms enable you to use a form and a subform to store and edit values in two related tables at the same time.

## Understanding the need that subforms fill

The most useful type of relationship is the *one-to-many* relationship. In this type of relationship one record in the main table can be related to multiple records in the detail table. If you want to create a form that shows the related information, you need

 ✔ A main form that shows the *one* side of the relationship
 ✔ A subform that shows the *many* side of the relationship

Say you have a form that shows the various foods that are available from an online store. In the main form you can select the category of food, such as cheeses, meats, or beverages; in the subform you can select the specific foods in one category such as bleu cheese, Swiss cheese, or cheddar cheese. In a nutshell, subforms greatly increase your ability to logically organize information in your forms.

## Getting to know the subform place

As the name implies, subforms are usually displayed inside a main form. Subforms can be displayed by using any of the standard Form views, and the view you select for the subform does not have to be the same as the view you use for the main form. In most cases, however, the subform is shown in the standard Form View or in Datasheet view.

Figure 10-1 shows a typical arrangement for a form and a subform. In this case, the subform has a very different background color than the main form, making the subform a little easier to identify in the figure.

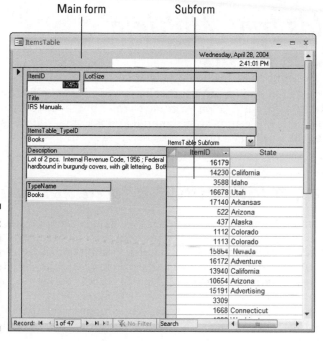

**Figure 10-1:**
The subform inside the main form is shown in standard Form View.

Subforms can also be displayed as a separate form window that pops up when the main form is opened. Unfortunately, this *Linked Form* view is somewhat confusing for users so you may want to avoid using this option.

It's important to understand the connection between a main form and a subform. Because the two forms typically show the records from two tables in a one-to-many relationship, you navigate through the records in the two forms in a different manner than you do in a single-table form. Think of the main form as a query that feeds the subform. The record you select in the main form determines which records you can view in the subform. When you move to a different record in the main form, a different set of records is displayed in the subform.

You can also nest more than one subform within a main form; you can nest subforms as deep as seven levels by placing subforms within subforms. Frankly, even though this is possible, you need to do some awfully heavy-duty planning to keep the whole mess understandable — much less to find room for the gigantic main form you'd need to hold such deep nesting. Just because you *can* do something doesn't mean that you *should*.

# Adding Fields from Multiple Tables to Your Forms

If you're interested in finding out the mechanics of adding fields from more than one table to your forms, you've come to the right section. Using fields from more than one table adds some complications compared to using fields from a single table (or from a query).

## Verifying relationships and adding fields

To build a form with a subform, you begin by making sure that the tables you want to use as the record sources have the proper one-to-many relationship established. You can choose the Database Tools⇨Relationships to display the Relationships window so that you can verify and establish relationships before you begin building the form.

If you aren't sure whether a relationship is a one-to-many relationship, choose Edit Relationships from the Design section of the Ribbon. The dialog box identifies the type of the relationship.

After you're sure that the tables have the proper one-to-many relationships, you can add any of the fields from those tables to the form. You add the fields from the *one* (or *master*) table to the main form and the fields from the *many* table to the subform. It's far easier to use the Form Wizard (More Forms on the Create section of the Ribbon) to add the fields because the wizard automatically adds the fields to the proper places on the forms.

Because Access understands how to *synchronize* the main form and the subform based on the table relationships, you don't have to include the fields that are used to create the table links unless you want those fields to appear on the forms. Even so, it's important to include the fields that will help users understand which set of records they're dealing with when they use the form. For example, if you're creating a form that shows order details in a subform, make sure that the main form displays the information that enables the users to identify whose order is being shown.

# Adding subforms with the Form Wizard

You can use several methods to create forms with subforms. The most straightforward method is to use the Form Wizard and add the related tables and fields by using the wizard. It's also possible to create your main form and subform separately and then add the subform to the form.

To create a form with a subform by using the Form Wizard, follow these steps:

1. **Open the More Forms option on the Create tab.**

2. **Click Form Wizard.**

   The Form Wizard dialog box appears.

3. **Select one of the tables whose fields you want to include from the drop-down Tables/Queries list box.**

   Which of the tables you add first doesn't make much difference; you can specify the *master table* shortly (in Step 7).

4. **Add the fields from that table to the Selected Fields list.**

5. **Repeat Steps 3 and 4 to add the next table and its fields to the Selected Fields list.**

6. **Click Next to continue.**

7. **Select the *master* table as the way you want to view the data, as shown in Figure 10-2.**

   You can only select the Form with Subform(s) option if you've selected the correct master table — otherwise your only option is to show all the data on a single form.

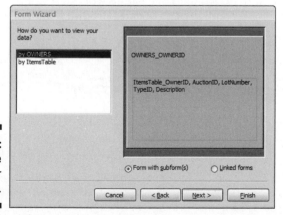

**Figure 10-2:** Choose the master table.

8. **Make sure the Form with Subform(s) option is selected and click Next to continue.**

If you select the Linked Forms option, your subform is created as a separate form that isn't embedded in the main form. Many users find the results of choosing this option to be confusing, so I don't recommend choosing it.

9. **Choose the layout option for your subform and click Next.**

For now, the default Datasheet view is okay — I show you how to modify the subform view in an upcoming section, "Choosing the Best Subform View."

10. **Select the appearance you prefer and click Next to continue.**

11. **Specify the titles you want for your form and subform.**

12. **Click Finish to view the finished form.**

## Adding a subform after the fact

If you don't want to create the form and subform at the same time, you can still add the form you want to use as a subform to the main form later. To do so, follow these steps:

1. **Open the main form in Design View.**

2. **Make certain that the Control Wizard icon is selected in the Ribbon (Design section) and drag the subform from the Forms list onto the main form.**

3. **Clean things up.**

You probably need to do a bunch of cleanup work in order to produce acceptable results, depending on how carefully you planned before you added the subform to the main form.

# Choosing the Best Subform View

If you've ever tried to enter or edit data by using the Access Datasheet view, you're probably wondering why it is the default view selection for subforms. It is hard to imagine a more difficult subform view to use, and yet, that's what Access gives you.

## Linking forms to external databases

Chapter 4 discusses using external database tables in reports, and Chapter 5 follows up with a discussion of using external database tables in queries. You can link an external table to the current database to ensure that you're using the most recent data, or you can simply import the external table so that you lose the currency of the data but you gain independence from the external database file. You can also create a multiple-table form that accesses data in an external database table, either by linking or importing the data.

Your decision to link to the database or import database information depends on your specific project. However, I generally recommend that you link to the database if you can. When you're working with a form, you probably have the expectation that you're working with live data; that is, if you make a change to some data by using a form, you almost certainly expect that the information in the database is updated to match the changes that you've made. This only happens if the external table is linked rather than imported.

With the exception of making certain that your external table is linked rather than imported, using an external database table in a form is no different from using a local table, regardless of whether you're using multiple-table forms or single-table forms.

Fortunately, you can change the subform view into something that's far more user-friendly than the Datasheet view. The setting for doing so is just a bit difficult to find, however, because it's not really where you might expect to find it.

## Making the switch from Datasheet view to another subform view

You can change the subform to a different view in one of two ways:

- ✔ The best method is to open the subform in Design View without having the main form open. When the subform is open in Design View, right-click the subform and choose Properties from the pop-up menu to display the Properties dialog box for the subform.

- ✔ The second-best method is to click the Properties option on the Ribbon to display the Properties dialog box for the subform. In the Properties dialog box, click the Format tab, and then choose the view you want to use for the subform from the drop-down Default View list box, as shown in Figure 10-3.

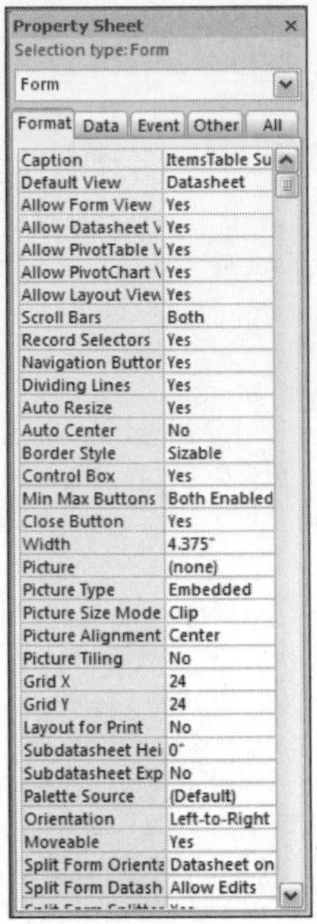

**Figure 10-3:**
Choose the
view
settings for
the subform
on the
Format tab.

Figure 10-4 also hints at the reason why opening the subform in Design View and setting its properties by using its Properties dialog box is the preferable method for setting the view for the subform. Although the drop-down list box partially covers the four options immediately below the list box, the labels for these properties are still visible. The four important options are Allow Form View, Allow Datasheet View, Allow PivotTable View, and Allow PivotChart View. You can set each of these options to either Yes or No so that you can lock out views that you don't want users to select. This is a great little feature because it enables you to reduce the possibility that a user will mess up the subform by selecting an inappropriate or confusing view.

Access also offers an option for displaying a subform in its own window. Choose Design➪Subform in New Window to enable this option. But use this display option sparingly (if at all) because displaying a subform in its own window may prevent users from seeing a clear relationship between the main form and the subform.

Figure 10-4 demonstrates the other option for changing the Subform view. This option is available when the form and subform are open for entering or editing data — not when they're open in Design View. To use this option you right-click the subform to display the pop-up menu. Then you choose the view you want for the subform from the Subform submenu.

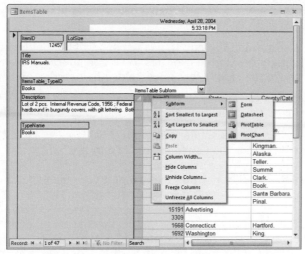

**Figure 10-4:**
When the
form and
subform are
open for
editing data,
you can
change the
view by
using the
pop-up
menu.

Users can also modify the subform view. As an Access application designer, you can probably imagine the panicked calls you might get from your users when all of a sudden "the form looks completely different, and I didn't do anything." Right. And I've got some swamp land and a bridge to sell you, too! So if you're worried that users may get confused and you want to head off panicked phone calls before they occur, lock the subform to the view you want by setting the Allow properties for those other views to No (refer to Figure 10-3).

## *Introducing your subform view options*

Even though the pop-up menu for the subform typically shows four options, you actually have five different view options available for subforms. That's because there are two different Form Views (but you can only choose between the two by using the Default View list box of the subform's Properties dialog box).

The view options for a subform include the following:

✔ **Single Form:** This is the standard view for ordinary forms, and it is arguably the best choice for subforms in a large percentage of situations.

✔ **Continuous Forms:** This is a strange combination of Form view and Datasheet view that displays multiple copies of the subform in a scrolling window on the main form.

✔ **Datasheet:** This is the standard Datasheet view and the one that appears by default.

This view is somewhat difficult to use because all the fields are displayed in a single row so the user has to do considerable horizontal scrolling if more than just a few small fields are included on the subform.

✔ **PivotTable:** This view shows the data summarized in a *PivotTable,* which is typically used for data analysis rather than data entry or editing.

✔ **PivotChart:** This view is similar to the PivotTable view, except that the data is charted rather than summarized in a table.

The PivotTable and PivotChart views really aren't very useful in most cases where you'd use a form, so I don't discuss them further.

The Continuous Forms view of the subform displays as many copies of the subform as necessary to show all the matching records from the many tables based on the selection in the main form. In addition, one extra, blank copy of the subform is added to the bottom of the set of subforms so that you can add additional records to the database. Users can view the individual copies of the subform by using either:

✔ The subform's navigator bar

✔ The scroll bar along the right side of the subform's section of the main form

The Continuous Forms view is the same as the Tabular view option offered by the Form Wizard.

Choosing the best subform view can be a real challenge. You need to

✔ Balance usability with efficiency.

✔ Consider the amount of space your form and subform combination will require in order to show all the required information.

# Adding Multiple Subforms

You can create forms with two or more subforms or even make forms with subforms that have their own subforms. The key to creating these complex types of forms is making sure that each level of the form has a one-to-many relationship with its subform through the underlying tables.

The most common example of this type of arrangement is probably that of an order tracking system. In this type of system, you have a Customers table that has a one-to-many relationship with an Orders table. The Orders table then has a one-to-many relationship with a Line Item table.

You add multiple subforms to a form with the same techniques you use to create a form with a single subform. That is, you add the first table and its fields to the design, and then you add the next table and its fields, and then the third table, and so on. If you have the proper table relationships set up, the Form Wizard creates the multiple subforms.

# Navigating Records in Multi-Table Forms

Whenever you have a form that draws records from more than one table, you need a method of navigating the records in each of these tables. To make this navigation possible, Access adds a *record navigator bar* to the bottom of each form and each subform.

## Choosing the right navigator bar

Figure 10-5 shows a form with a subform and the two record navigator bars. It also identifies the purpose of the navigation buttons.

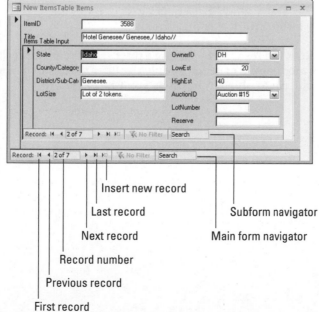

**Figure 10-5:**
The main form and the subform have separate navigator bars.

Users can sometimes get confused about which navigator bar to use — especially if you've been a little careless with your form design and forced users to scroll the form or the subform in order to see the navigator bars.

In Figure 10-5, the main form's navigator bar indicates that record 2 out of 7 records in the main table is visible in the form. The subform's navigator bar also shows that record 2 of 7 is visible.

In addition to using the buttons on the navigator bar, you can also move through the records by using the Page Up and Page Down keys. The insertion point for these keys must be in the section of the main form or the subform that you want to navigate.

## Finding records with filters

One method of finding records in a multiple-table form isn't very efficient. Scrolling through the records by using the main form or even the subform navigator bar gets old awfully fast. You could create a query, of course, but when you've already got the form, why start from scratch?

Figure 10-6 shows another way to locate records using an existing form — with *filters*. Simply right-click a field on the main form and enter a value. For example, I clicked the ItemID field on the main form in Figure 10-6 and chose Greater Than or Equal to 12457 as the value for the filter. After I did this, the form produced all the records in which the ItemID was greater than or equal to 12457.

A filter functions pretty much like a query except that filters are temporary and can easily be used with existing forms.

Figure 10-7 shows the results of applying a filter to the main form. Just as with the navigator bars, you need to apply the filter to the correct section of the form or subform to obtain the results you want.

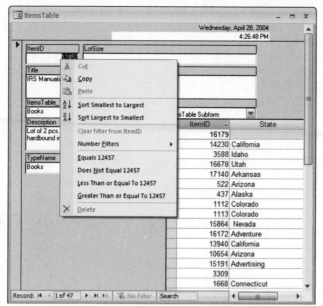

**Figure 10-6:**
Use a filter
to help you
find records.

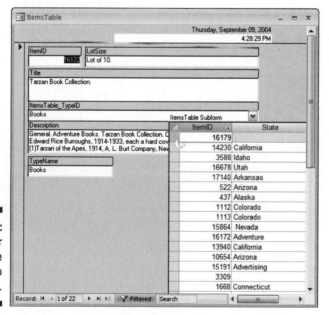

**Figure 10-7:**
The filter
limits the
main form to
22 records.

# Chapter 11

# Fixing Form Faults

• • • • • • • • • • • • • • • • • • • • • • • • • • • • • • • • • • • • • • • • • • • • • • • •

• • • • • • • • • • • • • • • • • • • • • • • • • • • • • • • • • • • • • • • • • • • • • • • •

*F*orms are the primary windows into your Access databases, so problems with your forms can cause a whole range of difficulties. If you control how users can interact with your forms and if you present the data in a clear and understandable fashion, you can save yourself a lot of trouble.

This chapter discusses several types of problems that you may encounter with forms and proposes solutions that may work for you. For example, this chapter shows you methods that you can use to help prevent users from entering invalid data. In addition, you see how to present data by using formats that reduce the possibility of error and confusion.

## Preventing Invalid Data with Input Masks

No doubt, you put a lot of time and effort into creating your Access databases. But all that time and effort can be wasted if someone is careless about entering data. Queries and reports end up being meaningless if they're loaded with invalid data.

You actually have several methods for controlling what data a user can place in your database:

 ✔ Your first line of defense comes when you design the table. When you define the function of the tables and the fields they contain, you can also

   • Define the type of data that can be entered into each field.

   • Create validation rules for the fields in the table.

✔ Another method of validating the data that the user enters is to create validation rules for the fields on a form.

This last method offers one important advantage over setting validation rules only in your tables: On a form, you can set validation rules for any control that accepts input even if that control is *unbound* (not tied to) a field in a table.

In addition, you can specify a message to display if users attempt to enter an invalid value.

## *Setting up an input mask with the wizard*

An *input mask* helps to prevent users from inputting invalid data by automatically converting the appearance of the data into the proper format so that the user can easily tell whether there's a problem. For example, you can use an input mask in a phone number field to let users know when they've typed an incorrect number of characters.

To set up an input mask for a field on a form, follow these steps:

1. **Open the form in Design View.**

2. **Right-click the field you want to modify.**

3. **Choose Properties from the pop-up menu.**

   The Properties dialog box for the selected field appears.

4. **Click the Data tab.**

   See Figure 11-1.

5. **Click the Build button to the right of the Input Mask text box.**

   The Input Mask Wizard dialog box, shown in Figure 11-2, appears.

6. **Select a mask and click Next to continue.**

   Some of your options include Phone Number, Social Security number, Password, and so on.

7. **Make modifications to the input mask if necessary.**

   One useful modification is that you can choose placeholder characters to indicate to users the number of characters that they should type.

8. **Click Next to continue.**

9. **Answer any additional questions on the remaining screens of the Input Mask Wizard dialog box and click the Finish button.**

   Different input masks require different information. For example, with a phone number mask you can specify whether you want placeholders to indicate the correct number of characters and whether you want the value formatted to look like a phone number.

**Figure 11-1:**
Use the
Input Mask
property of
the Data tab
to create an
input mask.

**Figure 11-2:**
Choose an
input mask
that suits
your data.

## Making an input mask from scratch

You can create your own input mask from scratch (or modify an existing
input mask) by using the characters shown in Table 11-1. Sometimes,
starting from scratch is the only way to create exactly the input mask you
want — given the limited choices that are available in the Input Mask Wizard
dialog box.

| Table 11-1 | Input Mask Characters |
|---|---|
| *Character* | *Purpose* |
| 0 | A number 0 to 9 is required, and no other characters are allowed. |
| 9 | An optional number from 0 to 9. |
| # | A number, a space, plus sign, or minus sign is optional. |
| L | An uppercase letter from A to Z is required. |
| ? | A letter from A to Z is optional. |
| A | Any letter A to Z or any number 0 to 9 is required. |
| a | Any letter A to Z or a number 0 to 9 is optional. |
| & | Any character or a space is required. |
| C | Any character or a space is optional. |
| . , : ; - / | Decimal placeholder and thousand, date, and time separators (based on the current settings in the Regional and Language Options area of the Control Panel). |
| < | Converts all characters to lowercase. |
| > | Converts all characters to uppercase. |
| ! | Displays the input mask from right to left, rather than from left to right. |
| \ | Displays the character that follows as itself (so you can show input mask characters). |

To create an input mask from scratch or to modify one, follow these steps:

1. **Open the form in Design View.**

2. **Open the Properties dialog box for the field you want to modify.**

3. **On the Data tab, enter the input mask by using the characters shown in Table 11-1.**

   For example, enter **00000\-0000** to create an input mask for a nine-digit U.S. postal code. This input mask displays an entry like 895216315 as 89521-6315.

# Limiting a User to Specific Values with Validation Rules

Although an input mask (which I describe in the previous sections) provides the user with some visual feedback, it's really difficult to create a good enough input mask to prevent a user from entering inappropriate values. For that, you need to create a *validation rule*.

If you've used Excel or another spreadsheet program, you'll probably find the task of creating a validation rule pretty familiar. Validation rules are created by using *expressions* that look very much like the formulas in a spreadsheet. Validation rules are actually somewhat more flexible than spreadsheet formulas, but the idea behind them is similar.

## Setting up your own validation rules

In an auction database, validation rules come in handy all the time. For example, you can create a validation rule that specifies that bids in an auction must be at least $100. The validation rule could also specify a maximum amount, of course, but I will keep the example simple.

To create a validation rule, follow these steps:

1. **Open the form for which you want to create a validation rule in Design View.**

2. **Open the Properties dialog box for the field that you want to validate.**

   In this case, I choose the WINNING BID AMOUNT field.

3. **On the Data tab, click in the Validation Rule text box to select it.**

4. **Click the Build button.**

   The Expression Builder dialog box, shown in Figure 11-3, appears. You can also type the rule directly in the Validation Rule text box if you prefer.

5. **Enter the validation rule, using the various tools in the dialog box.**

   In my example, I entered >99.99 in the upper box to specify that the value must be at least $100.

6. **Click OK to close the dialog box.**

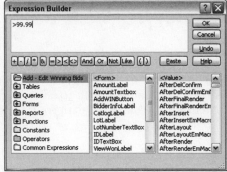

**Figure 11-3:**
Use the
Expression
Builder
dialog box
to create a
validation
rule.

7. **Enter the text that you want to appear on-screen if (when) a user enters an invalid value. Expand the size of the Property Field and type directly into the Validation Text text box (there is no Build option here).**

   In my example, I entered **Bids must be at least $100**. See Figure 11-4.

**Property Sheet** ×
Selection type: Text Box

| AmountTextbox | ▼ |

Format | **Data** | Event | Other | All

| Control Source | |
|---|---|
| Input Mask | |
| Default Value | |
| Validation Rule | >99.99 |
| Validation Text | Bids must be at least $100 |
| Enabled | Yes |
| Locked | No |
| Filter Lookup | Database Default |
| Smart Tags | |
| Text Format | Plain Text |

**Figure 11-4:**
Enter the
validation
text to
ensure that
users
understand
the rule.

8. **Switch the form to Form View and enter a value that does not meet the validation rule in the field where you just created the validation rule; then click in another field to see the results.**

If everything's been done correctly, Access displays a message box with your Validation Text message as soon as you attempt to move to a different field or to a different record. See Figure 11-5.

**Figure 11-5:**
Access displays a message telling the user that he's entered an invalid value.

 You can also specify validation rules by using expressions that check the values contained in other fields. For example, you can specify a rule that won't allow a bid to be accepted if it's below the reserve price for an item. Or, you can specify a rule that won't allow a user to enter a date that hasn't occurred yet or doesn't exist (say, November 31, 200-never).

Whenever you create a validation rule, be sure to also specify a validation text message so that users see a message they can understand. If you don't create a text message, Access displays a generic message (see Figure 11-6). This generic message is enough to confuse even experienced Access users, so you can imagine the effect it has on ordinary users! Also, a Property Sheet that seems frozen can usually be fixed by just expanding it to the left.

**Figure 11-6:**
You really don't want your users to see a message like this one!

 To get help, or to view the complete contents of one of the properties, such as validation text that is too long to fit the text box, press Shift+F2.

## *Remembering Access validation rules*

Creating your own expressions can be a bit confusing — especially if you can't quite get over what you've learned about creating formulas in Excel. One reason for this difficulty is that there are separate rules for *validation rule expressions* and expressions that you create to produce results in calculated controls:

- ✔ **A validation rule expression must not begin with an equal sign.** This type of expression is closer in concept to a conditional statement inside an Excel formula such as = IF (*conditional statement,* value if true, value if false).

- ✔ **An expression that calculates the value for a calculated control must begin with an equal sign (=).** This is essentially the equivalent of a complete formula in Excel.

Here are some points that can help you create expressions for validation rules with just a bit less frustration:

- ✔ **Use square brackets for field names, controls, and properties.** Place square brackets [] around the names of fields, other controls on a form, or any properties. This is a mandatory part of the process if the name includes any spaces, but good practice any time.

- ✔ **Use quotes for text strings.** Place double quotes (") around any text strings.

- ✔ **Use number signs for dates.** Use number signs (#) to enclose any date values.

- ✔ **Use periods to separate tables.** Place a period (.) between the names of tables and fields.

- ✔ **Use an ampersand (&) to combine the value of a field with a string value.**

- ✔ **Use *or* and *and* correctly.** Use *or* to specify that either of the conditions can validate the entry, and use the word *and* to specify that both of the conditions must be met to validate the entry.

## *Quick validation rules you can use*

Here are a few quick examples of validation rules to get you started:

- ✔ To specify that a date must be June 26, 2006, or later, use the following rule:

```
>=#6/26/2006#
```

✔ To specify that a numeric value must be between 75 and 99, use this rule:

```
>74 and <100
```

✔ To specify that an entry must have exactly five characters, use this rule:

```
Like "?????"
```

✔ To specify that the entry must consist of three characters, and that the last two of these characters must be numbers, use this rule:

```
Like "?##"
```

# Preventing Users from Changing Records

You may want to prevent users from making certain changes to complete records in your database. For example, perhaps you don't want users to delete records, or maybe you don't want them to add new records. To exercise this type of control over what users can do, you use the Properties dialog box for the form, as shown in Figure 11-7.

**Figure 11-7:**
You can control how users can modify records in a form.

The three options in question are:

- ✔ **Allow Edits:** Set this option to No to prevent users from modifying existing records.
- ✔ **Allow Deletions:** Set this option to No to prevent users from deleting existing records.
- ✔ **Allow Additions:** Set this option to No to prevent users from adding new records.

Even though the Allow Filters option appears just above these other three options, it has no effect on whether a user can modify the records in the database. The Allow Filters option simply controls whether users can apply a filter so that only specified sets of records can be viewed through the form. If you're dealing with inexperienced and easily confused users, setting this property to No might be useful in preventing panicked calls about how a whole bunch of records suddenly disappeared all on their own. Otherwise, you probably want users to have as much freedom to sort records as possible.

You can also use the Data Entry property to Only Allow a User to Add New records by setting the property to Yes. See Chapter 9 for information about how to lock individual controls on a form.

# Looking Out for Poorly Formatted Data

Have you ever encountered information that was possibly accurate but so poorly presented that it was nearly impossible to understand? Almost anyone who has tried to read a badly translated user manual for a cheap piece of electronic gear has experienced this problem firsthand. Sure, the information is there, but unless you can understand it, you won't know if you push this button or that one to adjust the volume, or which button deletes all your files.

Okay, so maybe your Access forms aren't quite that bad, but presenting information in a clear and understandable format is crucial to reducing the number of errors people will make when using those forms.

## Knowing what not to do

Although I'm sure you would never make such mistakes on the forms you design, a few examples can give you an idea of how poor presentation of data on a form can cause confusion. I'm using the term *formatting* to mean more than simply choosing the proper Format property for a field. Bad formatting includes layout sins such as making text boxes too small to properly show the data.

Poor formatting could also include using text colors that are too close to the background color for easy readability, but these types of problems are extremely difficult to demonstrate in a figure. When in doubt, use common sense and not try to use pink text over a fuchsia background in your forms. Believe me — no matter how much you like those two colors, they won't work out!

In Figure 11-8, the `DateReceived`, fields all show the same information even though it's very difficult to tell that from what is displayed on the form. Here's a rundown of the errors shown in the figure:

> ✔ **Wrong field format:** The underlying field is a `Date` field, so choosing one of the time formats is clearly an error (using a time format could be the correct choice in some instances, but not if you want to display a date).

> ✔ **Yucky text box sizing:** In an attempt to make the form look neat, I set the size of all the text boxes to that of the narrowest one, cutting off a good section of the month name. But this also hints at another potential problem with the form. The `DateReceived` field is too narrow. Suppose that the date displayed in this field appeared as 2/28/2004 — would you be able to tell for certain if the date was February 28 or December 28?

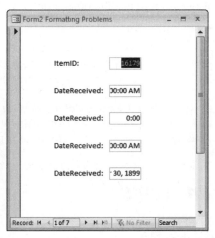

**Figure 11-8:** It's difficult to understand the data in some of this form's fields because of formatting problems.

Date fields aren't the only ones that suffer from poor formatting choices. Figure 11-9 shows a form that has five variations of the same field included on the form. Each copy of the field has a different numeric formatting property.

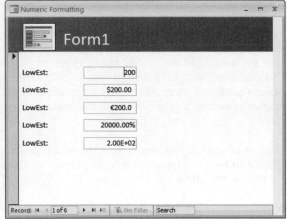

**Figure 11-9:**
Varying
numeric
formatting
can
produce
confusing
results.

Figure 11-9 shows these examples:

- ✔ The first copy of the field at the top of the form uses the default general number format. At first (and second, and third) glance, you may not notice whether the value shown in this copy represents a financial sum because there's no indication if this is in dollars, cents, or cow chips.

- ✔ The second copy of the field is set to currency with two decimal places, so determining that the value estimate is $200.00 is much easier.

- ✔ The third copy is formatted as Euros, but with one decimal place, so this value is also confusing.

- ✔ The fourth copy is set to percentage, and the last is displayed in scientific notation — clearly very bad choices to represent currency values.

I could go on, but I think you get the picture by now. Consider the type of information that you want to convey and apply proper formatting choices so that anyone using the form can easily understand what the data represents.

## *Formatting data on forms*

You use the Format tab of a field's Properties dialog box to set the display format for the field, as shown in Figure 11-10. The options available from the Format drop-down list depend on the data type in the associated field.

You may need to resize the Properties dialog box so that when you click the Format List Box drop-down list, the dialog box is wide enough to display the format samples that appear to the right of the selected property's name.

| Property Sheet | ☒ |
| --- | --- |
| Selection type: Text Box | |

LowEst ⌄

| Format | Data | Event | Other | All |

| Format | General Number |
| --- | --- |
| Decimal Places | 0 |
| Visible | Yes |
| Display When | Always |
| Scroll Bars | None |
| Can Grow | No |
| Can Shrink | No |
| Left | 1.25" |
| Top | 0.2917" |
| Width | 1" |
| Height | 0.2188" |
| Back Style | Normal |
| Back Color | #FFFFFF |
| Special Effect | Flat |
| Border Style | Solid |
| Border Color | #C0C0C0 |
| Border Width | Hairline |
| Fore Color | #000000 |
| Font Name | Calibri |
| Font Size | 11 |
| Font Weight | Normal |
| Font Italic | No |
| Font Underline | No |
| Text Align | General |
| Reading Order | Context |
| Keyboard Languag | System |
| Scroll Bar Align | System |
| Numeral Shapes | System |
| Left Margin | 0" |
| Top Margin | 0" |
| Right Margin | 0" |
| Bottom Margin | 0" |
| Line Spacing | 0" |
| Is Hyperlink | No |

**Figure 11-10:**
Use the
Format
property to
set the
display
format.

Numeric formats have an associated Decimal Places property. By default, this value is set to Auto, but often you can choose a different value for better results. For example, if you choose the Currency format, you ought to select 2 (to tell Access to format numbers with two decimal places) as the number in the Decimal Places property.

The display formats you choose for the form fields have no effect on how the data is stored in the database. These formats only modify the way that the information is shown on the form.

# Part IV
# Designing Great Reports

The 5th Wave                    By Rich Tennant

"Once I told Mona that Access was an 'argument' based program, she seemed to warm up to it."

# In this part . . .

Reports enable you to present the information from your databases to the world. Whether the viewer is your banker, your boss, or a customer, a great report makes that information far more useful and easy to understand. This part shows you how to create great reports that look good and that provide a wealth of understandable information.

# Chapter 12

# Adding Fancy Touches to Reports

· · · · · · · · · · · · · · · · · · · · · · · · · · · · · · · · · · · · · · · · · ·

· · · · · · · · · · · · · · · · · · · · · · · · · · · · · · · · · · · · · · · · · ·

*I*f forms are the objects that Access users probably see most often, reports are what Access users are most likely to share with others. You aren't likely to haul your laptop to the bank to show your banker an Access form when you want to demonstrate that your business is worthy of an increased credit line; you'd probably create (and print) an Access report that shows how well things are going.

Standard reports are just that — standard, ordinary, or even boring. If you want to make an impact, there's nothing like adding a little pizzazz. With a fancy touch here and there, your reports can display the professional appearance that gets noticed and tells viewers that you're serious about what you're doing. This chapter shows you how to add just the right bits and pieces to your Access reports without going overboard about it.

The Access Report Wizard adds some elements to reports that at least attempt to make the reports a little more presentable than a plain old print-out of raw information, but those wizards certainly don't have art degrees. By understanding the options that are available you can easily surpass the results that are produced by the wizards.

## Adding Descriptive Titles to Your Reports

A good title says a lot about a report. A title should tell busy viewers enough about the report that they know instantly whether they need to read it. A poor title leaves people wondering about both the content of the report and also about the amount of effort the report's designer put into it.

There are three primary types of titles on Access reports:

- ✔ Report titles appear once, at the beginning of a report.
- ✔ Page titles appear once per page on the report.
- ✔ Group titles appear at the beginning of each grouping of similar records in a report.

Each of the title types is optional, and you can vary their placement by using the associated header to make the title appear ahead of the information or by using the footer to make the title appear after the information. Even the term *title* can be a bit deceptive, because you can include items (such as dates and page numbers) that don't ordinarily fit the strict definition of a title. But, hey, this is your report, so you can do what you want with it.

## Getting title basics down

By default, the Access Report Wizard gives a report the same name as the table or query that is the basis for the report. Figure 12-1 shows a very basic report design with the totally unimaginative name, Items Table – Simple Grouping — which, of course, is also the name of the table.

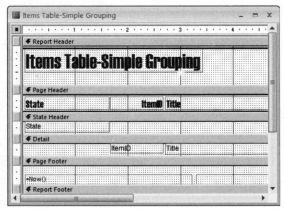

**Figure 12-1:**
Access isn't very imaginative in naming and titling reports.

The titles that the Report Wizard places on a report are *unbound controls* (see Chapter 9 for more about controls). They're not connected to any database fields or other objects. As a result, you can easily modify the titles as much as you want without worrying about hurting anything else in your database.

You can probably come up with good report titles without much help from me. After all, it doesn't take too much imagination to realize that "Items in Inventory" is a better, more descriptive title than "Items Table – Simple Grouping."

## Modifying existing titles

Access gives your reports pretty ordinary default titles that correspond to the names of tables. If you don't like the default title, you're by no means bound to keep it. You can modify a title two ways:

✔ Double-click the label and type directly in the label itself.

✔ Right-click the label and choose Properties from the pop-up menu to open the Properties dialog box for the label. In the Properties dialog box, click the Format tab and type the new title into the Caption text box (see Figure 12-2).

**Figure 12-2:**
The Caption property stores the text for the report title.

Even the Caption text box can be kind of restraining, so I like to press Shift+F2 to open the Zoom dialog box, as shown in Figure 12-3. The Zoom dialog box provides far more room to work than any of the property text boxes possibly can:

1. **Delete the boring default title in the Zoom dialog box.**

2. **Type your new title.**

3. **Click OK when you're done.**

**Figure 12-3:**
Use the
Zoom dialog
box to
greatly
expand your
working
area.

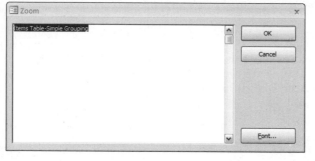

Although the Zoom dialog box is great, it doesn't do everything. In fact, despite all indications, it doesn't do formatting — at least not in your report. Don't waste your time trying to format the title by using the Font button in the Zoom dialog box. Any changes you make with that button only apply to how the text is displayed in the Zoom dialog box. They aren't carried over to the title in your report.

## *Formatting your report titles*

You can greatly modify the appearance of a title by using the various formatting options that are available on the Format tab in the Properties dialog box. You can find many of the formatting options on the Arrange section of the Ribbon, as well.

The Font list box (Home section of the Ribbon and also the Property Sheet) displays the font names, and on most systems it uses the actual font, so getting a feel for the font you're choosing is pretty easy. The fonts may not appear in the actual font on some older versions of Windows.

Most of the formatting options are pretty familiar, but a few may not be. For example, the property called Fore Color (Property Sheet) is the color of the text. Colors in Access are expressed with a really strange numbering system that won't make any sense no matter how long you work at it, so I suggest these steps:

1. **Click the Build button (not the down arrow) after you select the part of the report you want changed.**

2. **Select Fore Color property.**

   The Color dialog box appears.

3. **Pick either an existing color or a custom color.**

Another property that might seem a little odd is the `Font Weight` property. Font weight is usually a choice between normal and **bold**, but the Font Weight property list box gives you nine different choices ranging all the way from Thin to Heavy. You just have to experiment with this property to see what works best for your titles.

# Getting Dynamic with Your Titles

For a completely different type of report title you aren't likely to read about anywhere else, you might want to consider a *dynamic* title — that is, a title that you build by using an expression. This type of title can include information that you probably never knew was available, let alone put into a report title.

## Understanding how to use expressions in your titles

Before you can create dynamic titles (see "Using expressions to create dynamic titles," later in the chapter), you need to understand how expressions work.

Dynamic report titles require you to use a *calculated* control, which returns the value of an expression instead of simply displaying fixed text. Using an unbound text box, you can create a calculated control that looks like this:

```
="Inventory Item Report for "&[CurrentProject].[Name]
```

Here's the basic anatomy of an expression:

✔ First, the expression begins with an equal sign (=). The equal sign is necessary to set the value of the calculated control equal to the result of the expression.

✔ Next, the expression includes a text string that's enclosed in double quotes. Notice that there is a space before the closing double quote mark to ensure that the result of the rest of the expression is spaced properly.

✔ To concatenate the text string and the calculated result you use an ampersand (&).

✔ The CurrentProject item is a built-in Access object that refers to the current database. This object name is enclosed in square brackets for consistency because square brackets are required if the object name includes any spaces (and Access automatically adds square brackets if you forget to type them).

✔ The period between the two sets of square brackets tells Access that the next item in the string is a child of the previous item (CurrentProject).

In programmer-speak, this period is what is known as *dot notation*, and it is common in all modern *object-oriented* programming languages.

✔ Finally, Name is a property of the CurrentProject object, and it refers to the name of the currently open database.

For more information on the various properties in the CurrentProject object, see the section, "Using properties to control your expressions," later in this chapter.

## Using expressions to create dynamic titles

To create a dynamic report title, you use a different type of control than the ones you're probably used to. You need a *calculated* control because this type of control returns the value of an expression instead of simply displaying fixed text. You create this calculated control by using an unbound text box (just ignore any warnings Access tries to give you about the fact that the text box is unbound — that's exactly how you want it to be, unbound).

For example, say you want to create a dynamic title that combines some static text with the name of the database file so that the report title shows both the purpose and the source of the report. Although you could just enter the name of the database when you create the report, using a calculated control offers a great advantage. The name of the report is automatically updated if the database file is ever renamed.

To create a dynamic report title, follow these steps:

1. **Open the report in Design View.**

2. **Click the Text Box tool in the Design section of the Ribbon to select it and then drag out a large rectangle in the report header area of the report design (you may need to expand the header area first).**

   The rectangle should be large enough to hold the complete title, but you can always resize the text box later if necessary.

3. **Right-click the Title text box and choose Properties from the pop-up menu.**

   Alternatively, click the Properties button on the Ribbon to display the Properties dialog box.

4. **Click the Data tab to display it.**

5. **Click the Control Source text box to select it (you may need to close Expression Builder).**

6. **Press Shift+F2 to display the Zoom dialog box. You need the extra space it affords to easily enter the expression.**

7. **Enter an expression.**

   I entered =`"Inventory Item Report for "&[CurrentProject].[Name]` for my example, as shown in Figure 12-4.

**Figure 12-4:** This expression creates a dynamic title that shows the current database name.

8. **Click OK to close the Zoom dialog box.**

9. **Click the Close button to close the Properties dialog box.**

10. **In the Report design, click the label for the text box to select just the label and then press Delete to remove the label.**

11. **Save your work and then switch the report to Print Preview view to view the results.**

    The result of your expression looks something like Figure 12-5.

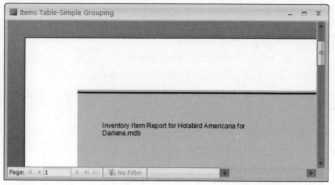

Inventory Item Report for Holabird Americana for
Darlene.mdb

**Figure 12-5:**
This is the
title that
results
from the
expression.

You can spice up the appearance of your dynamic title, using the same formatting options that you use on any ordinary title.

## Using properties to control your expressions

You can use other properties of the CurrentProject object in addition to the Name property. To use any of these properties, simply replace Name with the name of the property you want:

- ✔ **FullName:** This property returns the complete name of the open database file including the path with the drive letter and all folder names.

- ✔ **Path:** This property returns the complete path but without the database name. It is identical to the FullName property with the Name property stripped off the end.

- ✔ **FileFormat:** This property returns a number that refers to the Access file format of the open database file. This number is equivalent to the internal Access version number, so the Access 2007 file format returns a value of 12. This property probably isn't too useful in most cases, but it's there if you're curious.

The CurrentProject object has quite a few other properties, but they're not available in a calculated control. Those additional properties are only useful in VBA procedures.

## Getting rid of the .mdb document extension

Even though I don't find the .mdb extension on the end of the calculated title (refer to Figure 12-5) objectionable, you may. If so, you can use a couple of the functions that are built in to Access to strip it off the end result. The two functions are

- ✔ The Left function, which returns a specified number of characters from the beginning of a string
- ✔ The Len function, which returns the length of the string

To apply this fix to the example, replace the calculation in the expression

```
[CurrentProject].[Name]
```

with the following:

```
Left([CurrentProject].[Name],Len([CurrentProject].[Name])-
    4)
```

This expression uses both functions in this order:

1. The Len function determines the number of characters in the current database name

2. The Left function returns the name minus the last four characters — which happen to be .mdb.

   Your title now appears without the extension at the end of the result.

# Coming Up with Page Title Ideas

Page titles help readers keep track of multiple report pages. As with report titles, page titles can appear at the top of the page in the page header or at the bottom of a page in the page footer.

Most often, you place page numbers, dates, or even a brief report name in a page title. Page numbers and dates are covered in the section "Adding Dates and Page Numbers," later in this chapter.

You can use the same types of formatting options to spruce up your page titles that you use with report titles, but because page titles typically appear on each page of the report, you may want to be a bit conservative on the size of page titles to cut down on wasted paper.

By default, any page headers or page footers you define appear on every page of the report. However, you can choose other options to control where these items appear. You use the Page Header property (see Figure 12-6) or the similar Page Footer property of the report to adjust these settings.

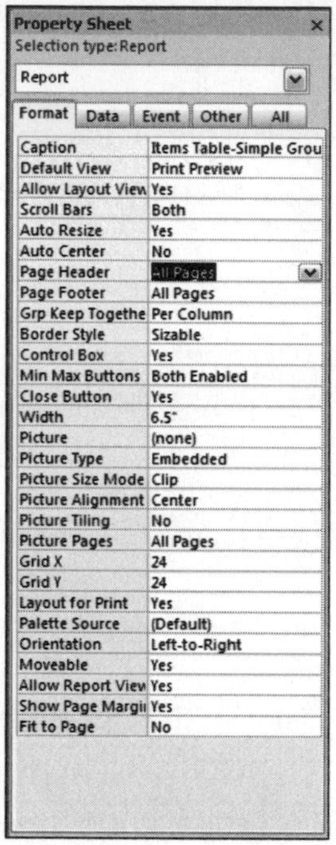

**Figure 12-6:**
The Page Header and Page Footer properties control where the page titles appear.

These two properties are just a bit cryptic, so a brief description is in order:

- ✔ **All Pages:** This option prints the page header (or footer) on every page of the report and is the default setting.

- ✔ **Not with Rpt Hdr:** This option prints the page header (or footer) on every page except the first page where the report header appears.

- ✔ **Not with Rpt Ftr:** This option prints the page header (or footer) on every page except the last page where the report footer appears.

- ✔ **Not with Rpt Hdr/Ftr:** This option prints the page header (or footer) on every page except the first page where the report header appears and the last page where the report footer appears.

If you don't want to include the database name in the report title, you might want to use the calculated control idea that I discuss in "Getting Dynamic with Your Titles," earlier in this chapter to add the database name to the page title.

# Adding Dates and Page Numbers

Date and page numbers are important report elements that probably seem like kind of throwaway pieces. But if you've ever dropped a big stack of report pages and had to figure out how to put the pages back in the proper order, you can easily understand the importance of page numbering. Likewise, if you've ever been faced with a situation where you ended up with several different copies of a report, you know that having the date and possibly even the time that the report was produced is the only way to be sure which copy is the current copy.

## Choosing the right place for dates and numbers

Where's the best place for dates and page numbers? Well, the flip answer would be somewhere on the report, but that wouldn't be a very helpful thing for me to say, would it?

Page numbers can only go in the page header or the page footer. There's simply no other place on a report for them. Your choice of placing them at the top or the bottom of the page is simply a matter of personal preference.

The report date, on the other hand, could easily be placed on the report header or footer in addition to the typical location on the page header or footer. I find that adding the date to the report header is a good way to start off a report, but that displaying the date along with the page numbers is also valuable.

## Getting fancy with date displays

It's very easy to add a date and time to a report. The simplest method is to choose Date & Time from the Design section of the Ribbon to open the Date and Time dialog box, as shown in Figure 12-7. Then you use the options in the dialog box to choose what you want to include.

**Figure 12-7:**
You can add
a date and
time by
using the
Date and
Time dialog
box.

You can also add the date to a report manually by using an unbound text box that is a calculated control. Generally, you use the expression =Now() to return the current date and time, but you can modify the expression if necessary. For example, if you need to print a number of reports in advance of a meeting and want all the reports to display the same date, you can adjust the date easily. For example, the following expression will display tomorrow's date on the report:

```
=Now()+1
```

You could also backdate a report with this technique, of course.

The Now() function returns a date and time serial number (if you use Excel, you probably are already familiar with the function). You can display the result as a date, as a time, or as a combination of the two, depending on the format you choose. Figure 12-8 shows the date and time format options that are available on the Format tab of the Properties dialog box.

In the Access date and time numbering scheme, a *time serial number* of 0 represents 12:00 AM, Saturday, December 30, 1899. If you need to represent a specific date and time on a report, add 1 for each full day and a decimal fraction representing the fraction of a day equal to the time you want. For example, if you want to show the date as June 26, 2006, and the time as 12:00 PM, use the following expression:

```
=38894.5
```

## Discovering some neat page number tricks

Page numbers are similar to dates and times in many ways. You can use the Insert Page Number button (Design section of the Ribbon) to add page numbers to a header or to a footer, or you can add page numbers yourself by using calculated controls. You can also use any of the formatting options to make the page numbers as fancy or as unobtrusive as you like.

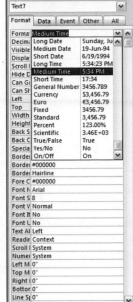

**Figure 12-8:**
Use the
Format
property to
decide how
dates and
times will
appear on
your
reports.

Access has two built-in objects you use to create page number expressions:

🖝 **Page:** This object represents the current page number.

🖝 **Pages:** This object represents the total number of pages in the report.

You might notice a very slight delay before a report begins printing when you have page numbers included in your report. That's because Access has to make two passes through the report in order to first determine how many pages it contains so that the Pages object holds the correct value.

Even though page numbers are usually used only in page headers or page footers, you can show the total number of report pages on the report header by adding an unbound text box to the report header and entering the following expression into the Control Source property for the text box:

```
="Total Report Pages: "&[Pages]
```

If you're the type of person who always wants to know how much work you still have in front of you, try using the following expression in an unbound text box in the page header or footer:

```
="Pages Left in this Report: "&[Pages]-[Page]
```

# Making Records Easier to Read with Alternating Bands of Color

The following sections offer some ways you can make the main parts of your reports a bit fancier. In the following sections you discover some techniques that are quite a bit different from the old tried-and-true methods that most Access users know. You can create some really unusual results.

You've probably seen reports that were printed on paper that has alternating bands of color. Those bands of color make it a bit easier to follow a line of data across a page, but they often don't line up very well with individual records. These steps show you how you to add alternating bands of background color that automatically line up perfectly with each record.

You already know that you can use the various formatting options to spruce up your reports, but you may not have considered using the color options, despite the fact that you may use a color printer. You don't have to do everything in plain old boring black text against a white background, and you can do color without *overdoing* color.

## Step 1: Picking colors and translating them to hex

You can set colors in Access in a couple of ways.

The most common method is also the least complicated:

1. **Select the object whose color you want to change.**
2. **Open the Properties dialog box.**
3. **Select the color property you want to adjust.**
4. **Click the Build button to display the Colors dialog box.**

   Figure 12-9 shows the Colors dialog box after you have clicked the More Colors button and then the Custom option.

After you choose a color, Access throws a really strange-looking number into the selected color property in the Properties dialog box. In the case of pure white, for example, the color is shown as 16777215.

**Figure 12-9:**
Use the
Colors
dialog box
to choose
colors for
objects.

Computers use a color model known as *RGB* — for red, green, and blue.
Every color is measured by how much red, how much green, and how much
blue is in the color. But computers use a different form of measurement called
*hexadecimal* (often shortened to *hex*) rather than the decimal (or base-10)
system most humans use. Hexadecimal is a base-16 system. The first 10 numbers are 0 to 9, and the numbers we think of as 10, 11, 12, 13, 14, and 15 are
shown as A, B, C, D, E, and F in hexadecimal.

So why is this important? You need to use the hexadecimal numbers to figure
out the equivalent decimal values that Access shows in the Properties dialog
box so that you can tell Access what colors you want it to use.

To further complicate things, the Colors dialog box shows the red, green, and
blue values in decimal, and you need to first convert those numbers to hex in
order to create the alternating colored records. Fortunately, this all sounds a
lot worse than it really is.

To figure out a color number manually, follow these steps:

1. **Open the Windows Calculator application.**

   You can find it under the Accessories submenu on your Start menu.

2. **Make sure the Calculator is in Scientific view by checking the
   View menu.**

3. **In Access open the Color dialog box.**

   Click the Build button in the Properties dialog box for one of the color
   properties you want to set.

4. **Make sure that the Color dialog box is fully expanded so that you can see the red, green, and blue values.**

5. **Choose a color you want to use.**

6. **With the Calculator in Dec (decimal) mode, enter the red value.**

7. **Click the Hex option button to convert the decimal value to a hexadecimal value.**

8. **Write down the value shown in the Calculator display.**

9. **Repeat Steps 5 through 8 for the green and then the blue values.**

10. **Clear the entry in the calculator and then enter the red, green, and blue values as a single hexadecimal value.**

    In the example shown in Figure 12-9, the value is 16777215 (#FFFFFF) for a stark white background.

11. **Click the Dec option button to display the equivalent decimal value.**

    My example for a lovely violet background works out to 12342445!

Go ahead and try several different color values by either.

- ✔ Changing the color selection in the Color model box
- ✔ Clicking in the color bands and then calculating the value that should appear in the Properties dialog box

    The numbers should match in every case if you don't make any mistakes entering the values.

# Step 2: Writing code to apply your color bands

In the previous section I show you how to find colors that look good as alternating backgrounds for the records in your reports. In this section, I show you how to achieve this by creating an *event procedure* — which actually is a bit of VBA code — in Access. Don't worry; even if you're not a programmer, this is a pretty painless process.

Here's what you need to do to add alternating bands of color to your report:

1. **Open the report that you want to modify in Design View.**

2. **Click the Detail band to select it.**

3. **Open the Properties dialog box and click the Event tab to make it visible.**

4. **Click the On Format property box to select it.**

5. **Click the Build button (choose Code Builder and click OK).**

   The code editing window in Microsoft Visual Basic appears, as shown in Figure 12-10.

**Figure 12-10:** Use this window to create the event procedure.

6. **Move the insertion point to the blank line just below the top line and enter** Private RowNumber As Long.

   This is a necessary step because in VBA you need to *declare* a *long integer variable* before you can use it in the procedure.

7. **Move the insertion point to the line below the one that begins with** Private Sub Detail_Format.

8. **Enter the following lines exactly as shown here:**

```
RowNumber = RowNumber + 1
If RowNumber / 2 = CLng(RowNumber / 2) Then
Me.Detail.BackColor = 16777088
Else
Me.Detail.BackColor = 8454143
End If
```

The numbers used in my example give alternating yellow and aqua bands. If you don't care for these colors, you can easily specify different colors by changing the two values 16777088 and 8454143 in Step 8. Use the procedures mentioned in the previous section to determine the values to use.

9. **Close the Microsoft Visual Basic window to return to your database.**

10. **Save your work and then switch the report to Print Preview view.**

   Switching to Print Preview view takes a bit longer than usual because Access is applying the formatting you asked it to add. Figure 12-11 shows how your report should appear.

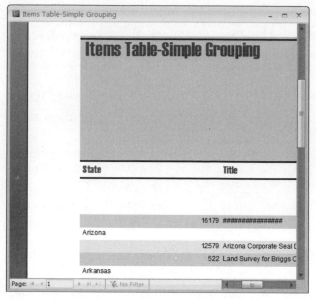

You can modify the event procedure by once again clicking the Build button to open the code editing window.

You can probably figure out most of the event procedure on your own, but a few things might throw you:

- The `CLng` function in the second line rounds a number to the closest integer value. This is how the procedure determines whether the current record is an even- or odd-numbered record, so this function controls whether the next line or the line following `Else` is executed.

- `Me.Detail.BackColor` is a programmer's method of referring to the background color of the current record in the Detail section.

- The procedure uses an `If` *condition* `Then` *statement if true* `Else` *statement if false* structure to control which statement is executed. As the `RowNumber` value is incremented, the two statements that set the background color are alternately executed as a result.

# Making Records Stand Out

One cool way to make certain records stand out is to use *conditional formatting* to apply special formatting to records that meet certain conditions.

Bonus: This method doesn't involve any VBA programming. For example, you could color all orders for a particular state by using a different color or you could use colors to flag records relating to products that are on sale.

To apply conditional formatting to a report, follow these steps:

1. **Open the report that you want to modify in Design View.**

2. **In the Detail section of the report, select the fields to which you want to apply the conditional formatting.**

   If you want, you can test the conditional formatting option with just one field. Building the conditional test is a little easier, of course, but only that field will have conditional formatting applied.

3. **Choose Conditional Formatting from the Design section of the Ribbon.**

   The Conditional Formatting dialog box appears, as shown in Figure 12-12.

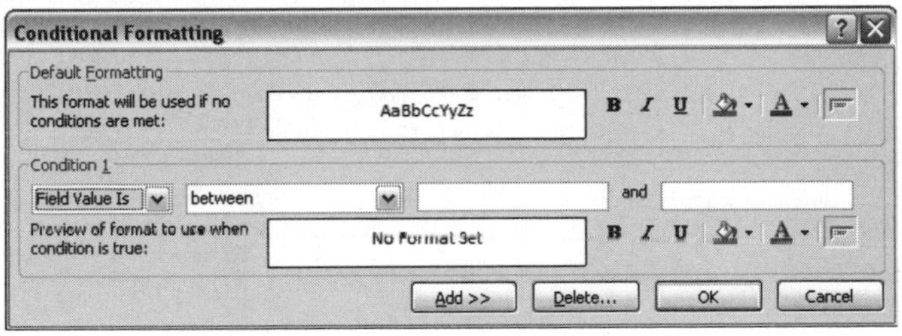

**Figure 12-12:**
Use the
Conditional
Formatting
dialog box
to specify
conditions
and
formatting
options.

| Conditional Formatting | ? X |
|---|---|
| Default Formatting | |
| This format will be used if no conditions are met: | AaBbCcYyZz    B *I* U 🎨▾ A▾ 🟰 |
| Condition 1 | |
| Field Value Is ▾   between   ▾   [            ]   and   [            ] | |
| Preview of format to use when condition is true: | No Format Set    B *I* U 🎨▾ A▾ 🟰 |
| Add >>   Delete...   OK   Cancel | |

4. **From the first drop-down list in the Condition 1 section, select Expression Is.**

   Making this selection hides two of the three remaining boxes on the same line.

5. **In the blank text box, enter the expression that defines the condition you want to test for.**

   In this example, I entered [State] = "CA" Or [State] = "California" to apply the conditional formatting if the value in the State field is CA or California.

6. **Select the formatting options you want to apply if the condition is met.**

   In this case, I chose a light blue text color. The dialog box looks similar to Figure 12-13.

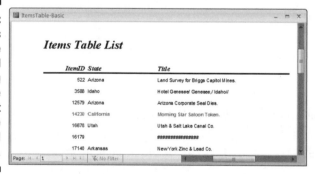

**Figure 12-13:**
The
conditional
formatting is
defined and
ready to
apply.

7. **If you want to specify any additional conditional formatting, click the Add button and repeat Steps 4 through 6.**

8. **Click OK after you specify all the conditional formatting you want to apply.**

   The Conditional Formatting dialog box closes.

9. **Save your work.**

10. **Switch the report to Print Preview view to view the results.**

    Access takes a bit longer to display the report when conditional formatting is applied. Figure 12-14 shows the results for my sample report.

**Figure 12-14:**
Access
applies the
conditional
formatting
to the
records that
meet the
specified
conditions.

*Items Table List*

| ItemID | State | Title |
|---|---|---|
| 522 | Arizona | Land Survey for Briggs Capitol Mines. |
| 3588 | Idaho | Hotel Genesee/ Genesee,/ Idaho// |
| 12579 | Arizona | Arizona Corporate Seal Dies. |
| 14230 | California | Morning Star Saloon Token. |
| 16678 | Utah | Utah & Salt Lake Canal Co. |
| 16179 | | ############### |
| 17140 | Arkansas | New York Zinc & Lead Co. |

Conditional formatting is applied only to the actual area occupied by the selected fields. If you don't want the color gaps between the fields to appear, either

✔ Make the fields large enough so they're against each other.

✔ Add an empty control like a blank label behind the other fields and apply the conditional formatting to the empty control.

It's not necessary for the field that you're testing in the conditional formatting expression to actually appear on the report as long as the field is a part of the table or query that supplies the data for the report. You could, for example, test the value in the State field even if the state never appeared on the report. This might cause some confusion among people reading the report, however, so you would want to explain the conditional formatting somewhere on the report — perhaps in the report footer.

If you print your reports in black and white, you can still use the color options discussed in the last two examples in this chapter. Just make sure that you substitute colors that appear as a light gray background in the printout so that the text is readable in print.

# Chapter 13

# Creating Reports That Summarize Data

●●●●●●●●●●●●●●●●●●●●●●●●●●●●●●●●●●●●●●●●●●●●●●●●●●●●●●

*In This Chapter*

▶ Grouping records

▶ Adding everything up

▶ Working with advanced summarizing methods

●●●●●●●●●●●●●●●●●●●●●●●●●●●●●●●●●●●●●●●●●●●●●●●●●●●●●●

A ll Access reports show data, of course, but sometimes that's all a report does — show raw data. In many instances, reports could be more useful if they went a bit further to analyze information and provide helpful summaries. Fortunately, Access offers a number of different options that enable you to create various types of summary reports.

Access offers a lot of tools for creating reports that summarize data. Many of them are fairly well hidden by the Report Wizards, but there's no reason why you can't take control and create your reports the way you want.

This chapter shows you how to group data to help organize your reports, how to add totals and subtotals to reports, and how to apply some more advanced report summarization techniques. Using the methods presented in this chapter, you can analyze the information that is contained in your databases so that the data is even more useful to you (and to others) than it already is. Do I smell a raise in your future?

## Discovering How to Group Records

Organization is absolutely vital in making information useful. Imagine how useless a large city's telephone book would be if the listings were simply added randomly without alphabetizing the records? Or consider how difficult shopping in a supermarket would be if the groceries weren't grouped into general categories such as produce, meats, dairy products, and so on. Information doesn't have much value unless it's organized in some way.

Access offers several ways for you to organize your data. Simple record sorting (see Chapter 12) is one of the most basic methods of organization, but record grouping bumps up the utility to the next level.

## Understanding your record-grouping options

When you *group* records in a report, Access arranges the records according to your specifications; but that's just the beginning of what's going on. Each group of records acts almost like a report within a report, meaning that you can create record subgroups using another field within the database. You can also create multiple groups within the same report. In addition, you can tell Access to summarize the records within each group so that you can view information, such as group totals, group record counts, or other more advanced forms of analysis.

Here's a look at the grouping methods available to you:

- ✔ You can group records based on an exact match of alphabetized values. People typically think of record grouping this way, but that's only one of the available options.

- ✔ You can group records that have similar but not precisely the same values.

- ✔ You can group records based on date or time ranges.

In most cases, you use a group header (and sometimes a group footer) to show how the records are being grouped. Generally, you place the field that is being used for the grouping in the group header so that the user can easily tell which group of records he is seeing. For example, if you group the records in a report by state, each group header shows the name of the state for the following group of records.

You might want to include a visual element such as a horizontal line in the group header or in the group footer to make the groups stand out from each other (the Format tab in the Property Sheet lets you create borders, and a line option appears in the Design section of the Ribbon).

# Creating your first report grouping

The simplest way to set up report grouping is to use the Report Wizard and specify that you want to group the records as you're building the report.

As you've seen in earlier chapters, the wizards aren't always as flexible as you might like. In addition, the wizards really only give you one shot at getting things correct — if you don't like the results, you must either start over from scratch or make the changes you want in Design View. Because of these limitations, I say you should bypass the wizard and instead create useful report groupings with the tools that you find in Design View.

## Grouping by date range

If you run a business, one thing you're always trying to find out is how your business is progressing. You may know it's progressing nicely, but a little evidence would be nice, wouldn't it? Are you getting more orders or making more profit as time goes along? Can you demonstrate to your banker that your business is growing steadily over time? These are some of the types of questions you can answer with a report that groups records by date.

Figure 13-1 shows an example of a report that shows the number of items received for an auction each month, along with the estimated total value of the items. This type of report uses grouping by a date range, so it can give you a good picture of how your business is doing on a monthly, quarterly, or yearly basis. If you really want to get an up-close look at progress, you can even track inventory, sales figures, and more on a weekly or daily basis.

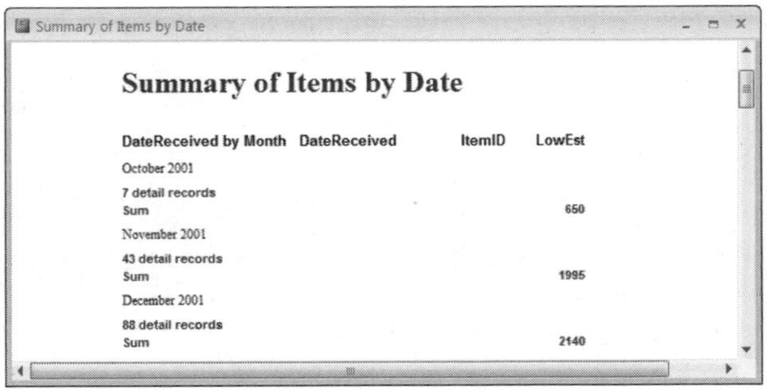

**Figure 13-1:** This report groups the records by month.

To add date grouping to a report, follow these steps:

1. **Create your basic report and open it in Design View.**

Make sure that the underlying table or query includes a field with dates that you want to use for grouping the records.

2. **Choose Sorting And Grouping by right-clicking the report or click the Grouping And Totals option in the Design section of the Ribbon.**

   The Group, Sort, And Total dialog box appears.

3. **Select the field that you want to use for grouping from the drop-down Field/Expression list box.**

   I selected the `DateReceived` field, and chose Oldest To Newest.

4. **Select the sorting method you want to use by choosing Ascending or Descending from the Add A Sort list box.**

5. **With Grouping still selected (click on the More arrow), choose headers, footers, time intervals, and the general appearance of the report.**

   Adding a group header or a group footer changes the associated field from simply being used for sorting to being used for grouping.

   In this example, I used a group footer to add the summary information, but I could have made the report even more compact by adding the information shown in the detail section to the group footer and eliminating the detail section.

   I selected `Month` to group the records by dates in the same month. Figure 13-2 shows how the Group, Sort, And Total dialog box should appear at this point. In the following sections you see how to use the group interval options.

### Specifying how groups are formed with the group interval

The Group, Sort, and Total dialog box includes an option labeled By Entire Value that you may find just a bit confusing at first. This option operates differently depending on the type of data that is contained in the field that you're using for grouping:

- ✔ **If the data type is text, then By Entire Value specifies the number of characters at the beginning of the text string to use to group the records.** For example, if you set the value to 3 (Custom), the report groups all records where the first three characters in the grouping field match; *Undercover* and *Underdahl* would be grouped together, but United would be in a different group.

- ✔ **If the data type is a numeric or date type, then By Entire Value specifies the number of values that will be consolidated.** For example, if you set the value to Quarter and the Group On value is a date, the report consolidates records for sets of three consecutive months.

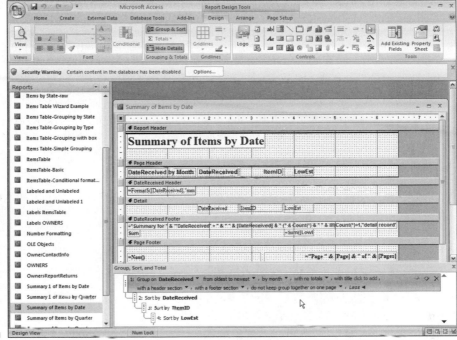

**Figure 13-2:**
Use the
Group, Sort,
And Total
dialog box
to set up the
grouping for
your report.

## Keeping records together

You've probably seen plenty of reports that used grouping but were still difficult to understand because the grouping simply wasn't very obvious. For example, it's simply not very intuitive to try to figure out what's going on in a report if a group header prints at the bottom of a page, but none of the records in that group appear until the next page.

The Do Not Keep Group Together On One Page option in the Group Sort, And Total dialog box is intended to help you control the location of the group headers, footers, and the related detail records. This option includes the following choices:

- ✓ **Do Not Keep Group Together On One Page:** Access makes no attempt to keep the group header, detail records, and group footer together on the same page. This is the default setting.

- ✓ **Keep Whole Group Together On One Page:** Access tries to keep the group header, detail records, and group footer together on the same page.

- ✓ **Keep Header And First Record Together On One Page:** Access starts a new page before starting the group if at least one detail record can't follow the group header on the page.

Unfortunately, the Keep Together option is somewhat less than perfect in execution. Alas, that's just the nature of reports. Depending on the data that you're including in a report, it might simply be impossible to keep the group header, detail records, and group footer together on the same page. For example, if you have a report in which a single group of detail records needs several pages to print, there's really no way that Access can fit the group header, detail records, and group footer together on the same page.

If the number of records in your database simply makes the Keep Together options unworkable, consider adding the field that you're using for grouping to the detail band on the report to help identify which group each detail record belongs to.

Fortunately, Access does provide another option that you can use to improve the layout of your grouped reports. You can set the Force New Page property for the group using the Format tab of the Properties Sheet, as shown in Figure 13-3.

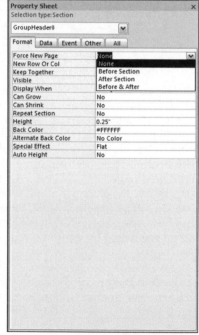

**Figure 13-3:**
Use the Force New Page property for additional control over how grouped records print.

The Force New Page property has four options:

- ✔ **None:** No extra pages are added, and the new group simply begins after the previous group ends.

- ✔ **Before Section:** Always starts each group at the top of a new page.

  ✔ **After Section:** Always starts the next group on a new page.

  ✔ **Before & After:** Begins each group at the top of a new page and forces the next group to advance to a new page.

All these options other than None should cause each group to begin at the top of a new page. You can set this property for any report section except for page headers and page footers.

## Making sure you get the right groups

Unfortunately, determining how to create the right type of grouping is not always easy. Making a report return the type of results that you want can be a tricky process. This is especially true if you want to summarize results using date or time intervals that are just a bit offbeat.

For example, suppose that you want to analyze your sales results from a number of years. Instead of showing the trend over time, you may want to know the number and amount of sales for each season or fiscal quarter. You could have your report show the total of all Quarter 1 results, the total of all Quarter 2 results, the total of all Quarter 3 results, and the total of all Quarter 4 results, regardless of the year. Getting this type of summary can be pretty tricky because even though you can group dates by quarter, you end up with four individual quarter groups for each year that's represented in your database. What you really want are four quarterly summaries where each summary totals all the results by quarter regardless of the year. Figure 13-4 shows an example of this type of report. In this case, the results for several years are combined into four quarterly summaries, and users can easily determine that demand for the business has been pretty seasonal.

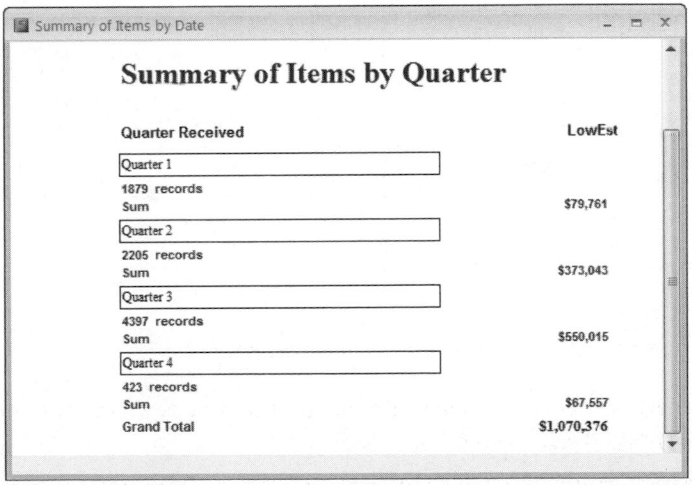

**Figure 13-4:**
This report groups the records by quarter regardless of the year.

| Summary of Items by Date | | – ☐ ✕ |
|---|---|---|
| **Summary of Items by Quarter** | | |
| Quarter Received | | LowEst |
| Quarter 1 | | |
| 1879 records | | |
| Sum | | $79,761 |
| Quarter 2 | | |
| 2205 records | | |
| Sum | | $373,043 |
| Quarter 3 | | |
| 4397 records | | |
| Sum | | $550,015 |
| Quarter 4 | | |
| 423 records | | |
| Sum | | $67,557 |
| Grand Total | | $1,070,376 |

The key to creating this type of summary is to use the functions built in to Access. The `DatePart` function enables you to group records based on specific pieces of date information without the chronological constraints that are imposed by the normal grouping options.

To use the `DatePart` function, you create an expression in the Expression Builder list box in the Group, Sort, And Total dialog box, as shown in Figure 13-5. The expression takes the place of the field name that you usually select from the drop-down list.

**TIP**

If you change from grouping on a field to grouping using an expression with the `DatePart` function, be sure to set the Group On option to Expression.

An expression using the `DatePart` function uses the following syntax:

```
=DatePart("date code",[fieldname])
```

Table 13-1 describes the date/time codes you can use with the `DatePart` function.

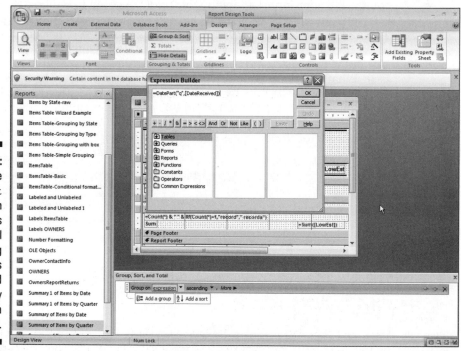

**Figure 13-5:**
The `DatePart` function provides additional grouping options compared to simply grouping on a field.

| Table 13-1 | Date/Time Codes for the DatePart Function |
|------------|-------------------------------------------|
| *Code* | *Meaning* |
| d | Day |
| h | Hour |
| m | Month |
| n | Minute |
| q | Quarter |
| s | Second |
| w | Day of the week |
| ww | Week of year |
| y | Day of year |
| yyyy | Year |

If you want to analyze your sales by month instead of by quarter, you replace the q with an m in the expression.

# Adding Subtotals and Totals

One of the big advantages of grouping records is that you can generate subtotals for each group in addition to overall totals for the entire report. In the report examples shown earlier in this chapter, you see how creating groupings can enable you to view the subtotaled results by month or by quarter.

You can use the Report Wizard to add subtotals and totals to your reports automatically. But adding these items yourself is also very easy.

## Understanding how subtotals and totals work

*Totals* and *subtotals* are actually the same thing. The only difference between the two has to do with where they're placed in a report. That may sound a little strange, but it's actually true because of the way Access groups records.

You can add a total or a subtotal to any footer on a report. (You can also add them to headers, but doing so tends to be a bit confusing for someone viewing the report.) When you run the report, Access calculates the totals and subtotals based on the report section where you placed the expression:

If you place the expression on the report footer, the result of the expression is a total of all matching records in the entire report. If you place the expression on the page footer, Access totals the records for each page individually. And if you place the expression on a group footer, Access creates the subtotals by group.

Essentially, Access treats totals and subtotals as (in programming parlance) *private* or *local* variables. That is, a subtotal for a group can only include the items that are contained within the single group. Any items that are in another group simply don't exist as far as the subtotal is concerned.

## Adding totals to groups and reports

You use the Sum function to create totals and subtotals.

The following expression placed in an unbound text box control would create a group subtotal, a page subtotal, or a report total for the values in the LowEst field, depending on where you placed the expression:

```
=Sum([LowEst])
```

Figure 13-6 shows a report design that includes both a group subtotal and a report total. The same expression is clearly used in both instances, but because the group subtotal only includes the items within each group, the expression produces very different results in each instance (reference Chapter 4 if necessary).

Be sure to set the Format property for any totals or subtotals (select them on the report first) appropriately (such as to Currency) so that the meaning of the total is easier to understand in the printed report.

Summary 1 of Items by Quarter
Report Header
Summary of Items by Quarter
Page Header
Quarter Received
LowEst
=DatePart("q",[DateReceived]) Header
="Quarter " & DatePart("q",[DateReceived])
Detail
=DatePart("q",[DateReceived]) Footer
Sum
=Sum([LowEst])
Page Footer
Report Footer
Grand Total
=Sum([LowEst])
Group subtotal
Report total

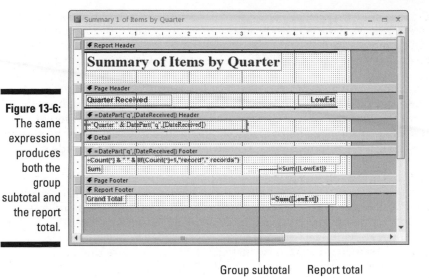

**Figure 13-6:** The same expression produces both the group subtotal and the report total.

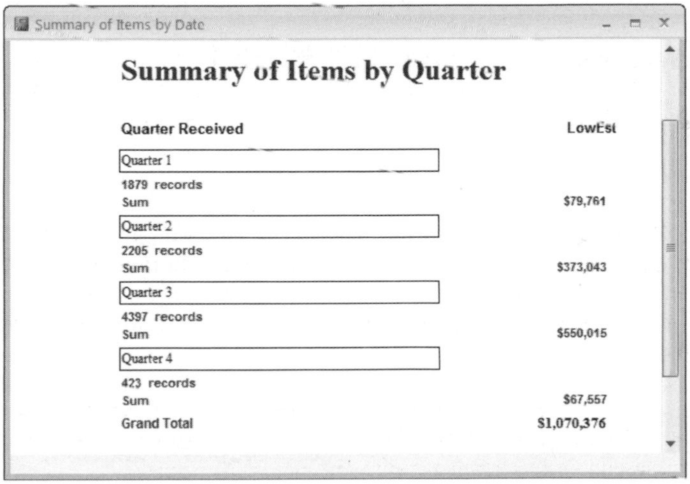

Summary of Items by Date
Summary of Items by Quarter
Quarter Received
LowEst
Quarter 1
1879 records
Sum
$79,761
Quarter 2
2205 records
Sum
$373,043
Quarter 3
4397 records
Sum
$550,015
Quarter 4
423 records
Sum
$67,557
Grand Total
$1,070,376

**Figure 13-7:** The same expression produces different results in different places in the report if the Format is incorrect.

# Using Some Advanced Summarizing Methods

Just as Excel really isn't much of a database application, Access isn't the best spreadsheet, either. Even so, Access does include a very large number of built-in functions that you can use in your reports. The latest version of Access actually includes more functions than most spreadsheet programs did a few years ago — although not all these functions are useful outside of VBA procedures.

Probably the easiest way to get a feel for the functions that are included in Access 2007 is to search the help file (the small question mark on the right) for *Functions by category* (type into Search). This listing is far more useful for you than an alphabetical listing of functions because you can find related functions based on their purpose instead of trying to figure them out by name. You can also view the list on the Web at `office.microsoft.com/en-us/assistance/HP011359591033.aspx`.

## Going beyond simple math

Even though Access has several built-in functions, you probably won't use more than a few of them in your reports. Still, if you don't know they're available, you could miss many of the functions that you might find awfully useful.

Although I can't list all the functions you might find useful, Table 13-2 shows a number of functions that you might want to use when you want a little more than just a simple sum. This table is far from comprehensive. For example, I have left out various financial functions that you're more likely to use in Excel than in Access.

| Table 13-2 | Some Useful Access Functions |
| --- | --- |
| *Function* | *Description* |
| Abs | Returns the absolute value of a number. |
| Avg | Calculates the arithmetic mean. |
| Count | Calculates the number of records. |
| DateAdd | Returns a date to which a specified interval has been added. |

| Function | Description |
|---|---|
| DateDiff | Calculates the number of time intervals between two dates. |
| DatePart | Returns a specified part of a given date. |
| Fix | Returns the integer value of a number. If the number is negative, Fix returns the first negative integer greater than or equal to the number. |
| Hex | Returns a string representing the hexadecimal value of a number. |
| IIf | Returns one of two values depending on the evaluation of an expression. |
| InStr | Returns the position of the first occurrence of one string within another. |
| Int | Returns the integer value of a number. If the number is negative, Int returns the first negative integer less than or equal to the number. |
| LCase | Converts a string to lowercase. |
| Left | Returns a specified number of characters from the left side of a string. |
| Len | Returns the number of characters in a string. |
| Log | Returns the natural logarithm of a number. |
| LTrim | Removes extra spaces from the beginning of a string. |
| Max | Returns the maximum value. |
| Mid | Returns a number of characters from a string. |
| Min | Returns the minimum value. |
| Now | Returns the current system date and time. |
| Nz | Converts a Null value to zero, an empty string, or a value you specify. |
| Replace | Replaces part or all of a string with a different string. |

*(continued)*

**Table 13-2** *(continued)*

| Function | Description |
|----------|-------------|
| Right | Returns a specified number of characters from the right side of a string. |
| Rnd | Returns a random number between 0 and 1. |
| Round | Rounds a number to a specified number of decimal places. |
| RTrim | Removes extra spaces from the end of a string. |
| Space | Creates a string consisting of the specified number of spaces. |
| Sqr | Calculates the square root of a number. |
| StdDev | Calculates the standard deviation for a population sample. |
| StdDevP | Calculates the standard deviation for a population. |
| StrConv | Converts string values to other forms. |
| StrReverse | Reverses the character order of a string. |
| Sum | Returns the sum. |
| Time | Returns the current system time. |
| Timer | Returns the number of seconds elapsed since midnight. |
| Trim | Removes extra spaces from both ends of a string. |
| UCase | Converts a string to uppercase. |
| Var | Calculates the variance for a population sample. |
| VarP | Calculates the variance for a population. |

The following sections pick out a few of the functions to show you how you can put them to use in a report.

## Converting string values

In Table 13-2, you see a list of several functions that process string values in some way. The LCase function converts all the characters in a string to lowercase, whereas the UCase function converts everything to uppercase. But suppose you're dealing with a database where some users have carelessly entered customer names in a variety of styles. Some names are properly capitalized, some are all lowercase, and some are simply weird.

Now imagine that you need to create a set of reports to send to your customers so that they can see a year-end summary of their orders. You wouldn't want to have the reports look sloppy with all that strange capitalization in the customer names, would you?

Well, the StrConv function (refer to Table 13-2) has several options, but its capability to convert strings so that the first letter of each word is capitalized (also known as putting words in *proper case*) is a real life-saver in this scenario. Although this function isn't perfect — names like O'Reilly and McDougal are still problematic — it works wonders for most of the messed up names in your database.

To convert strings to proper case, create an expression like this one (substituting the name of the field containing your customer names for *FullName*):

```
=StrConv([FullName],vbProperCase)
```

In the example, *vbProperCase* is a Visual Basic *constant* that tells the StrConv function the type of conversion you want to make. You could replace vbProperCase in the expression with the number 3 because that's the actual value of the constant, but using the constant makes your expression a little easier to understand. The Access help file lists several other constants you can use with the StrConv function.

## Finding the largest, smallest, and average values

You can probably think of several instances in which you'd like a report to show the largest, smallest, or average values — either in the report as a whole or in each record group. If so, some of the built-in functions can help.

The following expressions show the maximum, minimum, and average values in a field named `LowEst`:

```
=Max([LowEst])
=Min([LowEst])
=Avg([LowEst])
```

Where you place the expression is the key to how many records are analyzed. Place the expression in the group footer to give group results or in the report footer to give results for the entire report.

## Trimming off extra spaces

Extra spaces can creep into strings pretty easily. A user might accidentally press the Spacebar, or you might concatenate some values and inadvertently add some extra spaces along the way. Access offers several functions to get rid of the excess so that your reports look a bit neater.

✔ The `LTrim`, `RTrim`, and `Trim` functions are excellent candidates if the extra spaces you want to remove are at the beginning or end of the string.

✔ If you want to tighten up a report by removing extra spaces somewhere in the middle of a string, you use the `Replace` function.

The following expression looks in a field named `Description` for instances of two spaces; it replaces the two spaces with a single space:

```
=Replace([Description]," "," ")
```

In order to make this expression work correctly, make sure that you

✔ Include two spaces between the first set of double quotes and only one space between the second set.

✔ Separate the two sets of quotation marks with a comma (and no spaces).

## Rounding numbers

If you have values in your database that are the result of calculations, be aware that setting the display format of a number doesn't change the underlying value, and sometimes the underlying values don't quite match what's shown in a report. For example, suppose you create a report that generates customer invoices and the invoices include a 15% buyer's premium on each item.

# Having some fun with functions

The function I mention here probably won't be very useful on most of your reports, but it can provide a few moments of fun. You might find it especially handy for reports you print on April Fool's Day.

You can use the StrReverse function to reverse all the characters in a string so that *Underdahl* becomes *lhadrednU*. If you play this trick correctly and can keep a straight face, you might even be able to get the day off by claiming that you have to go and get some recharge fluid for your printer's "character order generator." After all, without a refill, everything comes out backwards.

Here's the expression to reverse the characters in the Description field:

```
=StrReverse([Description])
```

To pull off this trick successfully, you may also want to use the function on all the titles in the report, too.

It's entirely possible that the order total shown on the report won't exactly match the individual Item amounts shown on the report because numbers have been rounded. For example, if the bid is $125.75, a 15% buyer's premium is exactly $18.8625, but appears as $18.86 on the invoice. If you have three items like that, the total on the invoice won't precisely match the totals of the individual items as shown on the invoice. To fix this problem, use the Round function. This function rounds the values displayed on the report according to your specifications (to the nearest integer, to two decimal places, and so on). The following expression rounds the values to two decimal places for the WinningBid field after the buyer's premium is added:

```
=Round(([WinningBid]*1.15),2)
```

✔ The Fix and Int functions convert values to the nearest integer and can be useful in some instances. As noted in Table 13-2, these two functions differ in the way they treat negative numbers.

✔ The Abs function doesn't round numbers, but it strips off any negative signs, making all numbers into positive values.

# Chapter 14

# When Reports Go Wrong . . .

*A* report that has problems can be a real nightmare. You depend on reports to be accurate, but if something does go wrong with the report, you're lucky if it's only a small inconvenience. If you find an error, remember that things could always be worse — you could have sent out printed copies of a really messed up and incorrect report without knowing it!

A few miscues such as poor layout, bad formatting choices, and even too many labels can mess up your carefully created report designs if you aren't careful. It's important to take an objective look at your reports before you inflict them on anyone else so that you don't mislead readers or look like you haven't a clue.

This chapter focuses on helping you find and correct various types of report problems. These issues can range all the way from missing data to poor, confusing, or paper-wasting layouts. Even if you aren't having any report problems right now, read this chapter so that you can avoid problems in the future.

## Troubleshooting Reports

Troubleshooting is a process that requires a different type of thinking than you use when you're creating reports. When you're involved in the creative process, you're thinking about what you can do to make the report useful and attractive. But when you're troubleshooting, you're probably at least a little frustrated because things don't seem to be working quite the way you expect.

## Figuring out whether the report is really wrong

Keep one fact in mind when a report doesn't give you quite the results that you expected — perhaps there's nothing at all wrong with your report. Maybe you're expecting results that simply aren't supported by the data. For example, I'd love to have a report tell me that my business made a couple of million dollars in profits last month, but the report would have to be based on totally bogus data to show those kinds of results!

Before you set off to find out what's wrong with your report, step back and consider whether the report is correct but your assumptions aren't. One way to do this is to open the underlying table in Datasheet view and see what you find there. Alternatively, you might open a query (if your report is based on a query) and switch the query to Datasheet view. After you've verified the accuracy of the data, you're in a better position to determine whether you really need to do some report troubleshooting.

## Figuring out what's wrong with the report

If you've determined that nothing is wrong with the data but your report isn't producing the results that you expect, it's time to figure out what is actually wrong with the report. You can break down the problem into one of two areas — report layout errors or missing data.

### Correcting layout problems

Any number of layout problems can afflict your reports. You can end up with a report that is hard to understand, misleading, or even incomplete. Here are just a few of these types of layout problems:

- ✔ **Using the field names for labels:** This is fine if you've created field names that are a single, real word that accurately describes the contents of the field (something like Name is a fine label). But using labels like LowEst, CustName, or OrdDt probably isn't a very good idea — especially if you plan on showing the report to someone else (like your banker).

- ✔ **Using unlabeled fields:** This practice is a good way to save paper, but unless it's obvious which data is being displayed in each of the fields, expect that people reading the report will make errors and incorrect assumptions.

✔ **Not lining up field boxes with the correct labels:** If you've gotten creative in rearranging the report's layout, make sure that related field boxes and labels line up properly. Otherwise it's easy to associate the wrong label with a field. And don't forget that subtotals and totals should almost certainly be aligned with the data that they're summarizing in the detail section.

If you have many summary fields, you can always number them so that readers can tell at a glance what material is being summarized, and where the summary falls in the sequence.

✔ **Making field boxes that are too narrow to fully display the data:** You can mislead readers if data doesn't fit completely in the boxes meant to contain it. For example, if you have a text box that's only wide enough to show values under 100, readers won't know when there are values above 100 in the report.

✔ **Putting fields too close to the edge of the paper:** Most printers cannot print to the edge of a sheet of paper, so fields that are too close to the edge can be truncated. Access warns you if you try to print and some fields are too close to the edge, but most computer users are pretty good about ignoring warnings!

See the section, "Avoiding Bad Report Layouts," later in this chapter for some help resolving report layout problems.

### Correcting missing data problems

If you have a report that appears to be correct but simply isn't showing certain data when you run the report, there are a number of possible causes. If you've already checked the obvious one — that the data doesn't really exist, you might want to check the properties for the field, as shown in Figure 14-1. (You can display the Property Sheet by right-clicking the field and choosing Properties from the pop-up menu or by selecting the field and clicking the Property Sheet option in the Design section of the ribbon.)

What you want to see is that the field is visible.

Make certain that the `Visible` property is set to Yes. This setting can be a little confusing because even if the `Visible` property is set to No, the field still appears in Design View. It's only when you switch to Report View that the field disappears if the property is set to No.

The label for a field and the field itself both have a `Visible` property. As a result, the field label can appear when you run the report, but the data can be hidden.

| Property Sheet | | ✕ |
|---|---|---|
| Selection type: Text Box | | |

LowEst Grand Total Sum ⌄

**Format** | Data | Event | Other | All

| Format | Currency |
|---|---|
| Decimal Places | 0 |
| Visible | Yes |
| Display When | Yes |
| Scroll Bars | No |
| Hide Duplicates | No |
| Can Grow | No |
| Can Shrink | No |
| Left | 3.5417" |
| Top | 0" |
| Width | 1.25" |
| Height | 0.2083" |
| Back Style | Transparent |
| Back Color | #FFFFFF |
| Special Effect | Flat |
| Border Style | Transparent |
| Border Color | #000000 |
| Border Width | Hairline |
| Fore Color | #000000 |
| Font Name | Times New Roman |
| Font Size | 10 |
| Font Weight | Bold |
| Font Italic | No |
| Font Underline | No |
| Text Align | General |
| Reading Order | Context |
| Scroll Bar Align | System |
| Numeral Shapes | System |
| Left Margin | 0" |
| Top Margin | 0" |
| Right Margin | 0" |
| Bottom Margin | 0" |
| Line Spacing | 0" |
| Is Hyperlink | No |

**Figure 14-1:**
Check the
`Visible`
property for
the field.

# Avoiding Bad Report Layouts

Throughout this book, I mention the various report layout issues that you need to be aware of. In the following sections, you get a quick look at a few points that you might have missed along the way.

## Considering the purpose of your report

Sure, it's pretty obvious that the primary purpose of any report is to present some data. After all, why even bother going to all the work to create and print a report if the report doesn't say anything?

What I'm talking about here is something beyond simply presenting some data in a report. That is, I'm suggesting that you consider both the ultimate goal of producing your report *and* the target audience.

Here are some examples of what I mean:

 ✔ **Going overboard with formatting and style is a bad idea.** If you're creating a report that will serve a very formal function, don't create a report that uses a different page layout from the rest of your proposal.

Perhaps the report is just a single component of a business plan that you are presenting to your banker or other potential backers. If you have a cover letter that's printed in standard portrait mode, format your Access report so that it fits into portrait mode, too (Orientation on the Page Layout section of the ribbon).

✔ **Orienting the page layout to landscape can make all the difference.** A report that you create for a business brainstorming session might need to include more information than many other types of reports, so using the landscape printing option could be your best choice. This layout also enables better note taking (or doodling) during the meeting.

✔ **Cutting to the chase is usually a good idea.** Remember that people are often busy, so you might want to create a summary report that skips most of the fine details. This is especially true if you're dealing with the type of executive who just wants to know the bottom line without being bothered with the trivia.

The real point here is simply that a report layout that is perfect in one case could be a bad choice in another. Consider your audience when designing your reports.

## Avoiding text box data overflow

As I mention earlier in this chapter, creating an otherwise perfectly good-looking report that contains deceptive field boxes can be a disaster. Figure 14-2 shows an example of a report that contains two text boxes that are both bound to the same database field. You've got two very different views of the same record.

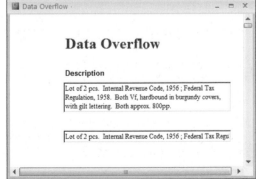

**Figure 14-2:**
Both text boxes are bound to the Description field.

In this example, the upper text box can display the entire contents of the field, but the lower text box can't. Figure 14-3 shows why the lower text box cannot show the entire value.

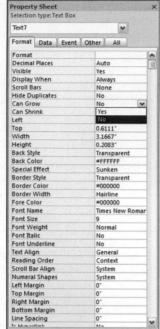

Figure 14-3:
The Can
Grow
property
controls
vertical
expansion
for a report
field.

If the Can Grow property is set to the default of Yes, the text box (or any report control or section) automatically expands vertically if necessary to display the entire contents of the field.

There is no property that allows a control to grow or shrink horizontally. As a result, fields with numeric values can be truncated even if the Can Grow property for the field is set to Yes.

The related Can Shrink property allows the text box to contract vertically.

## Avoiding page overflow

You can have problems with data overflowing the edges of the report if your design is too wide to fit the paper. As Figure 14-4 shows, getting too close to the edge is easy to do if you try to fit too many fields into a tabular report design — even if you switch to landscape layout. In many cases, this can also result in blank pages when you print.

If you use the Report Wizard, be sure that the Adjust the Field Width So All Fields Fit On A Page check box is selected to reduce the chances of your report design being too wide.

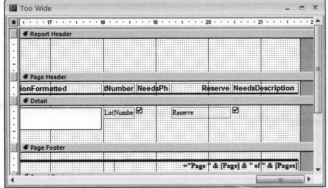

**Figure 14-4:**
This report
design is too
wide to print
properly.

One way to avoid making your report design too wide to fit the paper is to stack fields vertically. Unfortunately, this solution can create more problems if you're not very careful with the layout. Here are some considerations:

✔ If you have fields that might need to expand vertically to fit the data, place those fields so that no other fields are directly below them in the design.

✔ If you allow several fields to grow vertically, be sure to place them across the page so that they won't interfere with each other.

## Formatting data in reports

Your Access databases can contain a number of different types of data, of course. In most cases, this diversity causes no problems, but because a few of the data types have alternative formatting options, it's possible to cause real confusion by choosing inappropriate formatting.

Here's the rundown on the properties to keep an eye on:

✔ **Format property:** The Format property's most confusing data types are Number, Date/Time, and Currency. If you choose the wrong format for a text box that displays one of these data types on a report, you could confuse or even mislead anyone who reads the report.

Figure 14-5 shows the formatting options that are available in the Property Sheet drop-down list on the Format tab.

✔ **Decimal Places property:** This property controls the number of digits that are shown to the right of the decimal point. An inappropriate choice can be awfully confusing.

Although you can specify up to 15 decimal places, if your values are set to the Currency data type, your numbers are only accurate to 4 decimal places. Displaying more than 4 digits to the right of the decimal point for Currency values could imply that values are being calculated to a higher degree of accuracy than is actually the case.

**Figure 14-5:** Choosing the wrong number format can cause real confusion.

# *Eliminating Unnecessary Labels for Tighter Reports*

Labels are report elements that you can love and hate at the same time. Sure, labels do help people to understand what they're seeing in a report, but labels can also eat up an awful lot of space, making reports use far more paper than is really necessary.

By default, Access labels all the fields you add to a report. The field names are used as the labels, but you can easily change the text to suit your needs. If you use a Report Wizard to create a report that uses grouping, the wizard places the labels in the group header directly above the position of the field box in the detail section.

# Deciding whether you really need all those labels

Labels aren't always necessary, and in some cases they're downright undesirable. On the left side of Figure 14-6, you can see the default, labeled layout created by the Report Wizard; a much more compact, unlabeled layout appears on the right side. As long as the data is readily understandable, most readers won't have any difficulty with the unlabeled data.

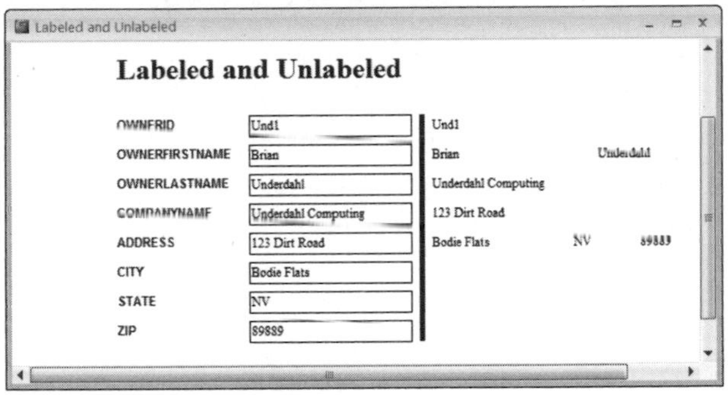

**Figure 14-6:** This report shows that labels aren't always necessary.

# Deleting labels

You may be surprised to discover that Access doesn't have a property that controls whether a field is labeled on a report. This means that deleting labels can be just a bit tricky. Because the field's label and the field's text box display the same text in Design View (unless you've modified the label, of course), you need to make sure you delete the right thing.

To delete a label (and leave the text box), follow these steps:

1. **Right-click within the label (which is to the left of the text box).**

2. **Choose Delete or press the Delete key.**

## *Moving labels to headers*

In some cases, you can save some space on a report by moving the labels to one of the headers. The page headers and any group headers are certainly good candidates for placing the labels in many types of reports. Both locations offer certain advantages. Determine which location works best by experimenting with the possibilities.

Your decision should be based on the functions of your report and the needs of your audience.

If you're used to rearranging your report designs by using drag-and-drop methods, you'll quickly discover that you're out of luck when you try this method to move labels from the detail section to one of the headers. That's because Access automatically moves the entire field — the label and the text box — as a unit when you use drag and drop.

To move a field to the header without taking the text box with it, you need to use the cut-and-paste method.

# Part V
# Way Cool Advanced Queries, Forms, and Reports

The 5th Wave                    By Rich Tennant

"Yes, I know how to query information from the program, but what if I just want to leak it instead?"

## In this part . . .

This part takes your Access skills and bumps them up to a whole new level by showing you advanced techniques for queries, forms, and reports. Here you discover some really cool tricks that take Access well beyond the ordinary. In addition, this part shows you a number of Access add-ons that can solve many of the problems you may encounter while putting Access through its paces.

# Chapter 15

# Tricks for Finding Data with Queries

*Q*ueries can seem like magical things in the ways that they enable you to quickly find data that's hidden somewhere in a database. The old saying about finding a needle in a haystack really does describe the kind of power that you can wield if you know the right query tricks. For example, by moving beyond ordinary query techniques, you can find records that fall within a range of values, locate records that are similar, and create queries that politely ask you what you want to find instead of always returning the same set of records. You can even create queries that toss out the junk so you can focus on the truly meaningful results.

A few new tricks can help turn ordinary queries into powerhouses that do far more than you might expect. Bumping your queries up to the next level makes you far more efficient, enabling you to return a range of records, ask what you want, and finally pare down the results so you're not swamped with useless information.

This chapter shows you how to use these advanced techniques to create queries that can find those lost needles in your haystack of data. You are sure to find that these tricks end up saving you a whole lot of time and frustration in the future.

## Finding Just the Data You Need

Plain-vanilla, everyday queries are fine when your needs aren't very complex and you just want to find a simple set of records. But sometimes, your needs are more complex, and a simple query simply isn't going to do it. In the following sections, you see how to

- ✔ Create more complex queries that return a range of records instead of simply delivering a set of records that match a specific criterion.
- ✔ Tell Access that you want to find records based on some inexact criteria.

## Getting to know the operators

You can use a number of *operators* in expressions. Unfortunately, Access doesn't exactly make it easy for you to find the operators that you can use (or to understand how they work).

Table 15-1 explains several of the operators that you may find useful in your queries.

| Table 15-1: | Some Useful Operators for Queries |
|---|---|
| *Operator* | *Description* |
| − | Subtracts one value from another or makes a value negative. |
| & | Concatenates two strings. |
| * | Multiplies two numbers. |
| / | Divides one number by a second number. |
| \ | Produces an integer by rounding both numbers to integers and then dividing the first number by the second number, and dropping any fraction. |
| ^ | Raises a number to a power. |
| + | Adds two values. |
| < | Indicates less than. |
| <= | Indicates less than or equal to. |
| <> | Indicates not equal. |
| = | Indicates equal to. |
| > | Indicates greater than. |
| >= | Indicates greater than or equal to. |

| Operator | Description |
|---|---|
| AND | Returns True when both expressions are true. |
| Between | Determines whether a numeric or date value falls within a range. |
| Eqv | Returns True when both expressions are true or both expressions are false. |
| In(string1, string2...) | Determines whether a string value is one of a set of string values. |
| Is Null | Returns True if a value is Null. |
| Like "pattern" | Matches string values by using the wildcards ? and *. |
| Mod | Divides the first number by the second number and returns the remainder. |
| Not | Returns True when the expression is not true. |
| OR | Returns True when either expression is true. |
| Xor | Returns True when either expression is true and the other expression is false. |

You probably won't use all the operators shown in Table 15-1, but they certainly do give you many options. You can see a number of these operators in action in the examples that follow in this chapter.

## Selecting a range of records

You already know how to create a query that finds records that are an exact match for a specific value. But what if you want to find a range of records, such as all the orders you received between July 1 and the end of December? You can use several different methods for finding these records, but most of them are simply too much work. You may also run the risk of accidentally missing some of them if you try to locate them manually. Besides, why not let your PC do the work? That's what it's there for.

To find a range of records, you use an *expression*. You place this expression in the Criteria text box in the Query Design window. That is, your expression takes the place of the single value that you ordinarily place in the Criteria text box.

### Selecting a range of records with greater than and less than operators

As you might guess, there often is more than one way to create an expression to select a range of records. Figure 15-1 shows two different methods for specifying a range of values in expressions.

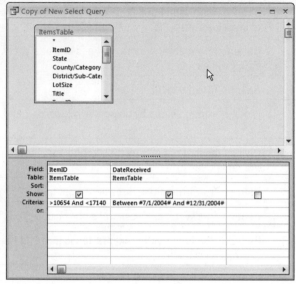

**Figure 15-1:**
This query
uses two
different
methods to
specify a
range of
values.

In Figure 15-1, the expression for the selection criteria for the ItemID field uses the greater than (>), AND, and less than (<) operators:

```
>10654 And <17140
```

In English, this expression means "the value must be greater than 10654 and less than 17140."

### Selecting a range of records with Between operators

The expression for the DateReceived field selection criteria uses the Between and the AND operators:

```
Between #7/1/2004# And #12/31/2004#
```

This second expression is easy to understand, but you need to be clear about a couple of items:

✔ **Date values must be enclosed in pound signs (#).** Otherwise, Access won't think you're entering a mathematical expression.

✔ **The `Between` operator works like the greater than or equal to (>=) and less than or equal to (<=) operators.** That is, the values that you specify with the `Between` operator are included in the range of values that are selected when you run the query.

Figure 15-2 shows the results of running the query shown in Figure 15-1.

| Item ▾ | DateReceived ▾ |
|--------|----------------|
| 15864 | 8/11/2004 |
| 15741 | 7/30/2004 |
| 14230 | 7/6/2004 |
| 15771 | 8/2/2004 |
| 14912 | 7/19/2004 |
| 15057 | 7/20/2004 |
| 15191 | 7/21/2004 |
| 15522 | 7/27/2004 |
| 15523 | 7/27/2004 |
| 15701 | 7/28/2004 |
| 14811 | 7/16/2004 |
| 14839 | 7/16/2004 |
| 15389 | 7/26/2004 |
| 16678 | 9/23/2004 |
| 16172 | 9/9/2004 |
| 16808 | 9/27/2004 |
| * (New) | 9/11/2006 |

Copy of New Select Query

Record: ⋈ ◂ 1 of 16 ▸ ⋈ ⋈ — No Filter — Search

**Figure 15-2:** Running the query selects a range of records that match both criteria.

In the figure, all the 16 selected records satisfy both the sets of criteria (the final row that shows `AutoNumber` in the `ItemID` field is not a record in the table — it is a placeholder for a new record with the default value of the current date). Should Datasheet view come back with only one result, the current date, both sets of criteria are not being met; it's not you!

## Switching between the AND operator and the OR operator

In the previous example, both sets of criteria have to be met in order for a record to be selected. That's the nature of the `AND` operator; both criteria expressions are on the same row of the design grid, so the two expressions are combined by using the `AND` operator.

The equivalent SQL statement shows how the two are combined:

```
SELECT ItemsTable.ItemID, ItemsTable.DateReceived
FROM ItemsTable
WHERE
    (((ItemsTable.ItemID)>10654
    And (ItemsTable.ItemID)<17140)
AND
    ((ItemsTable.DateReceived)
    Between #7/1/2004#
    And #12/31/2004#));
```

If you move the second expression down a row, as shown in Figure 15-3, you change the query to an OR query, where records that meet either criteria are selected.

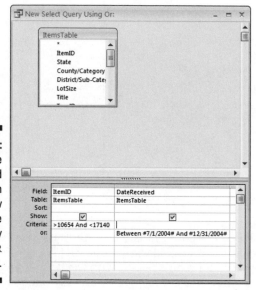

**Figure 15-3:** Moving the second expression down a row turns the AND query into an OR query.

This seemingly small change makes a big difference in the final results. As Figure 15-4 shows, the record counter now indicates that, instead of 16 matching records, 23 records now meet one or the other of the two criteria.

Here's what the modified query looks like. I've made only one small change — the AND in Line 6 is changed to OR:

```
SELECT ItemsTable.ItemID, ItemsTable.DateReceived
FROM ItemsTable
WHERE
    (((ItemsTable.ItemID)>10654
    And (ItemsTable.ItemID)<17140)
OR
    ((ItemsTable.DateReceived)
    Between #7/1/2004#
    And #12/31/2004#));
```

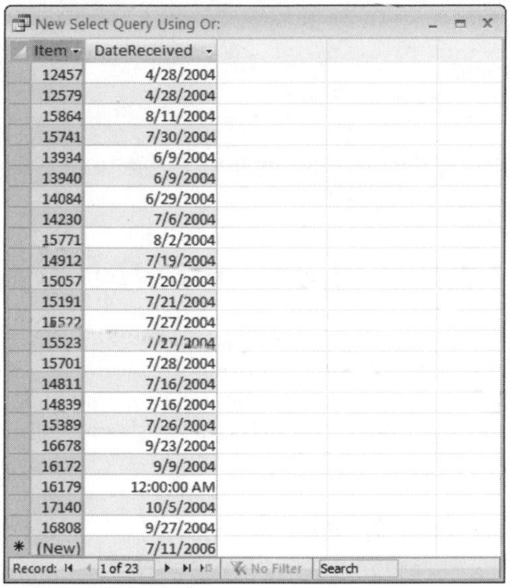

| Item | DateReceived |
|---|---|
| 12457 | 4/28/2004 |
| 12579 | 4/28/2004 |
| 15864 | 8/11/2004 |
| 15741 | 7/30/2004 |
| 13934 | 6/9/2004 |
| 13940 | 6/9/2004 |
| 14084 | 6/29/2004 |
| 14230 | 7/6/2004 |
| 15771 | 8/2/2004 |
| 14912 | 7/19/2004 |
| 15057 | 7/20/2004 |
| 15191 | 7/21/2004 |
| 15522 | 7/27/2004 |
| 15523 | 7/27/2004 |
| 15701 | 7/28/2004 |
| 14811 | 7/16/2004 |
| 14839 | 7/16/2004 |
| 15389 | 7/26/2004 |
| 16678 | 9/23/2004 |
| 16172 | 9/9/2004 |
| 16179 | 12:00:00 AM |
| 17140 | 10/5/2004 |
| 16808 | 9/27/2004 |
| (New) | 7/11/2006 |

New Select Query Using Or:

Record: 1 of 23  No Filter  Search

**Figure 15-4:**
Running the
OR query
results in
many more
matching
records.

You can continue to add additional sets of criteria as needed. For example, you can add another OR clause that also includes one or more AND clauses.

### Selecting the top set of records

Say you want to see a list of the top 25 orders for the year. The following SQL query statements can do the trick:

```
SELECT TOP 25
  Customer, OrderNumber, OrderDate
FROM OrdersTable
WHERE OrderYear = 2005
ORDER BY OrderAmount DESC;
```

This example uses a few SQL keywords you may not be familiar with. TOP tells Access that you want to see the top matching records, and 25 is a parameter that says how many of the top records to display. ORDER BY tells Access to sort the results, and DESC says to use descending order (you can use ASC to sort in ascending order).

You can add another SQL keyword, PERCENT, to tell Access that you want to see a *percentage* of the records instead of a *specific number* of them. The following modification to the query returns the top 10 percent of the orders:

```
SELECT TOP 10 PERCENT
  Customer, OrderNumber, OrderDate
FROM OrdersTable
WHERE OrderYear = 2005
ORDER BY OrderAmount DESC;
```

To find the bottom set of records, change the sort order to ascending.

# Finding data that's close but not exact

Maybe you've heard the old saying that goes something like, "Close only counts in horseshoes and hand grenades." Whoever made that one up didn't know much about finding information in databases, because I can think of many occasions when you might need to find data that's close, but not necessarily right on target.

### Understanding why close may be what you need

This may come as a bit of a shock, but many people are poor spellers, bad typists, or both. The end result can be errors in your databases; as a result, your queries that depend on exact matches may fail to find all the records that you want.

For example, suppose you have a customer named Dee Anderson, and she's asked for a listing of all her orders for an insurance estimate. You may know that her orders were entered by several people over the years, and you may not be sure that everyone always spelled her name the same way. What if some of the orders were listed under Dee Andersen, De Anderson, or even D Andersen? That's why you need to be able to find close matches — so that you can be sure to find all the possible variations.

### Using the Like operator with wildcards

To find close matches that aren't necessarily an exact match, you can use the Like operator along with the asterisk (*) and question mark (?) wildcards.

To find the variations on Dee Anderson, use the following criteria expression:

```
Like "D* Anders?n"
```

In this example both the asterisk and question mark wildcards help you create an inexact match. Here's how each of the two wildcards function:

- ✔ The asterisk matches any number of characters.

  All these names would be caught by the asterisk: Dee, Deborah, Deeana, Derek. It doesn't matter how many letters are in the name.

- ✔ The question mark matches exactly one character.

  In this instance, it catches any record that has the last name Anderson, Andersen.

- ✔ Together, the two wildcards work like the AND operator.

  All the Deborahs, Deeanas, and Dereks are eliminated from the search if their last names aren't Andersen or Anderson.

Now, suppose you wanted to find every customer whose name included the word *auction* somewhere in the company name. The following criteria expression would do the trick:

```
Like "*auction*"
```

Access isn't *case sensitive*. When you run a query by using inexact matching, `Like "*auction*"` produces the same results as `Like "*Auction*"`.

### Using other operators for inexact matches

You can use other operators to create inexact matches, too. For example, suppose you want to find all orders from customers whose company name doesn't include the word *auction*. The following expression does the trick:

```
Not "*auction*"
```

You could also find all customers whose last name starts with the letter U or any letter coming after it in the alphabet using the following expression:

```
>="U"
```

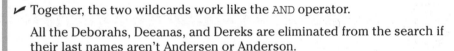

In this example you don't need to use a wildcard, because the expression already says *find all records that are greater than or equal to U,* automatically including any records where additional characters follow the beginning U.

# Creating Queries That Ask What to Find

Creating a great query that finds the set of records you want isn't too difficult after you get the hang of it, but most queries suffer from one problem — they're set up to always return a set of records that matches predefined criteria.

After you create a query, that same set of criteria is used every time you run the query until you open the query in Design View and edit the criteria. That's probably not a very good option for queries that you're setting up for use by the average Access user.

To get more flexibility in your searches, try parameter queries.

## Understanding parameter queries

As an alternative to using a query that uses specific, set criteria to select a group of records, you can create a *parameter* query. As Figure 15-5 shows, when a user runs a parameter query, Access displays the Enter Parameter Value dialog box and prompts the user to specify the criteria to use in the query.

**Figure 15-5:**
A parameter query asks which records you want to find.

You aren't limited to asking the user to enter the criteria for a single field in a parameter query. You can request as many parameters as necessary.

Parameter queries enable you to make a query flexible, but this flexibility comes at a price. Parameter queries only accept exact, matching values, so they return empty results unless you enter a value that completely matches the value in the field for one or more records. You can't use wildcards or expressions in the Enter Parameter Value dialog box. Access won't display an error message if you do use wildcards or expressions — it simply won't return any records.

## Building your very own parameter query

You can turn an ordinary query into a parameter query pretty easily. You may even have done so inadvertently in the past when you were experimenting with queries and wondered why that darn Enter Parameter Value dialog box popped up when you tried to run the query.

To make a query into a parameter query, enter the prompt that you want to display (enclosed in square brackets) in the Enter Parameter Value dialog box in the Criteria text box of the query design.

Figure 15-6 shows an example of the query design that displays the prompt shown in Figure 15-5.

**Figure 15-6:**
Enter the prompt in square brackets in the Criteria text box to create a parameter query.

You may want to display the prompts in a different order. To do so, you use the Query Parameters dialog box (Design section of the ribbon), as shown in Figure 15-7.

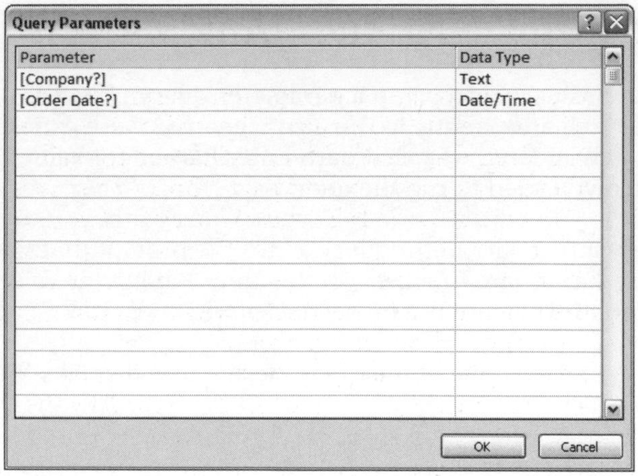

| Query Parameters | | ? ✕ |
|---|---|---|
| Parameter | Data Type | |
| [Company?] | Text | |
| [Order Date?] | Date/Time | |
| | | |
| | | |
| | | |
| | | |
| | | |
| | | |
| | | |
| | | |
| | | |
| | | |
| | OK Cancel | |

**Figure 15-7:**
The Query Parameters dialog box enables you to specify the order for the prompts.

To use the Query Parameters dialog box to specify the order for the prompts, follow these steps:

1. **First create the prompts in the dialog box.**

2. **Enter the prompts in the Parameter column exactly as you want them to appear.**

   Enter the prompts in the order that you want them to display when the query is executed.

3. **Choose the appropriate Data Type for each of the prompts.**

   This must match the data type that is used in the table.

4. **Click OK.**

   The Query Parameters dialog box closes, and you're returned to the Query design.

Chapter 17 shows another technique that might be even more useful in some cases than parameter queries. *Lookup lists* enable users to select a value from a list, thus eliminating the possibility of typing errors.

# Excluding Data You Don't Want

You've probably struggled with query results that were too inclusive. Sometimes having too many results is almost worse than not getting as many results as you might like. After all, when you're looking for a specific record, you don't want to have to wade through a couple of hundred of them that were returned by an overexuberant query.

## Eliminating duplicates from results

Most Access databases use *indexes* to prevent tables from being loaded with duplicate records. As a result, queries that include all the fields from a table typically don't return results that are complete duplicates across every field. The problem arises when you create a query that uses only some of the fields — in particular, in the type of query that you're most likely to create.

You might decide to eliminate duplicate results when you run a query for any number of reasons. Here are just a few examples:

- ✔ If you're trying to figure out where it would be most effective to advertise, you might want your query to display a list of cities where you have customers. You probably are likely to find this type of list most useful if San Francisco is listed once rather than 392 times.

- ✔ If you want to know which customers have placed orders in the past six months, a list with one result for each active customer is probably what you want.

- ✔ If you're sitting down with a consultant to brainstorm about what to include in your upcoming TV advertisement, you may want to give the consultant a list showing each type of item that's currently available for sale. Here, too, you'd want one result for each type, not one for every item.

- ✔ Finally, if your club is going to hold an election soon and you need a list of potential candidates, you might want to create a list that shows the names of members who have attended at least one meeting in the past year. You don't want to sift through multiple listings for your most active members.

## Finding duplicates with SQL queries

The easiest and most straightforward way to find the records you want without including all the duplicates is to use a SQL query.

You can use two SQL keywords to eliminate duplicates from the results:

- ✔ **DISTINCT:** Use this keyword to examine the fields that you've included in the query to determine whether the records are duplicates. Generally, you should use DISTINCT to return the smallest set of records.

The following example uses DISTINCT to return a list of cities where you have customers:

```
SELECT DISTINCT
City
FROM Customers
ORDER BY City;
```

✔ **DISTINCTROW:** Use this keyword when you want to examine all the fields, not just those included in the query, to determine if records are duplicates. Use DISTINCTROW when your query uses multiple tables.

Here's an example that lists the active members in your club, using DISTINCTROW to look at two tables, Members and Events:

```
SELECT DISTINCTROW MemberName
FROM Members INNER JOIN Events
ON Members.MemberID = Events.MemberID
ORDER BY MemberName;
```

TIP

If your database doesn't use an index and you find that it's a real mess due to duplicate records, you might want to use DISTINCTROW to find one instance of each of the duplicates and then use a make-table query to create a new table by using the unique records. Be sure to apply an index to the new table to prevent it from becoming loaded with duplicates.

## Modifying join properties to get the results you want

Sometimes you may need to modify the type of join that's used in a query in order to get the results you want. If you skipped over some of the earlier chapters, you might not realize why the type of join is so important to eliminating the records you don't want from the query results. See Chapter 8 for more on joins.

You can use any of the three types of joins in an Access query:

✔ *Inner joins* include all matching records from both of the joined tables. This is the default join.

✔ *Left outer joins* include all the records from the left-side table even if no matching records appear in the right-side table.

✔ *Right outer joins* include all the records from the right-side table even if no matching records appear in the left-side table.

Using the wrong type of join can lead to results that you don't want. You need to choose a join type that actually makes sense. If necessary, sit down and consider what results you want and see whether the join type that you specify returns those results. Access is perfectly happy to give you meaningless results if that's what you ask for.

Although you can use the Join Properties dialog box to change the relationships between tables, the most straightforward way to change the join type that is used in a query is to edit the SQL statements in SQL view:

1. **Open your query in Design View.**

2. **Switch to SQL View.**

   Either choose View⇨SQL View (Design section of the ribbon) or right-click the query and choose SQL View from the pop-up menu.

3. **Replace the join type that is specified in the SQL statements with the join type you want to use.**

For example, the following shows the members and events example (see "Finding duplicates with SQL queries," earlier in this chapter) changed from an inner join to a left outer join:

```
SELECT DISTINCTROW MemberName
FROM Members LEFT OUTER JOIN Events
ON Members.MemberID = Events.MemberID
ORDER BY MemberName;
```

# Chapter 16

# Tricks for Updating with Queries

*Q*ueries can do far more than simply find records that match specific criteria. You can also use queries to update data, add new fields, and fix certain problems in existing databases. You can even use a query to modify the data in a table, using information from another table. This chapter shows you the tricks and techniques you need to know to do all these tasks quickly and easily.

The queries I discuss in this chapter, action queries, make changes directly to your database. These changes can be to your data, to the structure of your tables, or both. Be very careful so that you don't put an important database at risk while you're trying out the tricks you discover in this chapter. In fact, why not back up your database right now.

## Creating New Fields with a Query

If you've worked with Access for any length of time, you've no doubt encountered many instances when you discovered that a particular table would be far more useful if only it had another field or two. Maybe you forgot to include a field to indicate whether a club member was active, or maybe you discovered that your Items table really needed a field to indicate products that are considered hazardous materials. Whatever the case may be, you can use queries to add these fields.

# Deciding whether using a query to add fields is worth it

If you've decided that a table needs a new field, the natural reaction is to simply open the table in Design View and add the field. That's easy enough to do, of course, but sometimes getting a bit creative and using a query instead is worth the effort.

For example, consider the following reasons why you might want to add the field by using a query instead of adding it in Design View:

- ✔ When you add a new field to an existing table in Design View, that field is empty for all the existing records. By using a query you can add default values to the field as you add it to the table.

- ✔ If the values in the new field result from a calculation that is performed when a user opens the record in a form, you can save time and effort. Instead of opening every existing record after you've added the new field in order to update the field values, write your query to perform the calculations and load the proper values into the existing records automatically.

- ✔ If the values for the new field already exist in another table, you can use a query to extract the values from the other table and add them to the proper records in the existing table.

If none of these conditions apply in your case, you'll obviously spend far less time if you choose to add the new field in Design View. You're also far less likely to make an error adding the field in Design View simply because of the various prompts that Access provides when you're modifying a table in Design View. Sometimes the simplest way of doing something really is the best way!

# Adding your first field with a query

To add fields to an existing table by using a query, you turn to SQL-specific queries.

If you need a bit of SQL review, take a look at Chapter 7 before continuing.

### Statements

Access SQL provides two different *Data Definition Language* statements that you can use to add fields to a table.

### CREATE TABLE

The CREATE TABLE statement creates a whole new table, and you use it for a make-table query.

Don't use the CREATE TABLE statement if the target table already exists. If you do, you'll destroy the existing table and any data that it contains — clearly not a move designed to make your day!

### ALTER TABLE

To add a field to an existing table, you use the ALTER TABLE statement, as shown in the following example:

```
ALTER TABLE ItemsTable
ADD COLUMN NewDesc TEXT(50) NOT NULL;
```

This SQL query tells Access to alter the table named ItemsTable by adding a field (column) named NewDesc. The new field will be a text field 50 characters long, and users must make an entry in the field when they add any new records.

You can only add one field at a time with the ALTER TABLE statement. You'll need additional queries if you want to add additional fields — this might be an excellent reason to consider mastering a bit of VBA programming (see Chapter 7) so that you can combine several ALTER TABLE and UPDATE queries into a single procedure.

See the section, "Adding Default Values by Using a Query," later in this chapter, to see how to add default values to the new field without overwriting any existing data.

Don't attempt to run the ALTER TABLE query more than once unless you remove the new field from the table's design between runs because you'll encounter errors if you try to run the query again. The reason for this odd Access activity is that you cannot apply the NOT NULL statement more than once to the same field.

## Other options

In addition to statements, you have several other options to add fields to tables.

### Make the new field a key field

You can also use the CONSTRAINT statement to make the new field into a key field so that the new field can be used in table relationships. Adding a constraint can be a little tricky because a table can have only one primary key — although it can have any number of secondary keys. A primary key does not, however, have to be a single field. You can create primary keys that combine the values in several fields.

### Build an index

Instead of adding a constraint, you may want to add an index for the new field you've added to the table. Adding an index can make table lookups faster because Access doesn't have to search all the records to find a value in an indexed field.

You use the `CREATE INDEX` statement to add an index. Here's an example of how to add an index that is sorted in ascending order for the new `NewDesc` field:

```
CREATE INDEX Index1
ON ItemsTable (NewDesc) ASC;
```

You can also create a unique index by adding the `UNIQUE` keyword between `CREATE` and `INDEX`. However, this may not be a wise choice in many cases because a unique index requires that each record contain unique vales in the field. That's probably not what you'd want for a 50-character text field because you may have more than one item with the same description.

# Adding Default Values by Using a Query

As you build upon your `ALTER TABLE` queries, you may reach a point at which you want to add default values to the new fields. By adding default values you can be sure that any rules you've established — such as requiring that the field not contain blank entries — are enforced.

## Getting to know what you can add

You can't add just any old value to a field by using a query. You do have to follow the rules even if it is your own database. Before you create a query to add values to a table, consider the following factors that might affect what you can do:

- ✔ **The data must be the proper type for the field.** You can't, for example, add text to a Date/Time field.

- ✔ **If you've set any rules restricting the values that can be entered in a field, your query must also follow those same rules.** You can't add data that is outside the range of acceptable values.

- ✔ **If you've set a field as a primary key or as a unique index, your data must be different for each record.** Trying to set default values for these types of fields by using a query isn't a good idea, simply because generating unique values is going to be really hard.

## *Adding default values to your very first field*

If you use a query to add a new field to a table, the new field will be empty in all the existing records. So your next step is to add a default value to the field. To do so, you can use a simple update query (use the Create section of the Ribbon for the query, then Design for the Update option), as shown in Figure 16-1.

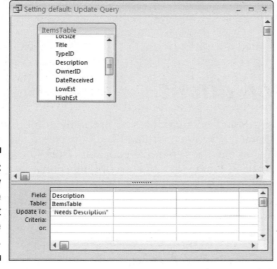

**Figure 16-1:**
This query sets the default value for the new field.

If you prefer to work in SQL view, the following SQL statements are the equivalent update query:

```
UPDATE ItemsTable
SET ItemsTable.Description = "Needs Description";
```

See Chapter 17 for tips on running queries by attaching them to buttons you add to forms. This can be an excellent way to ensure that both the ALTER TABLE and UPDATE queries are run consecutively.

## *Making sure you don't override real data*

Unfortunately, the query example shown in Figure 16-1 presents one little problem in the real world — you're overriding real data. You can remedy this situation by modifying the update query as shown here:

```
UPDATE ItemsTable
SET ItemsTable.Description = "Needs Description"
WHERE (((ItemsTable.Description) Is Null));
```

In this second version of the query, the Description field in the table ItemsTable is given a value of "Needs Description" only if the existing field is empty. You might be wondering why this query even bothers with the WHERE clause. You don't really need to use the WHERE clause if you run this second query immediately after the ALTER TABLE query, but suppose you get distracted for a few minutes between running the two queries and someone else begins entering values in the Description field. Oh, the horror! By including the WHERE clause you ensure that you don't destroy any existing values in the field.

# Performing Calculations

When you think of performing calculations, you probably don't think of Access queries first. In fact, if you're anything like many Office users I know, you likely start thinking about ways to move your data from Access into Excel to do calculations and don't even give a moment's consideration to doing them in a query.

## Determining whether to use a query for your calculations

So why should you buck the trend and use a query for calculations? Why not use your old tried-and-true method? Actually, I can offer several reasons why you might want to consider using a query:

- ✔ **Doing calculations by using a query is a lot less work than moving data to Excel and then doing the calculations.** Who needs extra work? Keeping your calculations in one application is so much faster.

- ✔ **Unless you're very careful, moving data between applications like Access and Excel increases the risk of errors.** This statement is especially true if you'll need to bring the calculated values back into Access.

- ✔ **If you're already comfortable with Excel, the expressions in Access are familiar.** In fact, the expressions you use for calculations in an Access query are almost identical to the formulas you create in Excel.

- ✔ **Finally, telling people that you're an Access expressions expert is just a whole lot cooler, isn't it?** Oh, the glory.

# *Writing your first query calculations*

You typically use calculations in queries to either modify existing values in a database or to supply new values where none currently exist. You can create calculations to serve many different purposes.

### *Adding days to date values*

Figure 16-2 shows an update query that uses an expression to add 90 days to the current date in the ServiceDate field if that last scheduled service date is earlier than the date when the query is run. This type of query can be very useful if you run a business and you need to schedule periodic service calls with your customers. You could then run a query daily to produce a list of customers you need to call to set up appointments.

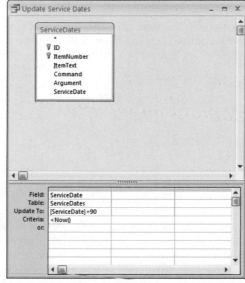

**Figure 16-2:**
This query updates values using a calculation.

 When you're working with dates in an expression, remember that integer values represent days and fractional (decimal) values are fractions of days — hours.

### *Modifying numeric values*

Another common way to use calculations is to modify a numeric value.

One example of this is to increase the prices of a certain class of products based on increased transportation costs. The following SQL query increases the price of all heavy widgets by 5 percent:

```
UPDATE Items
SET Items.Price = [Price]*1.05
WHERE ((Items.Class) = "HeavyWidgets");
```

Once again, this example uses criteria (the WHERE clause) to select the items to include in the calculation. Briefly switching to Datasheet view when you use criteria in a query is always a good idea. The switch helps you verify that your query will select the correct set of records.

### Summarizing Values

In some cases, you may want to create a calculation that returns a summary report of the values in your database. That is also quite easy to do.

The following example summarizes the values in the LowEst field of the ItemsTable table and shows both the total for each state and the maximum value for each state:

```
SELECT ItemsTable.State,
   Sum(ItemsTable.LowEst) AS [Sum of LowEst],
   Max(ItemsTable.LowEst) AS [Max of LowEst]
FROM ItemsTable
GROUP BY ItemsTable.State;
```

The following item:

```
Sum(ItemsTable.LowEst) AS [Sum of LowEst]
```

totals the values in the LowEst field and displays Sum of LowEst as the name at the top of the column. An AS clause always specifies how you want the information to be named in the output.

The last line in the statement

```
GROUP BY ItemsTable.State;
```

tells Access to group the results based on the values in the State field. The two summary values are summarized by state. If you don't include the GROUP BY clause in the query, the summaries include all the values in the table. You can see what this query looks like in Design View in Figure 16-3. You may need to click the Total option in the Design section of the Ribbon.

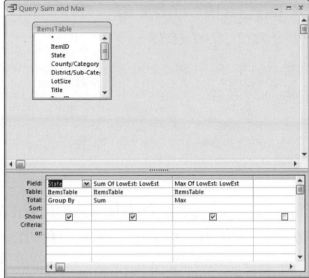

**Figure 16-3:** The summary query in Design View.

# Updating Records by Using Data from Another Table

Relational databases are efficient for many different reasons, and one of those reasons is that the data is typically split up over several related tables. Although this arrangement makes your Access database easier to maintain, it also makes sharing data with other applications, such as Excel, just a bit harder. So why not create a table that combines information from several tables if you intend to share that data?

Even if you don't need to share your Access data with other applications, you may well need to update records in one table with information from another table. Suppose, for example, that you sell a line of products that are manufactured by the Giant Kazoo Company, and the good people at Giant Kazoo just sent you a new Access database containing the latest legal disclaimer statements for each of the company's products. To avoid problems, you have to add those statements to the product descriptions in your database, but because you sell several hundred different Giant Kazoo products, updating everything manually is going to be awfully tedious. Well, this, too, is a perfect place to use a query that updates records in one table by using information that's contained in a different table.

## *Choosing the right type of query for your updates*

In order to update records in one table with data from another table, you need to use an update query. But this query must include both of the tables, and the tables must be properly joined.

If you aren't quite up to speed on using multiple tables in a query and making sure that they're properly joined, you may want to review Chapters 5 and 8 before you continue.

## *Updating data in one table with data from another without any conditions*

The simplest example of updating data in one table with data from another table occurs when you apply no conditions except that you want to update the correct records. Sure, this condition might seem obvious, but if you consider how the tables are joined, you realize that the join is the key to making sure that the correct records are updated.

To update records without any conditions, you create a query that adds the value from the `TypeName` field in the `TypeTable` table to the `Description` field in the `ItemsTable` table.

You might want to do something like this if you're creating a new table so that you can export the data for use in Excel or Word. Remember to link the two tables before you begin these steps.

To create the query, follow these steps:

1. **Click Query Design in the Create section of the Ribbon.**

   The Query editor and the Show Table dialog box appear.

2. **Add the `ItemsTable` and `TypeTable` tables to the Query design and then close the Show Table dialog box.**

   Make sure that the query design shows that the two tables are linked before you continue.

3. **Choose Update (Design section) to change the query from a select query into an update query.**

**4. In the first column of the Query Design grid, select ItemsTable.Description as the name of the field to update.**

This action places Description in the Field text box and ItemsTable in the Table text box.

**5. Enter the expression [TypeTable].[TypeName] in the Update To text box in the first column.**

Your query now looks similar to Figure 16-4.

**Figure 16-4:**
The finished query updates one table with data from another table.

**6. Save and name the query.**

**7. Click the large exclamation mark to run the update.**

Access displays a message box telling you how many records will be updated.

**8. Click Yes to update the records.**

This simple example updates all the records in the ItemsTable table, but that might not be what you want to do. Suppose that you only want to update the records where the State value is Nevada and the TypeName value is Mining. Now you have a slightly more complicated task because you need to specify two criteria that apply to two different tables. Because both criteria must be satisfied, you need to use an AND clause to join them.

TECHNICAL STUFF

## The SQL statement equivalent of what you just saw

If you prefer to work in SQL View, you can create the query listed in the previous steps (see the previous section, "Updating data in one table with data from another without any conditions") by using the following SQL statement:

```
UPDATE TypeTable
INNER JOIN ItemsTable ON
   TypeTable.TypeID =
      ItemsTable.TypeID
SET ItemsTable.Description =
   TypeTable.TypeName;
```

If you're a little confused by the SQL statement, don't worry. The layout of this statement simply demonstrates that you can accomplish the same goal in more than one way. Here's what you probably expected:

```
UPDATE ItemsTable
INNER JOIN TypeTable ON
   ItemsTable.TypeID =
      TypeTable.TypeID
SET ItemsTable.Description =
   TypeTable.TypeName;
```

In reality, both SQL statements do the same thing. When you have a multiple-table update query like this one, the first part of the SQL statement (everything before the keyword SET) simply defines the join properties for the query. So it doesn't matter which of the two tables is listed first as long as you build the join in the same order as the tables are listed. The SET portion of the SQL statement is where the real work gets done, and the order in that portion of the statement is extremely critical!

Figure 16-5 shows how to modify the query to add the two criteria. Notice that in this case, the criteria expression must specify both the names of the tables and the names of the fields because the criteria aren't based on the field that's being updated.

If you prefer to keep the query design a bit simpler, you can specify each of the criteria in its own column, as shown in Figure 16-6. Either way, the query returns the same results when you run it. (Access 2007 "corrects" the query, making it look like 16-6.)

In SQL View, the query now looks like this (it doesn't matter if you specify the criteria in the first column as shown in Figure 16-5 or in separate columns as shown in Figure 16-6 — the resulting SQL statement is the same):

```
UPDATE TypeTable
INNER JOIN ItemsTable ON
   TypeTable.TypeID = ItemsTable.TypeID
SET ItemsTable.Description = TypeTable.TypeName
WHERE ((ItemsTable.State="Nevada"
   And TypeTable.TypeName="Mining"));
```

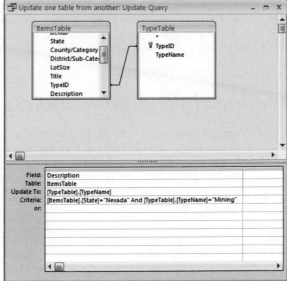

**Figure 16-5:**
The query now has two criteria that must be satisfied before a record is updated.

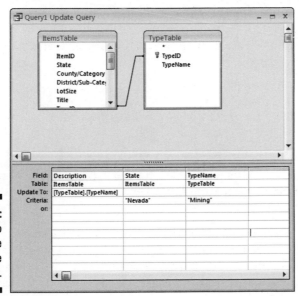

**Figure 16-6:**
You can also specify the criteria like this.

Although these examples originally left out the square brackets around the table and field names to keep the examples compact, using the square brackets is always safe, and the brackets are required if the table or field names include any spaces (Access 2007 adds them automatically).

## Making sure the right data is updated

In many cases, the field names in the table you want to update and the table where the updates come from are the same. There's nothing wrong with this duplication, but it can cause confusion and that can lead to updating the data in the wrong table if you aren't careful. Generally this is less of a problem if you're working in Design View than in SQL View because in Design View the Table row clearly indicates which table to update.

Before you run a query that updates data in one table with data from another table, be sure to verify that the correct table is shown in the Table row of the column that includes the Update To expression. If you're working in SQL View, check to be sure that the table you want to update is on the left side of the equal sign following the SET keyword.

# Chapter 17

# Killer Ways to Improve Forms

· · · · · · · · · · · · · · · · · · · · · · · · · · · · · · · · · · · · · · · · · · ·

· · · · · · · · · · · · · · · · · · · · · · · · · · · · · · · · · · · · · · · · · · ·

*Y*ou need stronger tools than the Form Wizard to create great forms that reduce input errors and make users more efficient. You also need to know how to apply some special tricks and techniques that really take your forms up a step from the ordinary.

That's what this chapter is all about. Here you discover how to give users a clearly defined, limited set of choices so that you can be sure of getting good input. You see how to add macro buttons to automate certain tasks such as printing a report. And you find how to help your users by displaying text prompts to remove confusion they may feel about what sort of input is expected.

You know what they say about an ounce of prevention. . . . Keeping bad data out of the database is a whole lot easier than trying to find it after it gets buried in there.

## Prequalifying the Data Entered

Let's face it — life would be a whole lot easier for you as an Access database developer if you didn't have to deal with all those darn users, wouldn't it? Imagine how sweet life would be if you never had to worry about someone making typing errors or coming up with yet another creative bit of data that might fit in the latest fantasy movie, but has no real relationship to reality. Well, that's the point of making sure that data is pre-qualified before it's entered into the database. *Prequalifying* requires setting up parameters that must be fulfilled before data is accepted into a form. If you give users a limited set of choices, you can be pretty sure that you'll end up with usable data. And you won't have to wonder what *maybe* means in the `Taxable` field, either! The two best ways of prequalifying data are to use lookup lists and to set default values.

## Creating lookup lists

A *lookup list* is a wonderful invention. Lookup lists enable a user to choose from a set of existing values so that you can be sure that the data that's entered is one of those values.

A lookup list is a control that lists data options. The lookup list is typically added to a form by using a combo box, as shown in the bottom of Figure 17-1; sometimes people use a list box as shown in the top of Figure 17-1 ( see Chapter 9 for a review of the differences between combo boxes and list boxes) for their lookup lists. The list of choices can come from a table, a query, or even be stored in the control itself. Choose a preexisting form or a Blank Form from the Create section of the Ribbon, change that form to Design View, and then choose your table. You can switch between Design View and Form View to get a good sense of what you are doing.

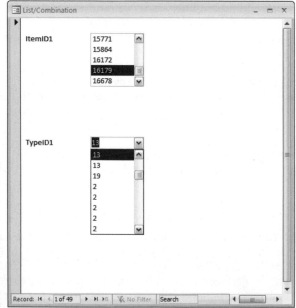

**Figure 17-1:**
The `TypeID1` field on this form is a lookup list that's in a combo box.

Regardless of the source of the list of values, users of the form can choose only one of those values, which is then typically stored in the field that's associated with the control.

It's also possible to store the selected value in a variable for use in an expression or a VBA procedure but, most of the time, you simply store the value in the underlying table.

### Choosing the source of lookup data

The list of values doesn't come from the table that's the form's record source. This concept can be one of the hardest to grasp because it seems so logical that you would get the data from that table; in reality, the list has to come from a different source. Part of the confusion probably arises from the way a combo box (or list box) works. When you move to a record that already contains data in the field that is the control source for the combo box, the combo box shows the existing value that's stored in the field. But even so, the combo box in the form also shows the other possible values that you can choose.

Here's a brush up on all the different kinds of sources you can set up as properties in the Properties dialog box:

- ✔ The *record source* is the table or query that feeds data to the form, and it's also where the data is stored as you enter or edit information on the form.
- ✔ The *control source* is the field where a control gets any existing value, and it's where data from the control is stored.
- ✔ The *row source* is where the combo box gets its list of choices to display.

Access offers a handy wizard that you can use to help you set up a lookup list when you add a combo box (or a list box) to a form. The following example shows you how to use the Combo Box Wizard to add a combo box:

1. **Open the form to which you want to add the combo box in Design View.**

2. **In the Ribbon, click the Combo Box icon to select it.**

    Make certain that the Control Wizards button in the Toolbox is selected.

3. **Drag the field that you want to use as a lookup list onto the form.**

    The Combo Box Wizard dialog box opens, as shown in Figure 17-2, offering you two options.

**Figure 17-2:**
Choose the
type of
combo box
you want.

4. **Choose the option that best suits your needs for the row source and click Next to continue.**

• If you choose the first option, the lookup list displays values from a table or a query.

This is the most commonly used (and useful) of the two options.

• If you choose the second option, you must enter a list of values to be stored in the control.

In this example, I chose the first option. The row source options display, as shown in Figure 17-3.

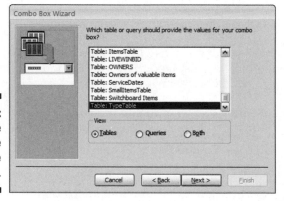

**Figure 17-3:**
Choose the
row source
for the
combo box.

5. **Select the table or query that you want to use as the row source and click Next to continue.**

The tables must be joined in order to use a table as the row source. The field selection options appear, as shown in Figure 17-4.

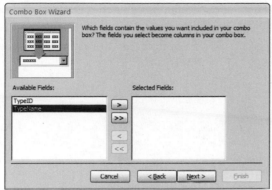

**Figure 17-4:** Choose the `row source` fields you want to display in the combo box.

6. **Add the fields that you want to appear in the combo box to the Selected Fields list with the > or >> buttons. Click Next to continue.**

7. **If you want to sort the items that are displayed in the lookup list, select the sorting options. Click Next to continue.**

   The column display and width options appear, as shown in Figure 17-5. For information about sorting, see "Improving lookup lists with proper sorting," later in this chapter.

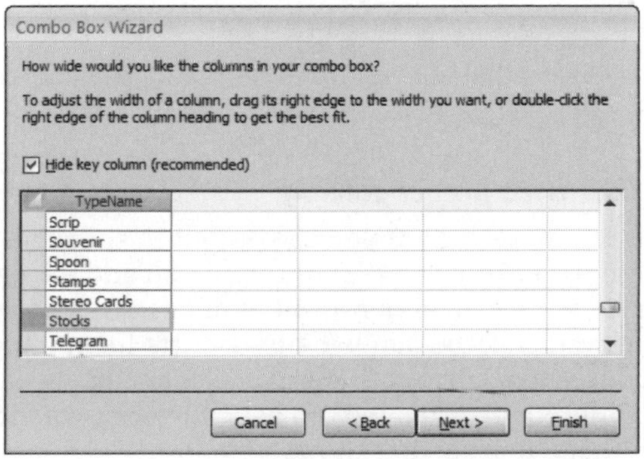

**Figure 17-5:** Adjust the column width if necessary.

8. **Adjust the column width by dragging the right side of the field name row. Click Next to continue.**

   You can also double-click the right edge of the field name row to automatically resize the column to fit the data.

Leave the Hide key column check box selected so that users won't be confused by the extra, unnecessary column.

The next dialog box gives you options for storing control source values, as shown in Figure 17-6.

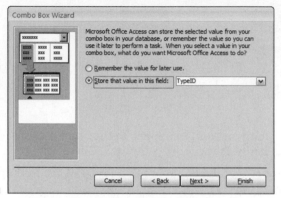

**Figure 17-6:**
Choose what you want Access to do with the value.

9. **From the Store That Value in This Field drop-down list, select the field where you want to store the data. Click Next to continue.**

10. **Enter the label you want to display next to the combo box and then click Finish.**

The Combo Box Wizard dialog box closes and adds the control to your form.

### *Improving lookup lists with proper sorting*

Although the Combo Box Wizard gives you the option to specify a sort order for the lookup list, you won't be given that option if you add a lookup list to a form by using the Form Wizard. In either event, you need to sort your lookup lists if you want to avoid the all-too-familiar, out-of-sorts lookup list shown in Figure 17-7. Logically organized lists prevent users from making careless mistakes! If you've encountered unsorted lookup lists on your own forms and wondered how to fix them, this section shows you how.

The key to fixing an unsorted lookup list is knowing where to look for the problem. When you create a lookup list that draws its values from a table, Access creates a SQL SELECT query statement in the control's Row Source property. You can modify that SQL statement to add an ORDER BY clause to specify a sort order for the value list.

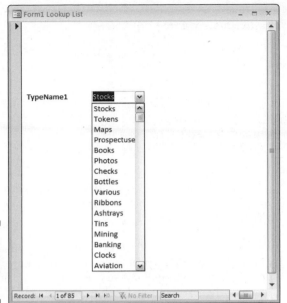

**Figure 17-7:**
An unsorted
lookup list is
hard to use.

You can modify the SQL statement in at least a couple of ways. Here's one that's easy and fast:

1. **Open the form in Design View and click the Combo Box to select it.**

2. **Right-click for Properties or click the Properties option on the Ribbon.**

   The Properties dialog box opens.

3. **On the Data tab, click the Row Source text box.**

4. **Press Shift+F2.**

   The Zoom dialog box appears, enabling you to view and edit the entire SQL statement.

5. **At the end of the SQL statement, move the insertion point just to the left of the semicolon, press the spacebar, and then enter ORDER BY and the name of the field you want to sort.**

   Figure 17-8 shows how the Zoom dialog box appears in my example.

6. **Click OK.**

   The Zoom dialog box closes, and your lookup list is now sorted in ascending order (from A to Z).

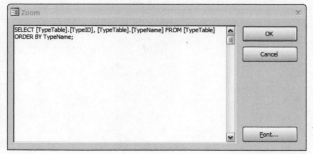

```
SELECT [TypeTable].[TypeID], [TypeTable].[TypeName] FROM [TypeTable]
ORDER BY TypeName;
```

**Figure 17-8:**
Use the
ORDER BY
clause to
sort the
lookup list.

You can add DESC to the ORDER BY clause to sort the lookup list in descending order (Z to A) if you don't like the default setting of ascending order. In Step 5, simply type **ORDER BY TypeName DESC**.

If you prefer a more visual approach to setting the sort order, you can open the Query Builder by clicking the Build (three dots) button after you've selected the Row Source text box in Step 3. Make the changes in the Sort row and save your changes when you close the Query Builder.

## Setting default values

Setting a default value for a field automatically enters that value in the field when a new record is created. This simple technique can make a database more convenient to use. Because the default value is the most commonly entered value, users often don't have to enter any information manually in the field when they create a new record.

You can, of course, use the Default Value property in a table design to set up the table so the same value is always entered whenever a new record is created. In most cases, this is the best way to set a default value, because by setting the default value in the table's properties, you ensure the value is automatically entered, no matter how someone creates a new record.

In some cases, though, you should set the default value for a field by setting the Default Value property for a control on a form, as shown in Figure 17-9. If you set the default value for a control on a form, that value is only entered when a new record is created by using the form.

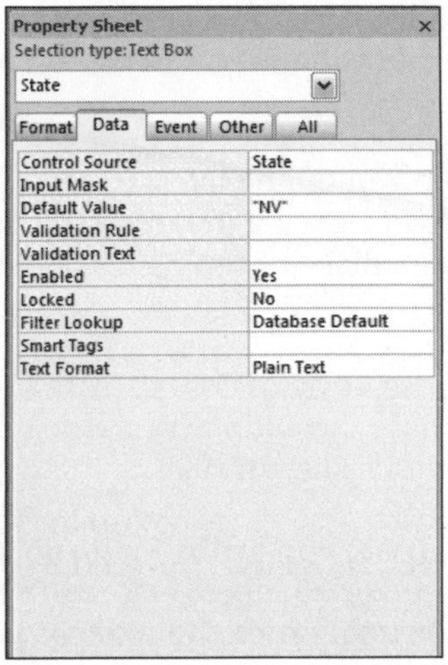

| Property Sheet | ✕ |
| --- | --- |

Selection type: Text Box

State ⌄

| Format | Data | Event | Other | All |

| Control Source | State |
| --- | --- |
| Input Mask | |
| Default Value | "NV" |
| Validation Rule | |
| Validation Text | |
| Enabled | Yes |
| Locked | No |
| Filter Lookup | Database Default |
| Smart Tags | |
| Text Format | Plain Text |

**Figure 17-9:**
Here the
State field
is set to a
default
value of NV.

The real advantage to setting default values for controls on a form (when compared to setting the default value for the field in the table design) is that you can create different forms, each with its own default value settings. This can be very useful if you have a database that tracks orders. By setting up different copies of the order entry form for each order taker, you can set the default value for each of their individual forms to automatically enter the order taker's name. That way, you can make sure that every order is automatically credited to the correct person.

# Crafting Forms That Are Easier to Use

You can easily create forms that do everything you want, but sometimes the downside of a form that does everything is that it isn't as easy to use as it should be. Making forms easier to use pays off in time saved and fewer errors. So after you have the basics down, put in a little extra effort working on usability.

## Making data appear in a logical order

People don't generally do very well when they're presented with a bunch of data that's in no logical order. That's why your telephone book is sorted by name, and your calendar shows the dates in chronological order. You can simply understand and find information more easily if it's arranged logically.

Access likes order, too. Unfortunately, the sense of order that Access likes isn't always the same as the sense of order that makes sense to humans.

When you create an Access table, you almost always include a field that's used as a *primary key*. This key could be something like a customer ID number, a product identification number, or even a membership number. The values in key fields are unique, which makes keeping track of the records easier for Access.

The one little problem with most database keys, of course, is that they're pretty unintelligible to people. You probably wouldn't try to look up a customer named Fred Holabird using a number like 1079999.

When you enter information into a database, you probably do so in a random order. Unless you have a database that never changes, you aren't likely to add all your customer records in alphabetical order. More likely, you will enter data as you receive it. For example, you may get an order from a new customer named Paul Johnson right after you finish entering one for John Mills. As a result, when Access creates the key values, Paul Johnson appears after John Mills. Sometimes (often, in fact) you may want to sort records by name. However, in general, you don't want to be stuck with a database that makes finding a specific customer's records awfully hard for the ordinary Joe.

## Controlling the order for displaying records

You can easily control the order in which a form displays records by setting the Order By property for the form, as shown in Figure 17-10. In the figure, the OWNERLASTNAME field value is used for sorting the records. The Order By property appears on the Data tab of the Properties dialog box.

When you set a property, such as the Order By property, for a form, that setting has no effect outside of the form. Sorting in a form does not change the record sort order in the table.

If you need to sort the records that are displayed in the form by more than one field, list the fields in the Order By text box separated by commas. Place the field names in order of importance. For example, if you want to sort by last name and then by first name, the Order By text box should look like this: LastName, FirstName.

**Figure 17-10:**
Use the
`Order By`
property of
the form to
set the sort
order for the
records
when
they're
displayed in
the form.

# *Adding command buttons for common tasks*

You do certain tasks quite often when you're working with your PC. Sometimes these are simple tasks, but you might have to press a half-dozen keys or click several times with your mouse to perform those tasks. Have you ever thought to yourself that you would like to click just once and have your computer take over and finish the job for you?

In Access you can use *command buttons* to run *macros* or VBA procedures that automate various tasks. (Macros are similar to VBA procedures, but not nearly as flexible or powerful. I discuss VBA procedures briefly in Chapter 7.)

## Setting a sort order for every occasion

Just as setting default values in forms sometimes makes using Access easier, setting the sort order in a form often makes more sense than trying to find a common sort order for every purpose. You may sometimes sort by customer name, sometimes by state, and maybe even by something like order size. By creating individual forms that display the records in their own, unique arrangements, you give your Access users tools to make their work easier and more efficient without requiring them to master the mechanics of queries and sorting.

### Knowing what you can do with command buttons

Maybe the title of this section should really be "Is there anything you can't do with command buttons?" The answer would have to be yes, but you can still do an awful lot that might surprise you with command buttons.

Here are a few examples of things that you can do with command buttons:

- ✔ Print a report
- ✔ Open a form
- ✔ Exchange data between your Access database and another application such as Excel
- ✔ Run a mail merger to generate personalized form letters or e-mails
- ✔ Export information to an accounting system such as QuickBooks
- ✔ Save the world from the plague of (insert the name of your favorite villain here)

Okay, so maybe you'd need a really complex VBA procedure to make that last one work, but you get the picture. Command buttons are great tools that help make Access databases easier to use.

### Creating your first command button

Access makes creating simple command buttons easy with the Command Button Wizard. This wizard offers a number of different common tasks that you can add to a command button.

Here's how to create a command button with the Command Button Wizard:

1. **Open the form on which you want to place a command button in Design View.**

   You might want to start with a new, blank form while you're experimenting with the wizard.

2. **Click the Command Button icon in the Ribbon (it is just called Button, and it is in the Design section) to select it.**

3. **Click in your form where you want the button to appear.**

   The Command Button Wizard dialog box appears, as shown in Figure 17-11.

4. **Choose the category of action you want the command button to perform.**

   As you select different categories, the Actions list displays the actions available in the selected category.

**Figure 17-11:**
Use the
Command
Button
Wizard to
create
simple
command
buttons.

5. **Choose the action you want and click Next to continue.**

   The next screen of the Command Button Wizard appears, as shown in
   Figure 17-12. In this example, I selected the Mail Report action in the
   Report Operations category, so the wizard in Figure 17-13 displays
   e-mail options.

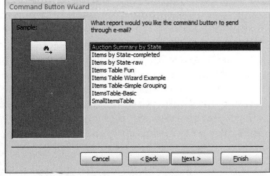

**Figure 17-12:**
If you select
the Mail
Report
action, you
must
choose
which
report you
want to
send.

6. **Select the report that you want the command button to e-mail and
   then click Next to continue.**

   The next Command Button Wizard screen appears, asking you to choose
   text or an image for the face of the button.

7. **Enter a name for the command button.**

8. **Click Finish to close the wizard.**

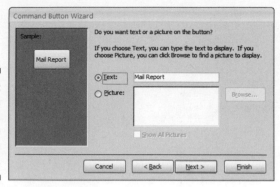

Although giving the command button a descriptive name may not seem important right now, keeping track of the objects (like controls you've added to forms) is far easier if you give them a name that means something to you. Remembering the purpose of a button that has a name that Access assigned (such as Command0) can be pretty hard.

### Creating command buttons that perform more than one task

If you're still wondering whether the Command Button Wizard is worth your trouble, consider how much more useful our command button could be if, in addition to e-mailing a copy of a form to recipients outside of your office, a single click of the command button performed a second action, such as printing the copies of the form for distribution within your office. Experiment with creating a couple of different command buttons that perform related actions such as e-mailing and printing a report. After you do this, open the code window and see how similar the VBA procedures are for the different buttons. As long as the actions you've assigned are similar enough, your VBA code won't look too different, and you can easily modify one of the buttons to perform more than one action.

Take the case of e-mailing a report and printing the same report. Because these actions are so similar, only one line of the following VBA code differs from the previous example. You can easily add that single line from one button's code to the other button's code and build a button that does both tasks simultaneously.

Here's all you need to do to modify the earlier example and do both jobs:

```
Private Sub EmailSummaryButton_Click()
On Error GoTo Err_EmailSummaryButton_Click

    Dim stDocName As String

    stDocName = "Auction Summary by State"
    DoCmd.SendObject acReport, stDocName
    DoCmd.OpenReport stDocName, acViewNormal

Exit_EmailSummaryButton_Click:
    Exit Sub

Err_EmailSummaryButton_Click:
    MsgBox Err.Description
    Resume Exit_EmailSummaryButton_Click

End Sub
```

The only change here is the addition of the line:

```
DoCmd.OpenReport stDocName, acViewNormal
```

Now you have a button that performs two actions with one click. Amazing what a little ingenuity can do!

## Creating a switchboard for better usability

If you're responsible for creating databases to be used by a variety of people, you probably want to make using the database as straightforward and obvious as possible. One thing that you certainly don't want is to have to explain how to perform basic tasks every time you get a new user (or when someone forgets for the 54th time how to print the same report). That's where a *switchboard* form comes in handy.

Switchboards are Access forms that aren't tied to a table, so they're not used to enter or edit any data. Rather, a switchboard is a form that contains a series of command buttons that open other forms, print reports, run queries, or perform any other common task that you might want to automate.

In most cases, you set up a switchboard so that it opens automatically whenever a user opens the database. One reason for this automated convenience, of course, is to keep you from repeatedly hearing (and answering) the question, "How do I open that switchboard thingy that lets me do stuff?"

TECHNICAL STUFF

# Getting up close and personal with the code behind your command button

Access actually goes to a lot of work when you create a command button. If you want to see how the command button works, right-click the finished button and choose Build Event from the pop-up menu to display the VBA procedure that the Command Button Wizard created for your button. You can also click the Code option to display the code window. Here's the VBA code that results from the e-mail a report example:

```
Private Sub
    EmailSummaryButton_Click()
On Error GoTo
    Err_EmailSummaryButton_Cli
    ck

    Dim stDocName As String

    stDocName = "Auction
    Summary by State"
    DoCmd.SendObject
    acReport, stDocName

Exit_EmailSummaryButton_Click
    :
    Exit Sub
```

```
Err_EmailSummaryButton_Click:
    MsgBox Err.Description
    Resume
    Exit_EmailSummaryButton_Cl
    ick

End Sub
```

The Dim statement sets up a string variable named stDocName so that the variable can be used to store the name of the report you want to e-mail. The DoCmd.SendObject command sends an e-mail message and is actually a very versatile command. You can even modify the command by adding additional arguments such as the e-mail address of the recipient, a message subject, or message text to explain the purpose of the report. You can find out more about the SendObject action in the Access Help files by searching for SendObject.

# *Creating your own switchboard*

The hardest part of the whole switchboard creation process is probably trying to decide which tasks you want to include on the switchboard.

Here's how to create a basic switchboard:

1. **Choose Database Tools (on the Ribbon)⇨Switchboard Manager.**

REMEMBER

In some versions of Access, you may see a message asking whether you'd like to create a switchboard. If you do, click Yes to continue. If not, you're sent directly to the Switchboard Manager dialog box (see Figure 17-14).

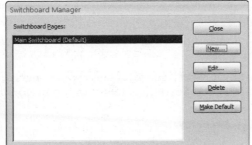

**Figure 17-14:**
Create a
new
switchboard.

**2. Click Edit.**

The Edit Switchboard Page dialog box appears, as shown in Figure 17-15, so that you can begin editing the switchboard.

**Figure 17-15:**
Begin
adding
items to
your
switchboard
using the
Edit
Switchboard
Page dialog
box.

**3. Click New.**

The Edit Switchboard Item dialog box appears, as shown in Figure 17-16.

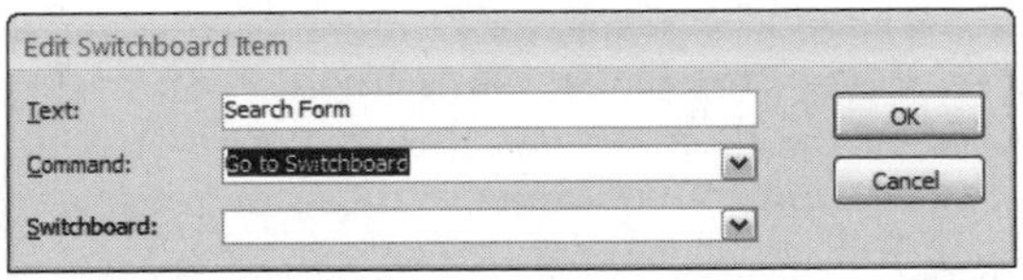

**Figure 17-16:**
Select the
items to
appear on
your
switchboard.

4. **Enter the text that you want to appear next to the first command button in the Text text box.**

5. **Choose the action you want the command button to perform from the Command drop-down list.**

6. **Select the corresponding switchboard, form, report, macro, or VBA function from the drop-down list closest to the bottom of the dialog box.**

The name associated with the box changes depending on your selection in the Command list; the third box disappears if you choose the Design Application or Exit Application choices in the Command list.

7. **Click OK.**

   The Edit Switchboard Item dialog box closes, and you return to the Edit Switchboard Page dialog box.

8. **Repeat Steps 4 through 8 for each command button that you want to add to the switchboard.**

9. **Click Close when you finish adding command buttons.**

   You return to the Switchboard Manager dialog box.

10. **If your switchboard does not show (Default) after its name, click the Make Default button.**

    This action makes your switchboard open automatically whenever a user opens the database.

11. **Click Close.**

    The Switchboard Manager dialog box closes.

Figure 17-17 shows a very simple switchboard I created for this example. You can get quite a bit fancier with your switchboard by opening it in Design View and editing the design just as you would modify the design of any other form. For example, you may want to add a company logo or some simple user instruction to the switchboard.

## Presenting data for information only

Sometimes you need to protect people from themselves. Or maybe the more accurate way to say it is that sometimes you need to protect your data from meddlers who don't realize how much damage they can cause.

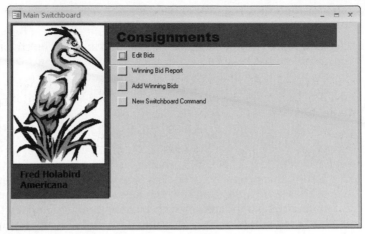

**Figure 17-17:**
The finished switchboard helps people use your database.

If you want to provide your users with a bit of extra information and still protect your data, you're well advised to follow some simple techniques to prevent people from changing certain information. For example, say you have a form that's used to enter the winning bids for items. You probably don't want anyone to change the descriptions of the items. Or, if you have a form that allows users to enter the descriptions of items you've recently logged in to inventory, you aren't likely to want someone to change the item inventory numbers.

## Making read-only fields

You can prevent someone from changing values that are displayed in a form by using a couple of different properties. In addition, there's one property that can fool you into thinking that it might help prevent changes, but it doesn't.

Found on the Other tab, the Tab Stop property may seem like it would prevent users from entering the field, but it really doesn't. A user can simply click in the field and edit away even if you set the Tab Stop property to No. Don't even think about using this property to protect your data!

To prevent changes to values in a field, follow these steps:

1. **Select the field in Design View.**

2. **Click the Properties option on the Ribbon.**

3. **Consider the following property settings:**

- `Enabled`: This property, found on the Data tab, can be set to No to prevent the field from being selected. It grays out the field for users so that they know that they're being shut out. The values are still shown, but users can't change them in the form. This is the best way to present data in a form without allowing it to be modified.

- `Locked`: This property, also on the Data tab, can be set to Yes to prevent changes to displayed values, but it doesn't prevent the field from being selected.

Setting this property to Yes is a sure way to confuse users because users see no indication that the field is locked (aside from the fact that nothing happens when they select the field and try to type in it). I recommend simply avoiding the `Locked` property for that reason.

## Giving users help with text prompts

You can display text prompts to help users understand the purpose of a form control. These handy little messages save you all sorts of support calls, and because they're so seldom used, people will think you're an Access wizard if you add them to your forms.

You can choose from two flavors of text prompts:

- ✔ **Status bar text** is information that appears in the status bar at the lower-left corner of the Access window when the field is selected.

- ✔ **ControlTip text** is information that pops up when the mouse pointer is held over a control for a few seconds.

It may seem like a bit of overkill to use both Status bar text and ControlTip text, but if you go to the trouble of adding one of them, you may as well add both. After all, some people navigate forms exclusively with the keyboard, so they never see the ControlTip text. And some people get so focused on the form that they ignore any messages that appear in the status bar. Unfortunately, this probably means that a certain percentage of your users won't really notice either of the efforts you put into adding text prompts, but you can't do anything about *those* people.

To add text prompts, follow these steps:

1. **Open the form in Design View and click the control that you want to modify to select it.**

2. **Click the Properties option on the Ribbon to display the Properties dialog box for the control.**

3. **Click the Other tab to display it.**

   See Figure 17-18.

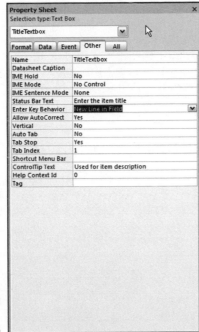

**Figure 17-18:**
Use the
Other tab
of the
Properties
dialog box
to add text
prompts.

4. **Enter any text you want to appear in the status bar in the Status Bar Text box.**

   You can enter a prompt up to 255 characters; but depending on users' screen resolutions, only about 50 to 80 characters actually appear. Limit your remarks to a single, short sentence. This is not the place to draft the Great American Novel.

5. **Add any text you want in the pop-up list in the ControlTip Text box.**

   You can enter up to 255 characters, but you should keep this even shorter than the Status bar text.

# Chapter 18

# Expert Methods for Sharing Reports

**In This Chapter**

▶ Sharing details of your data with Microsoft Excel

▶ Merging report data with Microsoft Word

▶ Incorporating OLE objects

*I*n a perfect world, you would never have to share your Access data with another application because Access would simply do everything you'd need to do without any outside help. But we don't live in a perfect world, and besides, the time is sure to come when you need to send Access data to someone who hasn't jumped on the Access bandwagon.

This chapter shows you methods that make sharing data with both Excel and Word simple and efficient. In addition, this chapter fearlessly takes on a topic that strikes terror into the souls of many Access users — using OLE (Object Linking and Embedding) objects in your reports. Okay, so maybe *terror* is a bit strong, but despite the fact that many Access users find them more than a bit intimidating, OLE objects are a type of shared data that can be awfully handy.

## Sharing Data with Microsoft Excel

As powerful as Access is, an awful lot of people are simply more comfortable analyzing data in Excel when they have the option. Somehow that Excel spreadsheet just seems a bit more friendly and cozy than the various options in Access. Sure, the PivotTables and PivotCharts offer a glimpse of Excel's power in Access, but they're just not the same as truly moving over to Excel and mucking around with the data in that program.

Although you can exchange data between Access and Excel using several different methods, Access 2007 no longer supports exporting report data to Excel. This useful feature was available in earlier versions of Access, but it has been removed from Access 2007 (I mention it here so that those of you who have upgraded from earlier Access versions won't waste a lot of time looking for this option). You can open an Access table or query in Excel, but forget about exporting reports from Access 2007 to Excel.

# Sending Reports to Microsoft Word

You have a couple of choices for sharing Access data with Word. The method that you choose depends on what you want to do with the information after it is exported to Word:

- ✔ If you primarily want to make the data look a bit fancier or include it without too many changes in a Word document, you should probably send the output of an Access report to Word.

- ✔ If you want to create form letters or catalogs in Word, try the Mail Merge feature so that Word gets a table of data that it can draw from. Strictly speaking, you're not really sending a report to Word, but the process is important enough that I discuss it anyway.

Access has great difficulty dealing with the OLE Object field type when sending data to another application such as Word. See "Using OLE Objects in Reports," later in this chapter, for a discussion of OLE Objects.

## Sending report data to Word

Sending report data to Word is a relatively simple process. Basically, you create your report, select it, and then choose External Data⇨Word. Access then goes through the "printing" process that creates a Word.rtf (Rich Text File) document from your Access report.

The Word document you create by using the External Data option on the Ribbon looks very much like the Access report itself. That's because the Word document includes the report headers, report footers, the page headers, and the page footers from the Access report. Date fields and page numbering are also included (the Word document includes hard page breaks to make the document look even more like the Access report).

Figure 18-1 shows a report as it appears in Access 2007, and Figure 18-2 shows how a report looks after being sent to Word.

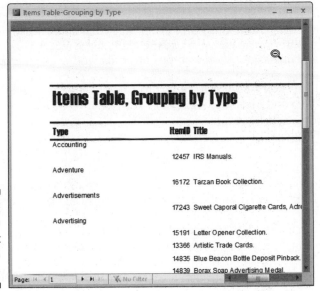

**Figure 18-1:** The sample report as it appears in Access.

**Figure 18-2:** The sample report after being exported to Word.

## Using the Word Mail Merge feature with Access

Word uses the term *mail merge* for any document that is automatically created from a data file, but that doesn't mean that you can only use this feature to create form letters. You can also use the Mail Merge feature to create personalized e-mail messages, various types of labels, and even catalogs.

You can't actually send an Access report to Word for use as a Mail Merge data source. Instead, you either

✔ Send the data as it exists in a table.

✔ Create a query to provide the data for the mail merge.

The basic idea here is that you provide Word with a table of the data for the merge, and the table must look similar to the Access Datasheet view:

✔ Each column must hold the data for a single field.

✔ The first row of the table must contain the field names.

✔ Each following row must contain the data for a single record.

You can choose one of two methods to create the Mail Merge file for Word.

✔ **Using Access features:** The first method works within Access and simply creates the Mail Merge file that you can use later in Word. That's the method I describe in this section.

✔ **Using Word features:** The second method creates the merge file and then immediately opens the Mail Merge Wizard in Word so that you can create your merged Word documents.

For information about using Word functions and features, take a look at *Word 2007 For Dummies* by Dan Gookin (Wiley).

Here's how to create the Word merge file in Access:

1. **Select the table or the query that you want to use as the data source for the merge file.**

2. **Right-click and choose⇨Export⇨Merge it with Microsoft Office Word to open the Microsoft Word Mail Merge Wizard, or use the More option from the External Data section of the Ribbon.**

   This will direct you to a dialog box, as shown in Figure 18-3.

3. **Select the Microsoft Word document from the File name and File of type drop-down lists.**

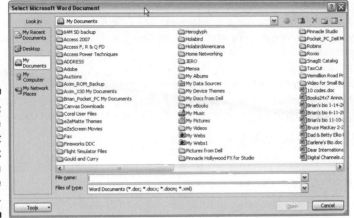

**Figure 18-3:**
Use the
Export
dialog box
to create a
Word merge
file.

4. **Make your choices and click Open.**

Access saves the Word file in the current directory, using the name of the table or query as the name of the Word file.

Word can use data from an Access table as the data source for a merge, but it can't use an Access query directly. That's one big advantage of creating the Word merge file in Access. Selecting specific groups of records by using an Access query is much easier than limiting the records with the options that are available in Word.

# Using OLE Objects in Reports

Most Access books either completely ignore OLE objects, or they dismiss them with a few quick sentences. The general attitude seems to be something like "OLE objects are bad, bad, bad, and you should avoid using them." I have a different take on OLE objects, and that's simply that they're only useful if you understand them.

## Understanding OLE objects

*OLE* stands for *Object Linking and Embedding* — one of those kind of nebulous terms that programmers seem to like to throw around when they're trying to snow everyone. *OLE objects* are simply documents that belong to another application that you use inside a document file. For example, you can embed a Word document into a field of an Access database. The Word document is the OLE object in this case.

Many different types of objects, from Adobe Acrobat documents to Excel worksheets, to bitmap images, and even wav sound files are available — but if you want to use them, the applications you have installed must be registered as OLE object sources.

## Linking versus embedding

OLE objects can be *linked* or *embedded:*

✔ A linked object is actually just a reference to the filename and location of the foreign document.

When you open a table, a form, or a report that contains a linked object, Access opens the linked document with the application that created the document, and it appears as if it is really a part of the database.

✔ An embedded object is contained within the database.

When you want to view the object in a table, a form, or a report, Access opens the embedded object by using the application that created it.

The difference between linked and embedded OLE objects is very important in some cases, but it's pretty much a wash in others. Here are some things to know about linking and embedding:

✔ Linked and embedded objects look the same in Access. You can't easily tell by viewing a table, form, or report whether the object is linked or embedded.

✔ Linked objects are updated if the original document file is updated, but embedded objects aren't.

✔ If the source document for a linked object is moved or deleted, Access won't be able to locate it, and therefore won't be able to open the file.

✔ Because embedded objects are a part of the database file, moving or deleting the original source document has no effect on Access. The embedded object can still be used in a report no matter what happens to the original source document that's outside of Access.

✔ Embedded objects are often nearly impossible to export from Access to another application. As a result, that embedded Word document that so nicely gives you formatted text within a field in Access really isn't going to play nice if you want to use the Mail Merge feature in Word to produce a catalog.

✔ Linked OLE objects are slightly easier to export to another application, but you'd better be ready to study VBA programming pretty extensively if you want to get too fancy. Even though Access is more than happy to let you add OLE objects to a database, it's awfully stingy about giving them back!

## Understanding the merits of using OLE objects in your database

Why would you even want to include a Word document in an Access database? When you create a report in Access, everything that's in a field on the report has the same formatting. In a Word document, on the other hand, you can format the document in any way you want. If you include a Word document as an OLE object in your Access database, all the formatting that you applied in Word appears when that field is used in a report. Suddenly you aren't limited to the lame formatting choices offered by Access. You could, for example, place the title of a book within a description in italics — which is generally considered to be the "proper" way of formatting book titles.

There are many different types of OLE objects, and your success in using them depends heavily on how much work the programmers of your applications did to make objects (documents) sharable. You have no control over how well the programmers did their jobs, but you can lessen the potential for frustration by trying out a few OLE objects from your favorite applications before you commit to using them on a full-scale basis in your Access databases. I've found that sometimes just switching to a different source program for my OLE objects makes a major difference in how usable those objects end up being.

## *Adding your first OLE object to your Access database*

Adding OLE objects to your database is the first step toward using OLE objects in reports. In this section, I show you how to add a couple of different OLE objects to your Access database and then use them in reports.

You must begin by adding a field that has the OLE object data type to your table (open your table in Design View and right-click Data Type to provide the OLE choice). For the purpose of these examples, I assume that you already have a table containing a field that is an OLE object type. In addition, I assume that you have created a form that has a box for the OLE object field.

Here's how to add OLE objects to your database:

1. **Open the form in Form View so that you can add items to the table.**

2. **Click the OLE object field to select it.**

3. **Right-click the field, and choose Insert Object from the pop-up menu.**

   The Microsoft Office Access dialog box appears, as shown in Figure 18-4.

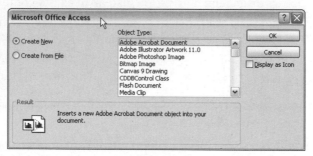

**Figure 18-4:**
Use this dialog box to add new OLE objects to your database.

4. **Select an object to embed:**

   • To create a *new object* to embed in the table, make sure that the Create New option button is selected and then choose the type of object you want to embed from the scrollable Object Type list. Click OK.

   The dialog box closes, and Access embeds the object. Access opens the selected application so that you can create the new OLE object.

   • To embed an existing object to the table, select the Create From File option.

   The dialog box that appears (shown in Figure 18-5) enables you to browse your system to find the file you want to add.

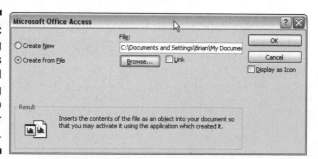

**Figure 18-5:**
This dialog box helps you add existing objects to your database.

5. **Enter the filename of the existing document in the File text box or click the Browse button to browse for the document file to add.**

6. **To link the object instead of embedding it, select the Link check box.**

7. **Click OK to add the object to the table and close the dialog box.**

8. **Repeat Steps 2 through 6 for each OLE object you want to add to a record.**

If the object appears as an icon in the form instead of as the content of the object, make sure that the Display As Icon check box is not selected in the Microsoft Office Access dialog box.

Figure 18-6 shows an example of a Word document that has been added to the database as an OLE object. The Word document, which appears in the `DescriptionFormatted` field, utilizes a number of different formatting options (color, boldface, italics, and various fonts) that aren't usually available in Access.

**Figure 18-6:**
This record
has a Word
document
as an OLE
object.

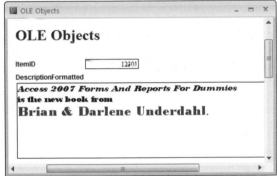

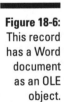

To control whether users can add linked, embedded, or both types of OLE objects, set the OLE Type Allowed property on the Data tab of the Properties dialog box for the OLE object field on the form (switch to Design View).

Figure 18-7 (Multiple Items in the Create⇨Forms section) shows how a report appears when you include multiple OLE objects in your database. In this case, the three visible records contain an embedded WordPad document, a linked bitmap image file, and a linked Word document file. Embedded and linked OLE objects look exactly the same, so you can choose the type of object that best suits your needs. You probably wouldn't use so many different options in your reports, but the figure does give you an idea of the possibilities.

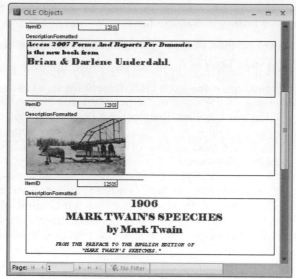

**Figure 18-7:**
This report
displays
three OLE
objects.

## Troubleshooting OLE objects so that they actually work

Using OLE objects in an Access database is easy on the surface, but sometimes things don't go quite the way you planned. Here are some tricks that
can help when things go wrong:

✔ **Problem:** You see an icon that says JPEG Image instead of the actual
image in a form or a report.

**Explanation and Solution:** Access doesn't like your choice of file type
for some reason. You need to convert the image to BMP or DIB. This
issue applies to several other types of image files, too, so if you can't see
the image, try converting it to BMP or DIB before you do anything else.

✔ **Problem:** You try to open an OLE object but only see a message saying
that the file can't be opened.

**Explanation and Solution:** Check whether the application that created the
object is already open. If it is open and it's waiting for you to respond to
a dialog box prompt, you won't be able to open a different object from
that application until you respond to and close the dialog box.

✔ **Problem:** An OLE object appears as an icon, and none of the earlier tricks in this list has solved the problem.

**Explanation and Solution:** Hmm . . . I don't know what's going on here. Try tinkering around in the Convert dialog box. Right-click the object. In the context-sensitive menu that appears, choose the *source application name* Document Object item (where *source application name* is the name of the program that created the object). The Convert dialog box appears. Deselect the Display As Icon check box.

✔ **Problem:** You absolutely have to export OLE objects from Access.

**Explanation and Solution:** Truth? Access doesn't really give you a good option. But you can export OLE objects from Access if you're willing to be creative (and spend a little money). You need to install Adobe Acrobat (not the free reader) or another application that can create *PDF* — Portable Document Format — files. Then create an Access report that includes your OLE objects; convert the resulting output to PDF. You may have to then convert the PDF file into another format (such as Word); but, at least, you can export the OLE object data and use it in another application. You're welcome.

✔ **Problem:** It still doesn't work.

**Explanation and Solution:** Sometimes stuff doesn't work, and all you can do is just move on. To be honest, just because an object type appears in the Object Type list in the Microsoft Office Access dialog box doesn't mean that it's going to work out well as an OLE object in your Access database. Access doesn't have any way to determine in advance whether objects that appear in the list are appropriate, so the only way to determine whether you really should insert the object is to try it and see what happens.

# Chapter 19

# Making Reports Look Better

• • • • • • • • • • • • • • • • • • • • • • • • • • • • • • • • • • • • • • • • • • • • • •

• • • • • • • • • • • • • • • • • • • • • • • • • • • • • • • • • • • • • • • • • • • • • •

*Y*ou want your reports to look good — otherwise, why even go to the trouble of creating a report? If appearance didn't matter, you could just hand everyone a copy of a datasheet printout and say, "The information you need is in there somewhere." No, that probably wouldn't cut it, now would it?

Improving the appearance of your reports actually involves using several subtle features that, individually, probably won't jump out and grab you. They are important, however, if you want to make a good impression. That's why I've assembled these little items in this chapter to make it easier for you to pick up some final, finishing touches that make your reports stand out from the crowd.

## Enhancing the Appearance of Important Information

Sure, all the information in a report is important, but some of it is more important than the rest. For example, you may want to be able to see at a glance the individual items that show profits; you probably also want to know which areas of your business aren't doing so well. In the end, that bottom line — how much you make (or lose) — is what you and the executives want to see.

Even though some information may be more important, the rest of a report should still be easy to understand and follow. Put some effort into making sure that your reports are clear and logical, adding emphasis to data that needs it.

## Sorting report data for clarity

When you create an Access report from scratch, the report displays the records based on how those records are sorted in the underlying table or query — unless you specify a different sort order. Usually, reports that don't specify another organization order records based on the table's primary index. Although this sort order may be useful for helping organize items in a table initially, it may not be the order that you want in your final report. For example, instead of sorting a report that shows the items for an upcoming sale by `ItemID`, you may want to sort the items by state, by value, or maybe even by their discount percentage.

You can choose one of four methods to control the sort order for a report, in order of importance:

- Use the Group, Sort, And Total dialog box to specify a sort order.
- Set the `OrderBy` property for the report.
- Base the report on a query that specifies a sort order for the records.
- Create an index for the underlying table.

Access doesn't stop you from specifying all four different sort orders (each with different parameters) for a single report. You can use all the methods mentioned without so much as a warning. Fortunately, Access does apply a pecking order to the methods so that you can be sure which of them wins out in the end. The Group, Sort, And Total dialog box sort order is the most important, followed by the `OrderBy` property, using a query, and, finally, by creating a table index. If you want absolute control, use the Group, Sort, And Total dialog box to set the report's sort order. Or, if you've tried to use one of the four methods to control the sort order and the report didn't sort the way you expected, check whether one of the more dominant methods is controlling the sort order.

### Using the OrderBy property

Even though a sort order specified in the Group, Sort, And Total dialog box takes precedence over a sort order set using the `OrderBy` property, you may want to use the `OrderBy` property because removing a sort order that's shown in the Group, Sort, And Total dialog box has the potential to really mess up your report if you're not careful. See the following section, "Understanding Group, Sort, And Total dialog box caveats" for more information. Changing or removing the `OrderBy` property is always easy and safe.

To specify a sort order, using the OrderBy property, follow these steps:

1. **Open the report in Design View.**

2. **Open the report's Properties dialog box.**

   See Figure 19-1. You can click the Properties option in the Ribbon or right-click in the report to display this dialog box.

**Figure 19-1:**
Set the
OrderBy
property on
the Data
tab.

3. **Enter the field(s) you want to use to control the sort order in the OrderBy property text box on the Data tab, making sure to enclose the field names in square brackets.**

   You can specify multiple fields by separating them with commas, and you can specify a sort direction by adding ASC for ascending (the default) or DESC for descending after the brackets, like this [State] DESC.

Use the OrderBy property to temporarily override the default sort order for a report without making a permanent change. Simply set the OrderBy property, run your specially sorted report, and then delete the property setting to return the report to its original state (or set the Order By On property to No).

### Understanding Group, Sort, And Total dialog box caveats

Chapter 13 covers using the Grouping And Totals option (Design section of the Ribbon), shown in Figure 19-2, in detail, so I don't spend a lot of time on the subject here.

**Figure 19-2:**
The sort
order you
specify in
the Group,
Sort, And
Total dialog
box always
takes
precedence.

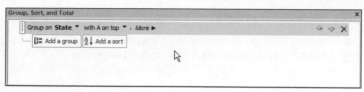

You need to be careful about using the Group, Sort, And Total dialog box for temporary report sorting purposes. As Figure 19-3 shows, Access warns you about potential damage to your report if you attempt to remove any of the entries in this dialog box — even if they have nothing to do with grouping.

**Figure 19-3:**
Removing
any entries
from the
Sorting And
Grouping
dialog box
displays this
message.

Of course, you can safely remove a line from the Group, Sort, And Total dialog box if the line doesn't have any grouping associated with it. But if you accidentally delete a line that sets up a grouping level, everything in the group header and group footer for that level is also removed. To avoid this risk, I recommend using the OrderBy property to control report sort order instead of using the Group, Sort, And Total dialog box.

## *Making data seem to jump out*

Chapter 12 discusses a number of fancy tricks that you can use in a report, such as incorporating conditional formatting and applying different colors to alternate report records. These tricks do, indeed, make data stand out, but they're probably not techniques that you'll want to use on every report. This section takes a look at some other options that you can use to make the data on your reports look a bit more impressive.

When you add a text box to a report, the Format tab of the Properties dialog box for that text box provides a whole bunch of interesting options for changing the appearance of your data. Figure 19-4 shows the Format tab of the Properties dialog box for a text box that displays the State field.

| Property Sheet | | ✕ |
|---|---|---|
| Selection type: Text Box | | |
| State | ▾ | |
| Format | Data | Event | Other | All |

| | |
|---|---|
| Format | |
| Decimal Places | 0 |
| Visible | Yes |
| Display When | Always |
| Scroll Bars | None |
| Hide Duplicates | No |
| Can Grow | No |
| Can Shrink | No |
| Left | 0.0417" |
| Top | 0" |
| Width | 1.6042" |
| Height | 0.1979" |
| Back Style | Transparent |
| Back Color | #FFFFFF |
| Special Effect | Flat |
| Border Style | Transparent |
| Border Color | #000000 |
| Border Width | Hairline |
| Fore Color | #000000 |
| Font Name | Arial |
| Font Size | 9 |
| Font Weight | Normal |
| Font Italic | No |
| Font Underline | No |
| Text Align | General |
| Reading Order | Context |
| Scroll Bar Align | System |
| Numeral Shapes | System |
| Left Margin | 0" |
| Top Margin | 0" |
| Right Margin | 0" |

**Figure 19-4:**
The Format tab of the Properties dialog box provides a wealth of appearance options.

Many of the properties, such as Format, Decimal Places, Visible, and so on are pretty easy to understand; if you're ever unsure about what a property does, watch the Access Status bar for an explanation of the property. Here's some information about some really useful properties you may not be aware of:

✔ **Hide Duplicates:** Use this property to prevent your reports from showing a value if it's the same as the previous record. This is handy if you group records but don't display the group header.

✔ **Back Style and Back Color:** You can set the background as transparent or change the background color.

✔ **Special Effect:** You can select an appearance such as raised or sunken to give text boxes a 3D effect.

✔ **Border Style, Border Color, and Border Width:** Use these properties to control the lines around the text box.

✔ **Fore Color and Font attributes:** You can change the text color, typeface, size, and so on of the fonts used to display the data.

✔ **Text Align:** You can set the alignment of the data within the text box.

✔ **Reading Order:** If necessary, you can change the order of the characters for languages that read right-to-left.

✔ **Scroll Bar Align:** You can set any scroll bars to the right or left side of the text box.

This option is more useful in forms than it is in reports.

✔ **Numeral Shapes:** You can choose how numbers appear in the text box.

✔ **Margin attributes:** You can control how far the text is from the edges of the text box.

✔ **Line Spacing:** You can increase and decrease the space between lines of text to improve readability.

Figure 19-5 demonstrates how some of the formatting options change the appearance of the data that's presented in a report. Notice that some of the options really need to be used with care because you can easily create an unreadable report. In this case, the Fore Color example shows how a poor choice makes the data invisible.

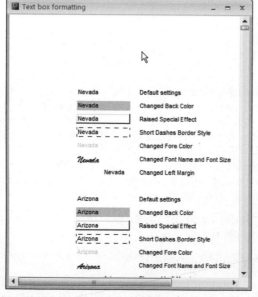

**Figure 19-5:**
This report demonstrates how several of the formatting options change the appearance.

# *Printing on Standard Labels*

There's really only one practical way to create Access reports that print on standard labels such as mailing labels, and that is to use the Label Wizard (Create section of the Ribbon). Sure, you can create this type of report from scratch, but doing so is an awful lot of work, and you won't end up with anything as good as what the Label Wizard can do, anyway.

People generally think of mailing labels when the idea of printing on labels comes up, but mailing labels are only a start. You could, for example, print out a set of labels, each containing an item number and brief item description for everything in your inventory.

You could use Avery 5385 Rotary Cards to print out a set of index cards for all your suppliers. From there, you can create a rotary file for a new employee. Or, maybe you want to create index tabs for the file folders you use to track each customer's orders.

To create a report designed to print on standard labels (or other related products like rotary index cards), follow these steps:

1. **In the Create area of the Ribbon, click Labels from the Reports section (after selecting the table or query you want to use as the record source).**

2. **The Label Wizard appears.**

   See Figure 19-6.

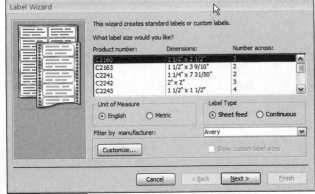

**Figure 19-6:** Choose the label stock you want to use.

3. **Select the label type you want to use.**

   If you use a generic brand of labels, you may have to search the instructions that came with the labels to discover which standard label number they're equivalent to (virtually all labels use the same specs as one of the standard label types). You won't have to set up custom labels unless you have something really weird! Click Next to continue and display the font options as shown in Figure 19-7.

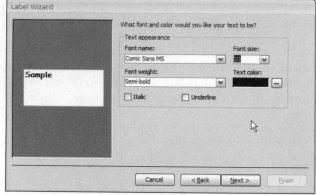

**Figure 19-7:**
Select the font options for your labels.

4. **Choose the font options that you want to use and click Next.**

The layout options, shown in Figure 19-8, appear. Keep in mind that depending on the options you choose, some data might not fit the label and will be cut off.

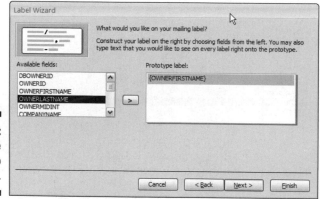

**Figure 19-8:**
Add the fields to your labels.

5. **Add the fields to build the labels the way you want them.**

Remember to leave spaces between fields and add any punctuation that you need. Click Next to continue.

6. **If you want to sort the labels, use the next screen of the Label Wizard to specify a sort order. Click Next to continue.**

   You can sort by using any combination of the fields you want even if you haven't used those fields on the labels.

7. **Enter a descriptive name for your labels and then click Finish to close the Label Wizard.**

If you have trouble making your data fit the labels, try using a smaller font size or a more compact font. You don't have to throw away the report you've just designed — simply open the report in Design View and make the necessary modifications.

Print a page or two of your report on plain paper to check the layout and alignment before you print the labels on expensive label stock.

Labels that have blank lines in the middle of the data look pretty unprofessional. Perhaps you have some customers who have a second address line that goes below the first address line and above the line for city, state, and zip code. You don't want that second address line to be a blank line for the majority of labels where the line isn't needed. The key to removing blank lines from your labels is to make certain that the Can Shrink property on the Format tab of the Properties dialog box for the text box is set to Yes. The Label Wizard automatically sets the Can Shrink property to Yes, so if you end up with blank lines in your labels, check to make sure this property wasn't somehow changed to No.

# Keeping Related Data Together

Reports can be difficult to understand if related data doesn't appear together. Think about how confusing an address list would be if Fred Holabird's name appeared at the bottom of one page and his address and phone number appeared at the top of the next page. Now imagine how much more confusing a report broken like that might be to someone like your banker or that elderly client who is trying to understand the commissions on items she consigned to auction with you. Clearly, you want to avoid confusion whenever possible.

## Understanding why Access splits records

Every report represents some sort of compromise. In order to make information fit right, you may have to limit the number of characters and thus cut off part of a long field entry. Or you may decide to allow a field to grow as much as necessary, only to have a very long entry split across a page boundary. If you want to limit the number of pages in a report so that you can complete the printing in a reasonable length of time and not have to spend a fortune on postage, you have to make difficult choices about what stays and what goes. Each of these compromises can work against you if you're trying to keep related data together.

In Chapter 13, you discover methods for grouping records in a report. Frankly, you're much more likely to have problems keeping related records together with grouped reports than you are with simple sorted, but ungrouped, reports. Not only do you have to cope with the variable number of records in each group, but also the group headers and footers tend to play havoc with your carefully designed page layouts.

## Tricks you can use to avoid splitting grouped records

Although you simply can't keep related records together in every instance, Access offers some tricks you can use to minimize the problem as much as possible. If your report uses grouping, the Format tab of the Properties dialog box for the group header (or footer) has some useful properties relating to this task (see Figure 19-9).

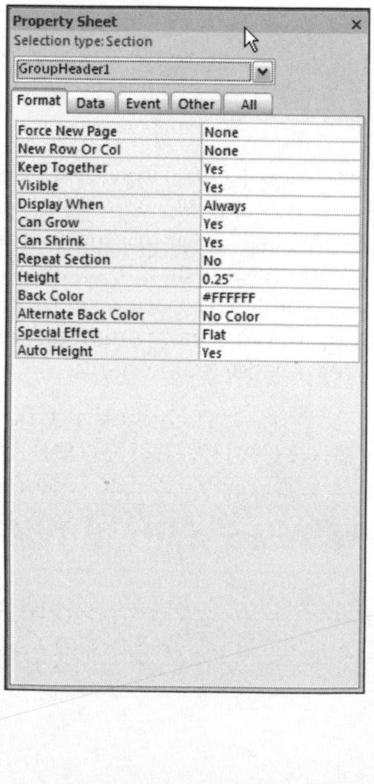

**Figure 19-9:**
Use the Format tab to set group properties that help keep groups together.

The properties that can help keep a group together include:

- ✔ **Force New Page:** Use this property to make Access start new groups at the top of a page.

- ✔ **Keep Together:** Use this property to make Access print each whole group on a single page if it fits.

- ✔ **Repeat Section:** Set this to Yes to print the group header at the top of each page.

You can use a combination of these properties to attempt to keep groups together, but keep in mind that the compromise for keeping records together is that you use more paper. That is, setting these properties to anything except No (or None for Force New Page) can use up a lot of paper when you print the report. Still, the compromise might be worth the paper if you can guarantee readability and eliminate confusion.

## Tricks you can use to avoid splitting sorted records

If you aren't using grouping in a report, you aren't faced with quite as many layout variables, and keeping each individual record together on the same page is going to be a little easier. But you need to pick up a few tips and tricks:

- ✔ Make sure that the Can Grow and Can Shrink properties are both set to No for any fields that are in the Detail section of the report.

- ✔ Each report section has a Height property on the Format tab of its Properties dialog box. Add together the page margins (Arrange and Page Setup sections of the Ribbon) and the heights of each report section to determine the total height of the report with one detail section. If the height of the detail section is set to an exact multiple of the difference between that total height and the height of the paper, records won't break across pages. You may have to shave a very small amount off the height of one or more sections to keep records in check.

- ✔ Make sure that everything on your report — including any horizontal lines, dates, and page numbers — can't spill over into the right margin on the printed report. This spillover can cause Access to get very confused about the page layout; the result is that your report ends up with a number of nearly blank pages.

 Switching a report into Report View is an excellent way to determine whether your report layout modifications are doing what you expect them to without wasting a lot of paper printing samples.

# Adding Your Logo to Reports

If you want to add a nice touch of class to your reports, why not add your own logo? Most companies and organizations have logos they use to add an official-looking appearance to letterheads, business cards, and so on, so why not use your logo on your reports, too?

Using a logo on an Access report is pretty easy, but there are a few little ways that Access might try to trip you up. Here's how to add a logo that you've stored in an image file:

1. **Open your report in Design View.**

2. **Click in the Report Header section of the report.**

   Make sure that you click the report section where you want to add the image before continuing; otherwise, Access adds the image in whichever report section was last selected (probably the Detail section) and expands the height of the section to fit the image size.

3. **In the Design section of the Ribbon, choose the Logo option.**

4. **Select the image file you want to use and click OK to close the dialog box and insert the picture.**

5. **Make certain that the image is selected and click the Properties button to display the Properties dialog box for the image.**

6. **On the Format tab, select Stretch from the drop-down Size Mode list box.**

   This option enables you to resize the image without cropping it. The default setting for this property, Clip, crops the image when you attempt to resize it. The Zoom setting is similar to Stretch, but it's a little harder to control.

7. **Use the resizing handles along the sides and corners of the image to resize it as necessary.**

   You may also have to resize the Report Header to eliminate any extra height that Access added when you inserted the picture, and you may need to move some other objects, such as the report title, to get the appearance you desire.

Figure 19-10 shows an example of a report with an added logo. Doesn't it make you want to see the list of available products?

**Figure 19-10:**
The logo
makes this
report look
even more
professional.

In most cases, the Report Header section is the appropriate place to add a logo because you use a logo for visual impact. Including a large logo on every page or alongside every record dilutes its impact. On the other hand, if you have a very small version of your logo, you could include that small version in the Page Header section.

Any image that you add to a report as a logo is an example of an *unbound control* because the image isn't associated with the data in one of the database tables. Images that are stored in fields as either linked or embedded objects can also appear in a report by including a bound control in the Detail section of the report. There's no special technique required to add these types of bound image controls to your reports, but the same `Size Mode` property considerations in Step 6 of the previous list also apply to bound image controls.

# Chapter 20

# Adding Efficiency with Great Tools

*In This Chapter*

▶ Documenting your Access database

▶ Improving the performance of your database

▶ Sharing Access data

$A$ ccess has an awful lot of powerful features — probably many more than most Access users will ever need. But you aren't the average Access user; you want to get more out of the application than the ordinary, everyday functions. You want power!

This chapter is about adding some real power tools to your Access toolbox. These aren't the wimpy little hand tools that ship with Access. No, we're talking supercharged add-ons that enable you to take control and show Access who's the boss! These are tools that help you document your Access applications, boost their performance, and share your data in ways you never dreamed possible.

Most of the tools I show you in this chapter are *third-party* add-ons for Access. Sure, you're going to have to pay a little extra if you decide that you want to add them to your toolkit, but you can use this chapter, along with the free trial version that most of these applications offer, to figure out which ones are right for your needs (and worth shelling out money for). You certainly won't need all these tools, but by the time you finish this chapter, you'll have a far better idea about what is out there to give you a bit of an Access boost. Obviously, I don't have room to show you all the ins and outs of these tools in a few pages, but that shouldn't prevent you from finding some real gems.

I encourage you to visit the Web sites that are shown for each of the items to find the most current pricing information, as well as any available options.

# Using Cool Tools to Document Everything

Access databases can be awfully complex. If you've ever tried the documentation tool that's built in to Access (on the Database Tools section of the Ribbon), you know that getting useful information about your database can be a real struggle. And if you've ever had a database go belly up, you know even more clearly how important it is not only to know a lot about the structure of your database, but also to have some tools to help in the recovery process. The tools in the following sections provide that extra help you really need.

## Comparing Access databases with CompareWiz

One of the most frustrating experiences for anyone who creates applications is dealing with people who just can't help tinkering. Maybe a user thinks that changing this report or that form will somehow improve things, but often the tinkerer just creates a nightmare for you when someone else says, "It doesn't work," and you have to figure out what's wrong. No one, of course, will remember having made any changes, so it's up to you to try and determine what has been modified.

CompareWiz from Software Add-Ins, (www.softwareaddins.com) can come to your rescue when you find yourself in that sort of pickle. CompareWiz finds and documents the differences between two copies of an Access database. One copy, of course, may be your master copy, and the other is the production copy that's used daily. By locating the differences between the two with this tool, you can cut short your troubleshooting by hours and concentrate on fixing the problem.

An example of how helpful CompareWiz can be would be an Access database where the OwnerID field is a required field. If the AllowZeroLength property for the OwnerID field was changed from false (0) to true (-1), users could skip over the OwnerID field without making an entry; now queries, forms, and reports that depend on that value would fail. CompareWiz can detect such changes and alert you to a potentially huge problem.

CompareWiz is available for all versions of Access going back to Access 97, so even if you don't have the most recent version of Access, you can use CompareWiz.

Unfortunately, CompareWiz can't tell you who made the change so that you can go and give the offender a dope slap! Well, maybe that's a good thing.

## Comparing the data in Access databases with CompareDataWiz

Even if you don't have to worry about someone changing the basic structure of your Access databases, you can easily end up with copies of the database that contain different sets of data. Perhaps someone took a copy of the database home over the weekend to do a report and decided to edit a customer's record because it needed corrections. Or perhaps you experienced a crash and need to figure out which of your backups contains the best set of records.

Access doesn't offer an easy way to compare the data in two different copies of a database. Sure, you could get fancy by linking or importing external data, but the complications that are likely to result are a recipe for confusion and disaster. I shudder to even think about the possible consequences of overwriting current data with outdated information.

CompareDataWiz, from Software Add-Ins, (www.softwareaddins.com), is the tool that you need to compare the data in two different Access databases. This excellent tool shows you which records have been changed, which ones have been added, and even which records were deleted in one copy of the databases.

CompareDataWiz is available for all versions of Access going back to Access 97, so even if you don't have the most recent version of Access, you can use CompareDataWiz.

When you know exactly how the copies of your databases differ, you can more easily develop a plan for either consolidating the information or for choosing the correct copy to keep. Even better, you can come up with a solution in a few minutes instead of spending hours making sure that you've made the correct choice on your own.

CompareDataWiz also offers you the option to print or export the results of the comparison. Using the export option is an excellent alternative to the somewhat complex Access database replication feature — especially if you don't need to constantly combine copies of the database on an ongoing basis.

## Checking out your queries with Query Tree Editor

Query Tree Editor, from 4TOPS (www.4tops.com), may not be a tool that you need right now, but remember it for the future. Query Tree Editor helps you understand the extremely complex relationships that often occur in Access databases when one query builds on another, which, in turn, builds on another, and so on. With Query Tree Editor you can find the dependencies and successfully edit the related queries.

Programmers and developers are notoriously poor at explaining how the systems they develop function. A tool like Query Tree Editor can be a lifesaver if you've been asked to maintain or update an Access database application that someone else created. Often, in those cases, your chances of finding understandable information about what's going on under the hood are probably somewhere between "not a chance" and none.

Even if you don't quite need the power of Query Tree Editor yet, 4TOPS offers some other excellent tools for exporting data to Excel and Word. See "Bringing data from Excel with Excel Import Assistant" and "Merge data with Word by using Word Link for Access," later in this chapter for more details.

## Fixing database corruption with AccessFIX

Can you imagine a worse feeling than the one that accompanies an Access warning that informs you that it can't open your company's most important database because the file is corrupt? Well, maybe there is something that could be worse — the feeling that comes over you when you remember that you haven't quite gotten around to backing up your files for a while, either. Somehow, I don't think this is going to be one of those days you look back on fondly.

Several things can go wrong with your Access databases. A power failure while the database is in use, a hard drive failure, or even a computer virus can all result in a database that won't open.

AccessFIX from Cimaware Software (www.cimaware.com) is an application that can save your bacon when Access decides to get uncooperative. In just a few minutes, AccessFIX can recover the data you thought was lost and put you on the road to recovery. Cimaware also offers ExcelFIX for Excel files, WordFIX for Word files, and OfficeFIX to recover all three types of Microsoft Office files.

Cimaware offers a free downloadable demo version that you can use to determine whether your data can be recovered before you pay for a license.

The best thing you can do to avoid the panic and sense of loss that come with a corrupt database is to use preventive measures. Never run an important Access database on a PC that isn't protected by an *uninterruptible power*

*supply* — UPS. A UPS is cheap insurance against both power outages and power surges that can harm your computer and destroy your data. And always back up your files.

If you find yourself facing a corrupted Access database, nothing is going to be more comforting than a message from AccessFIX telling you that 53,308 records were recovered. Just imagine how long reentering those records by hand would take!

In some cases, a database file may be so corrupted that AccessFIX won't be able to recover the complete structure of the database by looking at the damaged file. You can tell AccessFIX to get the structure information from another file, such as an out-of-date backup of your database.

After your file is recovered, AccessFIX saves the database in a new file with a different name. You can even choose to save the data in text files suitable for later importing back into Access.

# Souping Up Your Database

Can you honestly say that your Access databases run as fast as you'd like and that they're as easy to use as they should be? If not, have a look at some tools that can help you add the extra zip and convenience your users really want.

## Optimizing your Access database with SSW Performance Pro!

Wouldn't it be great if you knew an Access expert who would be willing to sit down and take the time to go over your Access databases with a fine-toothed comb and then tell you exactly where you could make improvements? I'm not talking about just any so-called expert, either. No, how about someone who knows Access inside and out, who actually tests the performance and then gives you specific recommendations about what you can do to get faster performance?

Well, that's the idea behind SSW Performance Pro! from SSW (www.ssw.com.au). Instead of sending an expert Access developer to your office (which could be expensive because SSW is in Australia), SSW created the SSW Performance Pro! tool that runs on your PC and then gives you a report about the results. (Besides, it might be a little less embarrassing to have a piece of software, rather than a real person, tell you which of your forms need a little extra work.)

SSW Performance Pro! can also check all the field names and table names to make certain that none of them contain characters that cause problems if you decide to split your database into *front-end* and *back-end* applications by using the Tools⇨Database Utilities⇨Database Splitter command.

Databases that are split into front-end and back-end applications store the tables in the back-end application and store the forms, reports, and queries in the front-end application by using table links. Splitting a database is often done to improve the performance of a multiuser database on a network. Each user then has a local copy of the front-end part of the database, and only the data has to be sent across the network. Unfortunately, splitting databases brings some additional considerations and complications that aren't covered in this book.

## Enhance your Access forms with Selector

You simply can't plan for every possibility. When you create Access forms, you typically think about all the ways people want to use those forms and plan accordingly. For example, if you have a form that enables users to select customer orders, you probably choose between sorting the records by customer, by order number, or maybe by order date. The one thing you aren't likely to do is to figure out how to let users sort the records the way they want.

Selector from Peter's Software (www.peterssoftware.com) is one of a series of very useful tools offered by this company. Selector enables you to create forms that present users with a number of user-selectable sort options so that they can choose the method that best suits their needs. To change the sort order, users just click the column heading of the column they want to use for sorting — exactly the way they do when looking at files in Windows Explorer.

## Create better forms with ShrinkerStretcher

Have you ever spent a bunch of time carefully designing a form, only to discover that the form ended up partially off the screen when others try to use it? This ugly scene can result from designing forms with a higher screen resolution than your users have. You might have a nice 1280-x-1024 (or even 1600-x-1200) resolution on your snazzy LCD flat-screen monitor (lucky!), but Fred back in Receiving might be stuck with that old system that maxes out at 800 x 600.

You could, of course, simply make small-sized forms that fit even the tiniest of screens, but ShrinkerStretcher, from Peter's Software (www.peters software.com), offers you another alternative you may find more acceptable. ShrinkerStretcher makes your forms and the controls on those forms resizable to fit any screen. Objects like labels, text boxes, combo boxes, and so on shrink or grow as necessary so that controls aren't hidden.

## Creating forms from existing forms with OmniForm

One problem with Access forms that you aren't likely to resolve is the fact that they look like Access forms. Although this doesn't qualify as a serious issue for the vast majority of Access users, it can be a big problem if you work for an organization that has a whole bunch of "legacy" paper forms and a management team that insists that any electronic forms look exactly like the old forest killers.

If you find yourself in this type of situation, you have several options:

- ✔ You can keep on handing out the paper forms and then reenter all the data manually. Yippee.

- ✔ You can look for a job with an outfit that realizes that computers are here to stay.

- ✔ You can invest in OmniForm from ScanSoft (www.nuance.com) so that you can create exact electronic duplicates of those old paper forms. Hubba hubba!

I really can't tell you which option to choose, but if you decide on OmniForm, you can scan existing paper forms to create forms that look just like the paper versions, but that enable users to fill out the forms on their PCs. You can create forms for use on Web sites or any other place where you might want people to fill in some information. OmniForm even includes Fillers, which are standalone data-gathering modules you can send to people so they can fill out the form without having OmniForm installed.

OmniForm doesn't actually create Access forms. Rather, OmniForm creates a rudimentary database of the form responses, which you then import into Access. Still, this process would certainly be a lot faster than reentering all the data from paper forms manually.

# Using Software to Share Stuff

Information is generally far more useful when it can be shared. In the following sections, I show you some ways that you can share your Access data both with people who don't have Access and with some of the other programs on your PC.

## Using Snapshot Viewer for Access to send a report to non-Access users

Snapshot Viewer is a small application that enables people who don't have Access installed to view Access reports. Snapshot Viewer is available as a free download from the Microsoft Office Web site (office.microsoft.com).

You create a *report snapshot* by choosing the More option in the Export section (on the External Data section of the Ribbon) and selecting Snapshot Viewer from the drop-down list. This action creates the file that others can view with the Snapshot Viewer. As the name implies, the report snapshot is a static look at the report that doesn't change when the data in your database changes.

As an alternative to creating a report snapshot, you might want to consider creating a *data access page.* This is a Web page that links to your Access database and shows live (not static) data. A data access page is similar to an Access form, and you use similar techniques to create forms and data access pages. You can use the HTML Document option from the More list to create a data access page.

## Linking Access and PowerPoint by using Take-Off DATAPOINT

If you really need to share your Access data, nothing puts it up in front of a crowd quite like a PowerPoint slideshow. Of course, getting your Access data into a PowerPoint slideshow can be a real pain.

An excellent solution for this problem is DATAPOINT from Take-Off (www. presentationpoint.com). DATAPOINT is a PowerPoint add-on that enables you to create a slideshow using dynamic content from Excel worksheets, text files, or, you guessed it, Access databases.

Take-Off offers a free, 30-day trial version of DATAPOINT that you can download. This company also has several other related products that you might want to consider.

## Sending data to QuickBooks with accessBooks Updater

If you use both Access and QuickBooks, you're probably already quite aware that QuickBooks doesn't really play well with the other kids in the sandbox.

But if you're in a situation like one of my customers, you may have data in an Access database that would be awfully handy if it were also available in QuickBooks.

In this instance, the company has an Access application that tracks the bids for an auction, but the bookkeeping and invoicing are done with QuickBooks. Needless to say, reentering several hundred invoices into QuickBooks manually after an auction closes takes a lot of work and is prone to error; the situation is especially annoying because everyone knows that the information is already in the Access database, so close, and yet so far away.

Enter accessBooks Updater from Synergration (www.synergration.com). This program imports data from an Access database into a QuickBooks company file.

You need to do some pretty fancy footwork to move data from Access to QuickBooks even with help from a third-party program like accessBooks Updater. I was hired to move data from Access to QuickBooks and to keep that data moving on a regular basis. In order to bring the auction data from Access into QuickBooks, I had to create a number of very sophisticated SQL queries that are executed by a series of VBA procedures in order to populate the tables that accessBooks Updater needs. When these tables were filled with the data from the auction program, accessBooks Updater added the information to the QuickBooks company file. Did getting this set up take a lot of work? Yes, but the end result is that my client can now create several hundred invoices in QuickBooks in a couple of minutes instead of spending several days. And the company no longer worries about typing errors because the data is transferred directly without rekeying.

## Bring QuickBooks data to Access with Digital Cows Deluxe Exporter

QuickBooks is just as difficult about letting any of its data escape as it is about allowing you to import data from another application. Sure, you can export a few of the lists to those almost incomprehensible (and virtually useless to anything except QuickBooks) IIF files, but you are really limited in exporting useful information. Well, it's your data, so I say that if you want to bring it into Access, you should be able to do so with minimal fuss and bother.

Deluxe Exporter from Digital Cows Technologies (www.digitalcows.com) gives you the freedom to export any of your QuickBooks data to Access and a number of other formats.

One way you might use Deluxe Exporter is to create a customer list in Access to use for advertising purposes. With all the QuickBooks data as fair game, you have the option to do an awful lot more in targeting your mailings to specific types of customers than you could with the simple customer address list that QuickBooks is willing to export on its own.

## Bringing data from Excel with Excel Import Assistant

Access can import data from an Excel worksheet, but you face some limitations to the process that aren't much fun. For one thing, Access really isn't very happy if you have anything in the worksheet that isn't part of the data — especially if that extra stuff is above or to the left of the data you want to import. And if your data contains any errors, well, guess where they end up?

Excel Import Assistant from 4TOPS (www.4tops.com) simply blows away the problems of importing data from Excel by providing you with tools and options for dealing with pretty much anything you might encounter. For example:

- ✔ You can easily import different parts of the worksheet to different tables.
- ✔ You can correct incorrect data on the fly.
- ✔ You can set up data mapping so that when you import the same type of data in the future, you won't have to specify what goes where.
- ✔ You can import data and automatically apply *autonumber* keys (unique values) to the records.
- ✔ You can automatically skip duplicated data.
- ✔ You can suppress error messages during the import process and automatically create an error log, electing to correct the problems after the import process is finished instead of dealing with each error in real time.
- ✔ You can automate the whole process of importing a bunch of Excel worksheets — which is especially handy if you have to import the data regularly.

You can automate future imports by using the Save tab in Excel Import Assistant to save the settings of a complex Excel import session for later use.

## Merge data with Word by using Word Link for Access

In Chapter 18 I show you how to send Access data to Word by using the Tools⇨ Office Links⇨Publish It with Microsoft Office Word command in a process known as mail merge. Although the Office Links tools are fairly handy, they're not all that flexible. If you really want your Access data to put Word through its paces, you need something like Word Link from 4TOPS (www.4tops.com).

Word Link goes well beyond mere mail merge. By using the full power of the Office automation features, you can create documents in several different formats, add controls to Word documents, automatically reorient or resize Word documents that contain too much data, get data from users, and, oh yes, do a mail merge.

The A in the column to the right of the list of available Word Link features indicates one of the advanced features. You may want to hide these features by deselecting the Use Advanced Features check box while you're getting the basics of Word Link down.

# Part VI
# The Part of Tens

The 5th Wave                    By Rich Tennant

"Please answer the following survey questions about our company's performance with either, 'Excellent', 'Good', 'Fair', or 'I'm Really Incapable of Appreciating Someone Else's Hard Work.'"

## In this part . . .

This final part helps you to find additional and very useful Access-related information on the Web. It finishes up by making sure you know some very important bits of information about queries so that your forms and reports are even more useful.

# Chapter 21

# Ten Great Access Sites Online

*T*he Internet has really changed the way people deal with the world. That's especially true for people who develop computer programs and Access databases. You now have easy entry into a whole universe of other developers, tools, and samples just by visiting the right places on the Web.

Unfortunately, finding really good Access-related Web sites isn't always easy. The name Microsoft chose for its database software doesn't help. Because the word *access* is very common; any Web search turns up thousands of sites that have nothing to do with our favorite database, Microsoft Access. If you go searching, be sure to enter **"Microsoft Access"** in quotes to limit the results a bit.

In this chapter, I share some of the really good Web sites I've found that actually do have useful information on Microsoft Access. I couldn't fit them all in, and to be honest, I left out sites that I mention in Chapter 20 simply because I had to draw the line somewhere.

Oh, and don't try to draw any conclusions about the rankings of these sites based on where they appear in the chapter. I purposely list them in alphabetical order to avoid giving any clues to my personal rankings.

# Access Database Tips

www.accessdatabasetips.com

The Access Database Tips site has many useful tips that can help you with tables, queries, forms, reports, and VBA modules. You can find a discussion of macros and VBA as well as various samples that are available for downloading. You can even subscribe to an online newsletter if you want to keep up with the latest news from this site.

# Access Monster

www.accessmonster.com

The Access Monster site has so many articles, tools, tips, and tutorials that you can probably spend days finding new things you didn't know about Access. There is also an extensive list of frequently asked questions. Because the resources are vast, you can probably find an answer for just about any problem because someone else has probably asked the same question before.

Access Monster also offers a large number of online forums where you can ask questions or simply browse to see what other Access users are talking about.

Always read the information for new users before you post a question in an online forum. Barging right in with the attitude that you don't have the time to learn the ropes — you just need an answer *now* — is a sure way to ensure that you quickly become extremely unpopular!

# Easy Access Database Directory

www.directory-base.com/access

The Easy Access Database Directory site offers tools, tips, downloadable samples, online magazines, and a whole lot more. Other Access users submitted many of the articles and samples, and the Easy Access Database Directory welcomes your submissions, too.

The Easy Access Database Directory site also provides links and ratings for a large number of Access add-ins. As a user community, this site enables you to find out what the other members think about the various listings; community members often leave feedback.

# Jamie's Software

`www.jamiessoftware.tk/home.html`

Jamie's Software is a site that might seem a bit sparse at first glance, but don't let that fool you. This site offers some free downloads that you won't find elsewhere, as well as a number of useful articles that can help you resolve some thorny Access issues.

Jamie's Software also has a message board that is sort of a free-form question-and-answer forum where users ask for help with various Access-related issues. This message board isn't really aimed at beginners, but if you've taken the time to gain an understanding of the issues, this site can be an excellent place to get just that little nudge you need to resolve your problem.

# Lebans.com

`www.lebans.com`

Lebans.com is the personal Web site of an Access developer named Stephen Lebans. The site shares hints, tips, and source code that you can use in your own Access projects. The site owner does not respond to programming questions, but all the samples are provided with the complete source code so that you can adapt them as necessary for your needs.

To find the various files you can download from the Lebans.com site, click the convenient Contents link. When you click the link, you can find each of the available files listed in a handy tree-structured list.

# Microsoft Office Online Access

`office.microsoft.com/en-us/FX010857911033.aspx`

The Microsoft Office Online Access Web site is Microsoft's official Access user site. Here you can find various articles, downloads, tutorials, and other information — straight from the horse's mouth.

One very interesting feature of this site is that you can typically order a CD with a trial version of the latest Access release. This is especially useful if you're still using an older, out-of-date version of Access and want to see if the newer version offers enough new features to make an upgrade worthwhile. You can order the CD, however, even if you don't already have Access.

If you get to a point where you feel that you really need to get some professional help with your Access problems, this site could be a great place to start. It contains lots of links to both companies and individuals who know Access inside and out.

The main Microsoft Office Web site (`www.office.microsoft.com`) frequently offers updates for Microsoft Office. Many of these updates correct serious security issues, so check for the free updates often.

# *MSDN — Microsoft Developer Network*

The Microsoft Developer Network is clearly aimed at professional application developers, but it also offers a wealth of extremely interesting and useful information for people who aren't quite pros yet. In fact, this site is so useful that I'm going to cheat a little and tell you about three interesting Access-related places at MSDN (but I'm only going to count them as one for the purpose of this chapter).

Although you can purchase a fairly expensive MSDN subscription, it's unnecessary to do so to gain entry to most of the useful Access info you can find here.

## *MSDN Access code samples*

```
msdn.microsoft.com/office/program/access/2003/download/
              default.aspx
```

This arm of the MSDN site offers various code samples that you can use with Access. The samples are listed by the Access version they were developed for, but you can generally use the samples for older versions in a newer Access release.

## *MSDN Access site*

```
msdn.microsoft.com/library/default.asp?url=/library/
            en-us/odc_2003_ta/html/odc_ancaccess.asp
```

At this area of the site, you can find technical articles, developer documentation, various downloads and code samples, and a link to *Smart Access,* a monthly newsletter aimed at Access developers and power users. You can also find some very handy links to things like the Microsoft Knowledge Base; the Knowledge Base offers incredibly useful and often esoteric answers to your problems with Access.

## Office Solutions Development

```
msdn.microsoft.com/library/default.asp?url=/library/
           en-us/odc_2003_ta/html/odc_ancoffsol.asp
```

Here you can find links to a vast number of useful articles, code samples, and downloads. This particular site is especially useful to expand your knowledge of Microsoft Office into the other applications beyond Access.

## Roger's Access Library

```
www.rogersaccesslibrary.com/TableOfContents3.asp
```

The Roger's Access Library site contains a large number of Access samples that you can download and use for free. These samples are intended to show you how to solve various problems with Access, and you can build upon them to create your own solutions. All the samples are listed alphabetically along with a brief description of their purpose.

Seeing how someone else approached a problem can often steer you onto the path of figuring out a solution for another, similar problem. If you don't see an example that is exactly what you need, be open-minded and look through the list on this site to see whether you can find related information. You may be surprised at how much you discover!

## The Access Web

```
www.mvps.org/access
```

The Access Web site is an FAQ *(Frequently Asked Questions)* site that is aimed at Access developers. As such, the topics tend to be quite technical, but also extremely useful. If you can't find the answer here, you probably aren't looking closely enough.

# Chapter 22

# Ten Things to Know about Queries (That Also Help You with Forms and Reports)

*In This Chapter*

▶ Queries are like tables

▶ You can use select queries safely

▶ Every query is an SQL query

▶ Be careful with action queries

▶ Joins are absolutely necessary if you want to use multiple tables in queries

▶ You must specify criteria

▶ Datasheet view is your friend

▶ Make-table queries are blank slates until you do something with them

▶ Don't forget to pick a record source

▶ Be sure you really want to use the delete query

*Q*ueries are really important tools in your form and report toolkit. In this chapter, I give you a quick look at some important things to remember about queries.

## Queries Act like Tables

One of the most important things to know about queries is that they act like tables in many ways. True, you can't store data in queries, but you can use queries as record sources for both forms and reports. You can even use a query as the record source for another query.

See Chapter 1 for more information.

# Select Queries Are Always Safe

Select queries are always safe to run because they never modify any data. Instead, select queries return a record set, which is sort of like having a temporary table full of the results of the query. See Chapter 2 for more on the types of queries.

Do your experiments with select queries and change the query type only after you're satisfied that the query is returning the correct set of records.

# All Queries Are SQL Queries

Every Access query is actually an SQL query. This means that you can always open a valid query in SQL view to examine or modify the query. The reverse does not hold true, however. SQL-specific queries generally cannot be opened in Design View because the Query editor has no way to represent some of the SQL-specific statements.

See Chapter 7 for more on SQL.

# Action Queries Can Harm Your Data

Action queries — make-table, update, append, and delete — actually make modifications to the data, which means that they can harm that data. Unless you've turned off the warning messages (which generally requires some VBA programming), Access warns you before you execute an action query. If you ignore the warnings, you have only yourself to blame for any damage that happens.

See Chapter 6 for more on action queries.

# You Need Joins to Use Multiple Tables in Queries

You can use fields from more than one table in a query, but only if you first create relationships *(joins)* between the tables. You can create those relationships in the Query editor or in the Relationships window, but there must be a valid relationship between the tables before you can run the query.

See Chapter 5 for more on using multiple tables in queries.

# Queries Select All Records Unless You Specify Criteria

If you don't want a query to return every record from the underlying table, you must specify criteria to narrow down the selection.

- Criteria you specify in a single row must all be satisfied (this is an AND condition).
- Criteria that are specified on separate rows require that only the conditions on a single row be satisfied (this is an OR condition).

See Chapter 15 for more on specifying criteria.

# Datasheet View Shows Results without Running the Query

Switching to Datasheet view displays the records that will be selected by the query without actually running the query. For action queries, this function safely shows you which records the query will act upon, but it won't show you how the records will appear after the query is executed.

See Chapter 2 for more on query views.

## Make-Table Queries Always Begin with an Empty Table

Make-table queries always create tables that contain only the records that are returned by the query.

- ✔ If you specify the name of an existing table as the target of a make-table query, any existing records in that table are wiped out before the new records are added.

- ✔ If you want to add additional records to an existing table without destroying what's already there, use the append query, not the make-table query.

See Chapter 6 for more on make-table queries.

## Queries Need a Record Source

Every query needs a record source — a table or another query — to supply the data for the query. In theory, you could create a single record table by using a make-table query that specifies each of the field values, but you'd be doing a lot of work for little purpose.

See Chapter 2 for information on choosing a record source.

## Delete Queries Are Forever

Access doesn't have a recycle bin. If you run a delete query and tell Access that you really do want to delete the records, those records disappear as surely as a July snowfall in Phoenix. If you're not absolutely sure that the records should be gone forever, make a copy of the records before you delete them. If you don't, how long do you think it will be before you realize that you shouldn't have deleted them?

See Chapter 8 for tips on avoiding data destruction.

# Index

## BUSINESS, CAREERS & PERSONAL FINANCE

Fundraising FOR DUMMIES
0-7645-9847-3

Investing FOR DUMMIES
0-7645-2431-3

**Also available:**

- Business Plans Kit For Dummies
  0-7645-9794-9
- Economics For Dummies
  0-7645-5726-2
- Grant Writing For Dummies
  0-7645-8416-2
- Home Buying For Dummies
  0-7645-5331-3
- Managing For Dummies
  0-7645-1771-6
- Marketing For Dummies
  0-7645-5600-2

- Personal Finance For Dummies
  0-7645-2590-5*
- Resumes For Dummies
  0-7645-5471-9
- Selling For Dummies
  0-7645-5363-1
- Six Sigma For Dummies
  0-7645-6798-5
- Small Business Kit For Dummies
  0-7645-5984-2
- Starting an eBay Business For Dummies
  0-7645-6924-4
- Your Dream Career For Dummies
  0-7645-9795-7

## HOME & BUSINESS COMPUTER BASICS

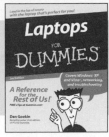

Laptops FOR DUMMIES
0-470-05432-8

Windows Vista FOR DUMMIES
0-471-75421-8

**Also available:**

- Cleaning Windows Vista For Dummies
  0-471-78293-9
- Excel 2007 For Dummies
  0-470-03737-7
- Mac OS X Tiger For Dummies
  0-7645-7675-5
- MacBook For Dummies
  0-470-04859-X
- Macs For Dummies
  0-470-04849-2
- Office 2007 For Dummies
  0-470-00923-3

- Outlook 2007 For Dummies
  0-470-03830-6
- PCs For Dummies
  0-7645-8958-X
- Salesforce.com For Dummies
  0-470-04893-X
- Upgrading & Fixing Laptops For Dummies
  0-7645-8959-8
- Word 2007 For Dummies
  0-470-03658-3
- Quicken 2007 For Dummies
  0-470-04600-7

## FOOD, HOME, GARDEN, HOBBIES, MUSIC & PETS

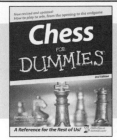

Chess FOR DUMMIES
0-7645-8404-9

Guitar FOR DUMMIES
0-7645-9904-6

**Also available:**

- Candy Making For Dummies
  0-7645-9734-5
- Card Games For Dummies
  0-7645-9910-0
- Crocheting For Dummies
  0-7645-4151-X
- Dog Training For Dummies
  0-7645-8418-9
- Healthy Carb Cookbook For Dummies
  0-7645-8476-6
- Home Maintenance For Dummies
  0-7645-5215-5

- Horses For Dummies
  0-7645-9797-3
- Jewelry Making & Beading For Dummies
  0-7645-2571-9
- Orchids For Dummies
  0-7645-6759-4
- Puppies For Dummies
  0-7645-5255-4
- Rock Guitar For Dummies
  0-7645-5356-9
- Sewing For Dummies
  0-7645-6847-7
- Singing For Dummies
  0-7645-2475-5

## INTERNET & DIGITAL MEDIA

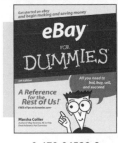

eBay FOR DUMMIES
0-470-04529-9

iPod & iTunes FOR DUMMIES
0-470-04894-8

**Also available:**

- Blogging For Dummies
  0-471-77084-1
- Digital Photography For Dummies
  0-7645-9802-3
- Digital Photography All-in-One Desk Reference For Dummies
  0-470-03743-1
- Digital SLR Cameras and Photography For Dummies
  0-7645-9803-1
- eBay Business All-in-One Desk Reference For Dummies
  0-7645-8438-3
- HDTV For Dummies
  0-470-09673-X

- Home Entertainment PCs For Dummies
  0-470-05523-5
- MySpace For Dummies
  0-470-09529-6
- Search Engine Optimization For Dummies
  0-471-97998-8
- Skype For Dummies
  0-470-04891-3
- The Internet For Dummies
  0-7645-8996-2
- Wiring Your Digital Home For Dummies
  0-471-91830-X

* Separate Canadian edition also available
† Separate U.K. edition also available

Available wherever books are sold. For more information or to order direct: U.S. customers visit www.dummies.com or call 1-877-762-2974.
U.K. customers visit www.wileyeurope.com or call 0800 243407. Canadian customers visit www.wiley.ca or call 1-800-567-4797.

## SPORTS, FITNESS, PARENTING, RELIGION & SPIRITUALITY

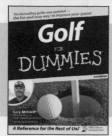
0-471-76871-5

0-7645-7841-3

**Also available:**
- Catholicism For Dummies
  0-7645-5391-7
- Exercise Balls For Dummies
  0-7645-5623-1
- Fitness For Dummies
  0-7645-7851-0
- Football For Dummies
  0-7645-3936-1
- Judaism For Dummies
  0-7645-5299-6
- Potty Training For Dummies
  0-7645-5417-4
- Buddhism For Dummies
  0-7645-5359-3
- Pregnancy For Dummies
  0-7645-4483-7 †
- Ten Minute Tone-Ups For Dummies
  0-7645-7207-5
- NASCAR For Dummies
  0-7645-7681-X
- Religion For Dummies
  0-7645-5264-3
- Soccer For Dummies
  0-7645-5229-5
- Women in the Bible For Dummies
  0-7645-8475-8

## TRAVEL

0-7645-7749-2

0-7645-6945-7

**Also available:**
- Alaska For Dummies
  0-7645-7746-8
- Cruise Vacations For Dummies
  0-7645-6941-4
- England For Dummies
  0-7645-4276-1
- Europe For Dummies
  0-7645-7529-5
- Germany For Dummies
  0-7645-7823-5
- Hawaii For Dummies
  0-7645-7402-7
- Italy For Dummies
  0-7645-7386-1
- Las Vegas For Dummies
  0-7645-7382-9
- London For Dummies
  0-7645-4277-X
- Paris For Dummies
  0-7645-7630-5
- RV Vacations For Dummies
  0-7645-4442-X
- Walt Disney World & Orlando
  For Dummies
  0-7645-9660-8

## GRAPHICS, DESIGN & WEB DEVELOPMENT

0-7645-8815-X

0-7645-9571-7

**Also available:**
- 3D Game Animation For Dummies
  0-7645-8789-7
- AutoCAD 2006 For Dummies
  0-7645-8925-3
- Building a Web Site For Dummies
  0-7645-7144-3
- Creating Web Pages For Dummies
  0-470-08030-2
- Creating Web Pages All-in-One Desk
  Reference For Dummies
  0-7645-4345-8
- Dreamweaver 8 For Dummies
  0-7645-9649-7
- InDesign CS2 For Dummies
  0-7645-9572-5
- Macromedia Flash 8 For Dummies
  0-7645-9691-8
- Photoshop CS2 and Digital
  Photography For Dummies
  0-7645-9580-6
- Photoshop Elements 4 For Dummies
  0-471-77483-9
- Syndicating Web Sites with RSS Feeds
  For Dummies
  0-7645-8848-6
- Yahoo! SiteBuilder For Dummies
  0-7645-9800-7

## NETWORKING, SECURITY, PROGRAMMING & DATABASES

0-7645-7728-X

0-471-74940-0

**Also available:**
- Access 2007 For Dummies
  0-470-04612-0
- ASP.NET 2 For Dummies
  0-7645-7907-X
- C# 2005 For Dummies
  0-7645-9704-3
- Hacking For Dummies
  0-470-05235-X
- Hacking Wireless Networks
  For Dummies
  0-7645-9730-2
- Java For Dummies
  0-470-08716-1
- Microsoft SQL Server 2005 For Dummies
  0-7645-7755-7
- Networking All-in-One Desk Reference
  For Dummies
  0-7645-9939-9
- Preventing Identity Theft For Dummies
  0-7645-7336-5
- Telecom For Dummies
  0-471-77085-X
- Visual Studio 2005 All-in-One Desk
  Reference For Dummies
  0-7645-9775-2
- XML For Dummies
  0-7645-8845-1